BRISTOL'S STAGE COACHES

The mail coach arriving at Bristol, 1826 (detail, see page 120).

Bristol's Stage Coaches

DORIAN GERHOLD

First published in the United Kingdom in 2012
by The Hobnob Press, PO Box 1838, East Knoyle, Salisbury, SP3 6FA
www.hobnobpress.co.uk

British Library Cataloguing in Publication Data
A catalogue record for this book is available from the British Library

ISBN 978-1-906978-15-0

Typeset in Minion Pro 12/16 pt. Typesetting and origination by John Chandler
Printed by Lightning Source

Cover illustrations:
Front: 'The Night Team', *c.1836 (detail from a painting by Charles*
Cooper Henderson).
Back: The Tam O'Shanter coach, c.1836 (detail, see p.218)

Contents

Acknowledgements

I AM MOST GRATEFUL to the many librarians, archivists and museum staff who have produced newspapers and documents, answered queries or arranged for photography. Nick Young kindly located photographs of buildings in Thatcham. Sally Laurence Smyth provided the great service of reading and commenting on the entire text.

Illustrations are reproduced by permission of the following: Richard Green Gallery, London, front cover; Bristol Museum and Art Gallery, frontispiece, 1, 30, 52, 87, back cover; Reece Winstone Archive, 2, 9, 50, 80, 96; Bristol Reference Library, 3, 4, 27-8, 39, 47-9, 79, 81, 82, 84, 86, 90, 91, 95, 99, 104, 106; British Museum, Prints and Drawings, 5, 31, 32, 38, 41, 46, 53, 57-9; © The British Library Board, 7, 11, 20; Oxfordshire County Council – Oxfordshire History Centre, 8; Slough Library, 10, 70; Bath in Time – Bath Central Library, 17, 63; Hounslow Libraries Local Collections, 18; Private Collection/ © Chris Beetles, London, U.K./ The Bridgeman Art Library, 22; Courtesy of the Huntington Art Collections, San Marino, California, 33, 34; Abingdon County Hall Museum, 37; Private Collection/ Photo © Christie's Images/ The Bridgeman Art Library, 53; National Portrait Gallery Picture Library, 56; Victoria Art Gallery, Bath and North East Somerset, England, 62; Iris & B. Gerald Cantor Center for Visual Arts, Stanford University, California, 67; Wiltshire Heritage Museum, Devizes, 68; Mrs Ann Spokes Symonds – photograph P.S. Spokes, 69; © Royal Mail Group Ltd 2011, courtesy of the British Postal Museum & Archive 2011, 72, 92; Berkshire Record Office, 73 (D/EX 1373/1,

f. 21); Cardiff Local Studies Library, 94; © *The Times* 1841, 105. The following were provided by the author: 6, 12-13, 15-16, 19, 21, 23-6, 29, 35, 36, 40, 42, 43, 51, 60, 64-6, 71, 74-8, 83, 85, 88, 89, 93, 97, 98, 100-3, 107-9. Attempts to trace the owners of any rights in the following have been unsuccessful: 44, 45, 55, 61.

Note on currency

There were 12 pennies or pence to a shilling and 20 shillings to a pound. Pounds, shillings and pence are referred to here in the following form: £2.6s.8d.

Abbreviations used in the notes

ABG	*Aris's Birmingham Gazette*
BD	Bristol directories (*The Bristol directory* (1785); William Bailey, *The Bristol and Bath directory* (1787); John Reed, *The new Bristol directory* (1792), W. Matthews, *Matthews's new Bristol directory* (later *Matthews's complete Bristol directory; Matthews's annual Bristol directory*; 1793-1862)
BG	*Bristol Gazette*
BM	*Bristol Mercury*
EFP	*Exeter Flying Post*
FFBJ	*Felix Farley's Bristol Journal*
Gerhold	Dorian Gerhold, *Carriers and coachmasters: trade and travel before the turnpikes* (2005)
Harris	Stanley Harris, *The coaching age* (1885)
NLW	National Library of Wales
PP	*Parliamentary Papers*
POST	Document reference in Royal Mail Archive
RLD	*Robson's London directory* (1832-9)
RO	Record Office or History Centre
TNA	The National Archives
Webb 1	William A. Webb, *The early years of stage coaching on the Bath road* (1922) [part 1]
Webb 2	William A. Webb, *Stage coaching on the Bath road* (c.1931) [part 2], typescript at Wiltshire Heritage Museum

1

Introduction

FOR A CENTURY or so before the railways stage coaches were
the country's main form of fast transport, rivalled only by the
more expensive post-chaises. They carried not just passengers but
also information in various forms – letters, parcels and London
newspapers. The stage coach system and the quality of the services
it provided were therefore highly important to social, economic and
political life. This book seeks to cast light on that system and how
it developed by examining one of England's most important coach
routes, Bristol to London, and one of its largest coach networks.

In 1700 Bristol was England's second city, with about 20,000
inhabitants, and was a major centre of both overseas and domestic trade,
as well as serving a wide area of England and Wales as a financial centre
and a cultural centre.[1] The Bristol-London route passed through Bath, the
country's most important spa and leisure town, which grew spectacularly
in the eighteenth century. Although Bristol lost ground relative to the
rising industrial cities of the Midlands and North in the eighteenth
and nineteenth centuries, it continued to grow strongly, reaching a
population of 125,000 in 1841.[2] Its coach network was correspondingly
large. It had more services to London in the 1830s than anywhere except
Birmingham, Brighton and a few places within 15 miles of the capital.
Its network of regional and local services was then outranked only by
those of Birmingham and Manchester.[3] Bristol therefore provides a good
vantage point for examining how the stage coach system developed.

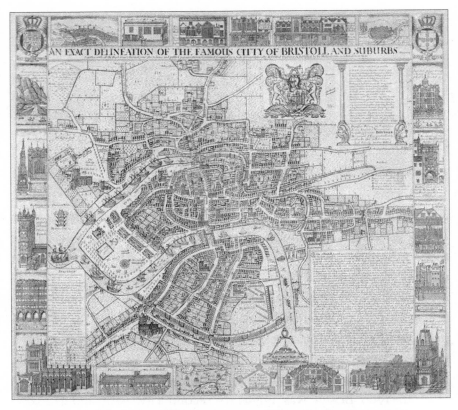

1 An exact delineation of the famous citty of Bristoll and suburbs, *by James Millerd, 1673. Bristol's main coaching inns were around the crossroads mid-way between the two bridges.*

There is already much written about stage coaches. These writings tend to follow a similar form: caricaturing only slightly, there is first the binding mud of the early stage coach period, with coaches apparently able to operate only in summer; then some speeding up as turnpikes spread in the eighteenth century and the transformation seemingly brought about by the mail coach in the 1780s; followed by a story of continuous acceleration and growth leading to the golden age of the 1820s and 1830s, with numerous anecdotes of coaching life in that period; and finally the decline of stage coaching as railways spread.[4] A good impression is usually given of what stage coaching was like in those final decades before railways, and what it was like then to be a coach passenger.

But something is missing. That something is an explanation of how stage coaching developed over nearly two centuries in order to become the much-admired system of the 1820s and 1830s, and exactly when, how and why the various changes took place. How different, for example, was stage coaching in the 1830s from that in the 1780s or the 1750s? Was there just a long, gradual improvement in coach services, or was change concentrated in short periods, and if so why? How did the trade-off between greater speed and the higher cost of going faster operate in different periods? Did coachmasters simply respond to improved roads, or were there other influences? What changes were there in the vehicles used, and in the way horses and teams were organised, and why? To understand these matters, we need to know among other things how coach speeds and fares

2 *The quays of Bristol, looking from Canon's Marsh towards St Stephen's Church, c.1870.*

changed over time – something in which both coachmasters and passengers were keenly interested.

There are good reasons for the gaps in our knowledge. Very few business records survive for stage coaches, and when they do they tend to be sharing accounts, covering income and the small proportion of costs which proprietors bore jointly, rather than the much more significant accounts covering the partners' individual expenses in providing horses. Plenty of information exists for mail coaches,[5] but again the contractors' own records have not survived, and the evidence is patchy for speeds and fares. One of the best articles on stage coaches, dealing with the coach network in south Hampshire, concluded that the most useful source was trade directories, which list the services from each town.[6] These can indeed, when handled carefully, indicate how and when the coach network grew, but they still provide limited information about the services themselves, rarely indicating speeds or fares.

The most important source for this book has been newspaper advertisements, supplemented by directories and other records. These have never before been thoroughly exploited for a particular coach route or network over a long period.[7] Coachmasters did not always see much point in advertising in newspapers, especially in the earlier period, and above all at times when there was nothing new to offer. Even when they did advertise, they were often maddeningly vague: frequently only departure times were given, or they added the arrival time without mentioning the fare, or vice versa. Often they proclaimed a reduction in fares without specifying either the new fare or the old one, or said 'Fares as usual'. Advertisements are least informative about timings before the 1770s (partly because timings then were usually given in days rather than hours), and least informative about fares in the nineteenth century, and they are relatively rare around 1800 (for reasons which will become clear).

ASTONISHINGLY CHEAP AND EXPEDITIOUS TRAVELLING TO LONDON.

BUSH COACH OFFICE, Corn-Street, Bristol.

THE AGE, a FOUR-INSIDE Post COACH, leaves the above Office every Afternoon (except Sunday) at Half past Two.—Fares: Inside, only £1 4s.—Outside, 12s.

LONDON ROYAL MAIL every Afternoon at a Quarter past Five.—Inside, £1 18s.—Outside, 18s

Parcels under 12 lbs. weight, 1s. each.—Heavy Luggage, 1d. per lb.

Bristol, Nov. 7, 1833.   TOWNSEND & SON.

WHITE LION & WHITE HART COACH OFFICES, *BROAD-STREET.*

Observe—LONDON COACH FARES GREATLY REDUCED!!

No Fees to Coachmen or Guards.

EMERALD (in 13 hours) 7 morn. £2. 2s. inside; 18s. out. MONARCH (in 14 hours) ¼ past 5 evening, £1. 18s. inside; 14s. out.

Celebrated fast Day Coach

REGULATOR, ½ past 7 morning, £1. 15s. inside; 15s. out.

NIGHT REGULATOR, 4 afternoon, £1. 10s. inside; 12s. out.

ROYAL MAILS and well appointed STAGE COACHES to all parts of the Kingdom, daily.

J. NIBLETT, Proprietor.

3 Advertisements for London coaches in 1833. (Bristol Gazette, 14 November 1833.)

268

MAIL AND STAGE COACH OFFICE.

BUSH, Corn-street.—John Townsend & Co.

ABERGAVENNY—(Telegraph) Mon. Wed. & Fri. at 10 morn.
arrives at Abergavenny at 5 in the even. where it meets the Brecon Mail.

BATH—12 times a day.

BIRMINGHAM—(Mail) every evening at 7 ; comes in every
morning at 6.—Through Newport, Glocester, Tewkesbury, Worcester,
Droitwich and Bromsgrove ; arrives at Birmingham at ¼ past 6 morn.

BIRMINGHAM——(Duke of Wellington) every morning at 6,
same route as the Mail ; arrives at Birmingham at 6 in the evening.

BRIGHTON—Mon. Wed. and Friday, at quarter before 7 morn.
—through Salisbury, Southampton, Chichester, Arundel, Worthing, &c.

EXETER—(The Times) In 11 hours, every morning, at 8—
through Langford, Cross, Bridgewater, Taunton, Wellington, White Ball,
and Collumpton ; arrives at the New London Inn, Exeter, at 7 evening.

GOSPORT—every Tuesday, Thursday, and Saturday morning
at 7—through Bath, Wolverton, Beckington, Warminster, Heytesbury,
Codford, Sarum, White Parish, Southampton, and Titchfield ; and arrives
at Gosport at 7 in the evening.

LEICESTER & NOTTINGHAM—every Tues. Thurs. and
Saturday morn. at 7—through Glocester, Cheltenham, LEAMINGTON,
Evesham, Alcester, Stratford, Warwick, Coventry, Hinkley, & Ealsham.

LONDON—(Mail) every afternoon at 4 ; comes in at 10 morn-
ing—through Bath, Chippenham, Calne, Marlborough, Newbury, and
Reading, and arrives at Glocester Coffee-house, Piccadilly, at 6, and the
Swan with Two Necks, Lad Lane, London, at ½ past 6 morning.

LONDON—(Regent) every day at 1 ; same rout as the Mail ;
and arrives at the same Inns in London, at ½ past 7 morning.

MILFORD and Waterford—(Mail) every morning at ¼ past 10.
through Newport, Cardiff, Cowbridge, Neath, Swansea, Pontardulais,
Llanon, Carmarthen, St. Clare's, Tavern Spite, Cold Blow, Narbarth, and
Haverfordwest, to Milford at 9 next morning, and at 11 the Packet sails
for Waterford.

NEW PASSAGE—Every Mon. Wednes. and Frid. morn. at 7 ;
and Sun. Tues. Thurs. and Sat. morning at 8 ; returns evenings at 5.

OXFORD—(Mail) every morning at 7 ; comes in at 5 evening.
—through Bath, Petty France, Dedmartin, Knockdown, Tetbury,
Cirencester, Fairford, Lechlale, Farringdon, and Kingston Inn ; arrives at
the Angel Inn, Oxford, at 9 in the evening.

PORTSMOUTH (Mail) every afternoon at 4 ; comes in at ¼ past
9 morning.—Same route as the Gosport Stage above.

SOUTHAMPTON—(Rocket Post) every morning, except Sunday at 7—through Bath, Woolverton, Beckington, Warminster, Haytes-
bury, Codford, Sarum, &c. ; arrives at Southampton at 4 afternoon.

SWANSEA—(Cambrian)—every Mon. Wed. and Friday, at 7
morning ; arrives in Swansea at 10 in the evening.

WEYMOUTH—every Tues. Thurs. and Sat. morn. at 7,—
thro' Bath, Frome, Upton, Bruton, Wincanton, Sherborne and Dorchester.

4 *The first part of the coach list in* Matthews's annual Bristol directory *of 1824. The
list reflected the information innkeepers chose to provide, and John Townsend was
unusual in providing arrival times.*

Bristol may well be the main exception here, together with Exeter. For most of the period from the 1770s onwards, Bristol coachmasters erratically but reasonably often provided departure and arrival times or the number of hours and inside and outside fares, sometimes with other helpful information, such as the type of vehicle, the route and the names and locations of proprietors. 324 advertisements or other sources giving journey times or fares or both have been identified for Bristol-London services from 1658 to 1842 (all but eight from 1750 onwards) and 573 for regional or local services from Bristol from 1744 to 1846. There is also, uniquely outside London, a good set of annual or (at first) near-annual directories for Bristol from 1793 onwards, which are particularly informative in the 1820s and 1830s, sometimes giving departure and arrival times (Fig. 4).[8] In addition, some valuable information is available from lawsuits in the courts of Chancery and Exchequer, in a few cases shedding light on the internal workings of firms. Travellers' diaries and the records of the Post Office are helpful too.

Together these make it possible to follow the story continuously in detail and to see what changed and when. We can observe the long transformation of the pioneering services of the seventeenth century, proceeding at around four miles per hour and taking two or three days between Bristol and London, into the coaches of the 1830s, some proceeding at just over ten miles per hour and taking only 12 hours. In the process it becomes clear that much of the established story of stage coaching, and especially the established chronology, is incorrect. Indeed the heroic age of stage coaching was not the 1820s and 1830s at all. The story of Bristol's coaches provides the key to understanding the stage coach system as a whole.

5 *Passengers inside a night coach, drawn by George Woodward, 1796.*

How to be a coachmaster

FIG. 5 SHOWS passengers asleep in a night coach in 1796, blissfully unaware that their coachman is asleep too. If we could read their thoughts in the moments when they were jolted awake, we would probably find them worrying about four things. Is the coachman driving safely? How much longer will the tedious journey take? Was the high cost of the journey worthwhile? And is there any way of becoming more comfortable? The coachmaster's success or failure depended on meeting their requirements at the least possible cost to himself, and especially on how he balanced speed against cheapness. That in turn determined how he organised his horses.

The horse dominated the economics and operation of stage coaches. Fig. 6 shows the breakdown of a coachmaster's costs in 1760-1. The single most important cost was horse provender – 66% in this example. Every other cost was minor. Costs which varied directly in proportion to the number of horses kept totalled 81%.[9] Later, when tolls had increased and heavy taxes had been imposed, horse provender's proportion declined, but it always remained by far the largest cost.[10]

6 *Costs of running John Hanforth's London to Manchester and Leeds machines in 1760-1, showing the dominance of provender costs. The only costs not directly proportional to the number of horses kept were tolls, coaches and harness and coachmen and postilions. (Source: TNA, E 134/8GeoIII/East10.)*

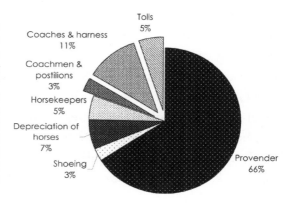

The physical capability of the horse was an important factor. If time was no object, the best speed for a horse drawing a vehicle – that is, the speed at which its labour produced the greatest result in terms of tons moved and miles covered – was about two miles per hour, and that was the speed at which carriers of goods travelled right up to the arrival of railways.[11] At the other extreme, once the horse's speed rises to about 11 miles per hour it can do little more than move its own body, with hardly any power left to draw anything.[12] Between those extremes, speed over two miles per hour could be achieved by incurring extra cost: through carrying smaller loads, through a larger stock of horses working fewer hours per week (usually in shorter stages) or simply through wearing out the horses sooner. The fact that greater speed resulted in extra cost and therefore higher fares, unless there was an external change such as better roads, underlies the entire story of stage coaching. Passengers were keen on greater speed, but not at any price, and the coachmaster therefore had to judge what speed they were willing to pay for.

In the short term, provender prices were the main influence on fares, and dearer provender meant either higher fares or reduced speeds. In the longer term, better roads, horses and vehicles made it possible to increase coach speeds without a corresponding increase in fares, and they did so mainly through their impact on the horse's labour and therefore on the number of horses which needed to be kept for a given speed.

The impact of the horse on stage coaching was more extensive still. Given the cost of feeding horses, teams and stages had to be organised so as to obtain the maximum possible work from them. Also, horses had to be fed whether they were working or not, and a completely idle horse still requires about half as much feed as one in heavy work,[13] so extra horses could not be kept just in case they might be needed. Therefore the frequency of service could be varied only if the proprietor bought or sold horses, and loss was incurred by doing so.[14] On the other hand, once horses were bought or sold and the frequency of service altered, total costs changed almost in proportion, though in the case of the Bristol to London road, where almost all services from the 1770s were daily or daily except Sunday, this was a drastic step. The importance of provender costs and other costs proportional to the number of horses, and the fact that overheads were minimal, meant that there was only a small difference between direct operating costs and total costs, and so the scope for competitive price reductions was limited, except when temporarily reducing fares below cost in order to force a competitor off the road.[15]

Furthermore, good judgment was needed in purchasing horses and obtaining provender at the best price, as well as in looking after the horses, and it was advisable for individual coachmasters to make those decisions themselves rather than being subject to the potentially imprudent decisions of others. And yet it was extremely demanding for one person to manage a frequent service over a long route. This resulted in the distinctive organisation of stage coaching, which can be glimpsed in the 1670s on some of the longest routes but seems to have been universal by the 1760s.[16] The usual arrangement was a partnership spread out along the route, with individual coachmasters 'horsing' the coach within their own 'district' of the road (usually a stage or two).[17] Each paid separately for the horses, horse provender and horsekeepers used within his district, while the partnership as a whole paid the other costs, such as vehicles, drivers, guards (if any) and turnpike tolls. Receipts left after those joint payments had been made were divided among the partners in proportion to the work done by each one's horses, expressed as a number of miles. This system provided the greatest possible financial independence and devolution of management to the local level which was consistent with maintaining a long-distance service.

Within his own district, therefore, the coachmaster needed to be skilful in purchasing horse provender, as well as being a good judge of horses and a diligent supervisor of his employees in the stables and on the road. Probably in few industries was slack management punished so quickly. The coachmasters had to make other decisions about the horses jointly, relating to the size of teams, the stages they were to run and the time they were to be allowed to do so. Other decisions also had to be made jointly: the type of vehicle, the frequency and departure times of services, the level of fares, whether guards were to be used, how the coach should be advertised and how competitors (especially any new ones) were to be responded to. Sometimes coachmasters were responding to external changes, such as improved roads or changes in provender prices, whereas sometimes they were themselves the agents of change, for example by putting on a new type of vehicle, challenging competitors with unusually fast or unusually cheap services or responding aggressively towards new competitors.

Success depended mainly on buying good horses, purchasing provender at reasonable prices, supervising men and horses diligently, striking the right balance between speed and cost, and filling the coach. Conversely, disaster could result from a sharp rise in provender prices not matched by higher fares, ill-judged purchases of provender and horses, keeping too many horses, disease among the horses, general slackness in management causing costs to rise and standards of service to decline, failure to attract enough passengers and aggressive price reductions by oneself or competitors.

All of these could affect the fate of individual coachmasters, but in the long term the decisions about speed and cost were especially important, changing over time the character of the coach trade as a whole. In essence, the story of stage coaching is about coachmasters achieving greater speed without significantly increased cost, resulting in a large increase in the number and range of services and thereby serving their passengers and a newly-industrialising country better and better. That is what this book is about.

Notes

1   W.E. Minchinton, 'Bristol: metropolis of the west in the eighteenth century', *Transactions of the Royal Historical Society*, 5th series, vol. 4 (1954), pp. 69-89; David Hussey, *Coastal and river trade in pre-industrial England: Bristol and its region 1680-1730* (2000).
2   *Census of Great Britain, 1851*, PP 1852-53 (1631), pp. cxxvi.
3   RLD 1836, pp. 1-43.
4   The best of this genre is Stella Margetson, *Journey by stages* (1967). Other useful works are Edmund Vale, *The mail-coach men of the eighteenth century* (1960); John Copeland, *Roads and their traffic 1750-1850* (1968); Brian Austen, *British mail-coach services 1784-1850* (1986). Of earlier works, the best are Stanley Harris, *The coaching age* (1885); Charles G. Harper, *Stage-coach and mail in days of yore* (2 vols., 1903).
5   In the Royal Mail Archive and among the *Parliamentary Papers*.
6   M.J. Freeman, 'The stage-coach system of South Hampshire, 1775-1851', *Journal of Historical Geography*, vol. 1 (1975), pp. 259-81. See also John H. Chandler, 'Stagecoach operation through Wiltshire', South Wiltshire Industrial Archaeology Society, Historical Monograph 8 (1980).
7   William C.A. Blew, *Brighton and its coaches: a history of the London and Brighton road* (1894) follows this approach, but not very revealingly. The same applies to

Webb 1 and Webb 2.

8   W. Matthews, *Matthews's new Bristol directory* (1793 ff). There are also Bristol directories for 1785, 1787 and 1792.

9   Based on TNA, E 134/8GeoIII/Easter 10. The figures in Fig. 6 differ from those in Theo Barker and Dorian Gerhold, *The rise and rise of road transport, 1700-1990* (1993), p. 17, because (i) a notional 3% is included for shoeing of horses and (ii) there is assumed to be only one coachman and one postilion.

10   See below, p. 173.

11   Dorian Gerhold, *Road transport before the railways* (1993), pp. 57, 59, 188-9, 194-6.

12   *Report from Select Committee on steam carriages*, PP 1831 (324), p. 56; R.H. Thurston, *The animal as a machine and a prime motor* (1894), p. 52.

13   W.A. Henry and F.B. Morrison, *Feeds and feeding: a handbook for the student and stockman* (1917), p. 671.

14   Gerhold, *Road transport*, pp. 80, 83.

15   *Ibid.*, p. 150.

16   Gerhold, p. 119; below, pp. 60-2.

17   The word 'partnership' is used here for convenience, but in legal terms these were not partnerships, as the coachmasters were not responsible for each other's debts.

2

The first century of stage coaching

If any be defirous to go to Bath or Briftol, let them repair to the Sign of the Coach and four Horfes at the lower end of Queens ftreet, and there they may be furnifhed every Munday and Thurfday with a Coach and Horfes by Roger Bulbank, and Henry Folbig.

7 *The first advertisement for a Bristol to London stage coach, 1657.* (Publick Adviser, *26 May 1657.*)

The pioneers

STAGE COACHES BETWEEN Bristol and London are first recorded in May 1657. They ran every Monday and Thursday from the appropriately-named Coach and Four Horses, Queens Street, London, under the ownership of Roger Bulbank and Henry Folbig (Fig. 7). Another coach, on Thursdays from the Red Lion, Fleet Street, was advertised in June 1657 by Onesiphorus Tapp of Marlborough, though the following year he described it as a London to Marlborough coach instead. In May 1658 there were coaches from the George without Aldersgate on Mondays and Thursdays, 'with good coaches, and fresh horses in the roads', and in August 1658 Edmond Poynes' coaches from inns at or near Charing Cross 'every Monday and Thursday throughout the year'. The Monday and Thursday departures in all these cases suggest three-day journeys (Monday-Wednesday and Thursday-Saturday, with no travel on Sunday), and therefore just 40 miles a day. All of these are likely to have passed through Bath, but somewhat later there is the first reference to a Bath coach, in 1667, running three times a week at 5 am, also taking three days.[1]

The first record of a Bristol stage coach is only a few years after the founding in April 1653 of what was almost certainly the first stage coach changing horses *en route* – that from London to York. Changing horses *en route* (the 'fresh horses in the roads' of 1658) was fundamental, as it made it possible to work them faster. The innovation spread quickly, to 20 separate destinations by the end of the 1650s. Bristol's first recorded coach is later than those of Exeter, Worcester, Lincoln, Cambridge, Southampton and Salisbury, but some of these are known only from chance references in diaries, and it is conceivable that there was an earlier Bristol coach which is not recorded.[2]

Stage coaches were an addition to travellers' existing options, which ranged from fast and expensive to slow and cheap. At one extreme were post-horses, by which up to about seven miles per hour could be achieved and 60 to 70 miles per day, for 3.3 pence per mile. Using one's own horses was slower, because the horses were not changed and became tired, but it was also cheaper; travellers typically covered about 40-47 miles per day, at about four miles per hour. Using one's own carriage was slower still unless changes of team could be arranged – the same four miles per hour but only about 30 to 36 miles per day. Apart from walking, travel by carrier's waggon was the cheapest and slowest option: about 20 to 25 miles per day at two miles per hour, for about 1.0 pence per mile. A few waggons were called coach-waggons or waggon-coaches, and evidently catered chiefly for passengers, but they could be little faster than ordinary waggons because they did not change their teams and were still heavy vehicles with large loads. They seem to have covered more miles per day than ordinary waggons (about 25 to 33), perhaps reflecting somewhat lighter loads, and to have been a little more expensive.[3]

How the stage coach differed from the waggon-coach was that it changed its horses, at least in summer, and was a lighter vehicle carrying smaller loads. Therefore it could travel faster, but at higher cost: a travelling speed of about 4.3 miles per hour in summer compared with about two miles per hour, and a fare of about 2.3 pence per mile compared with about 1.4 for waggon-coaches.[4] It provided journeys which could be almost as quick as those by post-horse at less cost and with somewhat greater ease and probably less risk, though with the disadvantages of fixed times and having to travel in close proximity to strangers – a novel experience in the seventeenth century.

8 David Loggan's engraving of a coach in 1675. This may well have been a stage coach rather than a private one, but there was probably little difference in this period anyway. The winter arrangement is shown, with a team of six and a postilion driving the leading horses.

Despite the enduring myth that the first stage coaches ran only in summer, there is abundant evidence on other routes, especially from advertisements and diaries, that in fact they ran throughout the year, though at lower speeds and with larger teams in winter. In one case they kept to the daily timetable even during heavy snow.[5] There is no direct evidence from the Bristol road until 1693,[6] but it is highly unlikely that the Bristol coaches were different in this respect, as buying and selling large numbers of coach horses twice a year would have been difficult and expensive. Edmond Poynes indicated his intention in 1658 to run 'throughout the year'.

Something is known about two of the earliest Bristol coachmasters. Henry Folbig was a London hackney coachman, at least in 1662, and this was common among the pioneers, who had evidently spotted an opportunity to extend their trade beyond the London area. Onesiphorus Tapp, less typically, was postmaster at Marlborough, and perhaps intended to use his coach to carry letters on his own account, as he was doing (illegally) in 1670. Apparently none of the Bristol coachmasters of 1657-8 were still involved in coaching by 1672. John Cressett, who was then seeking to have the stage coaches suppressed as a nuisance, argued that the coachmasters were largely licensed London hackney coachmen, carriers or innkeepers, and summed up the Bristol ones as follows: 'Bristol, Bath, Newberry, by Widdow Tooby, who is licensed [in London], Mr. Baldwin that hath an inn at Twiford, Mr. Wells innkeeper at Bath, Mr. Shute a baker and Mr. Drew innkeeper at Newberry'. The Bristol route had quickly developed the pattern which became normal in the eighteenth century: coachmasters based at inns along the route rather than at either destination. William Drew, who was a Bristol-London coachmaster from at least 1663 to 1690, is a particularly interesting example, because he seems to have worked out the best arrangement and changed his trade and location as a result: in 1663 he was a London hackney coachman, but by 1672 he was an innkeeper at Newbury. Not until 1765 was there a proprietor of Bristol-London stage coaches based at Bristol.[7]

After 1667 there are no more advertisements for Bristol or Bath coaches for 40 years, but in 1681 and 1690 there are lists of services which, very unusually, name the proprietors. Bristol appears at first sight to have had numerous separate services, because its coachmasters, unlike almost any others in this period, tended to use several different London inns for the same services, which were therefore repeated in the lists for each of those inns. In fact there were just two firms. One belonged in 1681 to William Drew and Mr Saunders (Drew, Saunders and Richard Barnes in 1690) and had three services a week. The other belonged in 1681 to Thomas and William Baldwin, Robert Toobey and John Booth (together with John Baldwin and Hugh Evans but without Thomas Baldwin by 1690). They had two coaches a week, with an additional summer-only service three times a week from a different inn. The latter were the flying coaches, taking two days instead of three. When they began is not known, but the term had been in use on other roads by 1666, and flying coaches (exceeding about 51 miles a day) were almost as old as stage coaching itself. Long-distance services from London were still few in

9 *The White Lion (left) and the White Hart (right) in Broad Street, Bristol. These were Bristol's two main coaching inns in the first half of the eighteenth century and remained important until the end of stage coaching. The two inns together formed Isaac Niblett's headquarters in the nineteenth century. They were demolished in 1866.*

1690, the nearest to Bristol being those of Gloucester and Taunton. Bristol was one of only three places over 100 miles from London with competing services, the others being Worcester and Norwich.[8]

Some of the coachmasters of the 1680s can be identified, such as William Drew at Newbury. One of the Baldwins was probably the Mr Baldwin who was an innkeeper at Twyford in 1672. William Baldwin, innholder of Reading, took the lease of the Crown at Slough (Fig. 10) in 1701, and his son Thomas succeeded him there in 1703 and took over the coaches, describing himself as a citizen and cooper of London. John Booth was a rare example (in this period) of a

10 The Crown Inn, Slough, in 1904. William Baldwin, one of the Bristol-London coachmasters listed in the 1680s, leased the inn in 1701, and it passed to his son, Thomas, in 1703, becoming the headquarters of his coach business. The inn was demolished in 1932.

London innkeeper involved in coaches on several different roads. He ran the Saracen's Head, Friday Street, one of the inns used by the coaches, and in 1681 was also involved, though only briefly, in Exeter and Taunton coaches. Robert Toobey was a coachman at Reading, and was probably the son of the widow Tooby mentioned in 1672 and of the 'Robert Tobey' who was among those petitioning for the incorporation of the London hackney coachmen into a company in 1635. Evidently Toobey junior, like William Drew, found it more convenient to live on the route than in London.[9]

For Robert Toobey there is also a probate inventory of August 1694 listing his possessions. Apart from his clothes (£7), about £20 in cash and £20 of debts owed to him, the coaches and harness (£48) and the horses (£184) were all he possessed. There were five coaches, distinguished by colour – yellow, grey, 'blew bodyed' and 'red bodyed', together with 'the swan coach', varying in value from £6 to £10. The 29 horses were each individually named and valued, at sums mostly from £3 to £10.10s.0d (the exceptions including 'the nagg called Masters Pad').[10] Clearly this firm already followed the practice of each partner separately owning his horses, and in this case his coaches too. Toobey's horses could have been formed into seven teams of four, whereas the firm as a whole needed about 14 such teams in summer,[11] so he may have had a half-share of the firm.

The next information is from 1707, when passengers to and from Bath were warned that Mr Bristoe, Mayor of Reading, who was concerned in the stage coaches,

> does, contrary to the rules of liberty and good manners, oblige all persons to light and lye at the Cardinal's Cap (his present habitation in Redding) under the penalties following: if ladies, to be charg'd with a constable; and if gentlemen, to walk in the dirt, with bag and baggage, to the gaol in the said town.

Presumably the coaches arrived late in the evening and Bristoe used his authority as Mayor to harass passengers who refused to stay at his inn and walked the streets looking for a better one. The accusation was of course indignantly denied in the newspaper's next issue.[12]

From 1709 to 1725 Thomas Baldwin advertised his service frequently (Fig. 11). The pattern was usually a three-day coach twice a week and a two-day flying coach three times a week in summer, as in the 1680s. In 1718 he announced flying coaches six days a week from 28 April, 'which is a performance never done before', but this was not repeated. He had evidently acquired the whole of the firm run by the Baldwins and others in the 1680s, though once he mentions a partner in the flying coaches, John Wilkinson of Bath. In 1724-5 he refers to rival coaches.[13]

Baldwin's last advertisement is from July 1725, and the coachmasters who advertised later the same year seem to have combined the two formerly competing Bristol firms. London

This is to give Notice, that the London, Bath, and Briftol Flying or Two Days Coaches, belonging to Thomas Baldwin, Citizen and Cooper of London, living now at the Crown-Inn at Slough, being the Bowling-Green-houfe, begin Flying on Monday March 15, 1724, and fets out from the Saracen's Head Inn in Friday-ftreet, and the One-Bell Inn, behind the New Church in the Strand, London, and the White Hart Inn in Broad-ftreet, Briftol; and the Bear Inn in Bath, Mondays, Wednefdays and Fridays. Likewife the Three Days Coaches fets out from the Places abovefaid on Mondays and Thurfdays. The Prices of the Flyers to Briftol are 25 s. to Bath 22 s. 6 d. and fo to London, and the Three Days Coaches to Briftol are 22 s. 6 d. and to Bath 20 s. and fo from Briftol and Bath to London. The Coachmens Names for the Flyer are John Baldwin and John Pinfolde, and the Three Days Coachmen are Anthony Somerhill and Robert Tiller: All which Coachmen drive quite through from London to Bath, and back again; which none of the other Stage Coaches do, but changes upon the Road; and Henry Gardener drives from Bath to Briftol; and back again.

11 One of Thomas Baldwin's advertisements, from 1725. It is unusually detailed, even indicating how he organised his coachmen. Baldwin was the only coachmaster from the first century of Bristol stage coaching who advertised frequently. (London Journal, 3 April 1725.)

directories suggest only a single firm from 1726 and that is confirmed by the *Bath and Bristol guide* of 1750. That firm was to dominate stage coaching between Bristol and London until the 1790s. By 1728 it had five partners: John Wilkinson (presumably Baldwin's former partner at Bath), John Pinfold (one of Baldwin's coachmen and later a Bath innkeeper), Henry Pratt (a coachman at Reading), William Dunt and John Eaton. The pattern of services in the early 1750s was similar to that in the 1680s and under Thomas Baldwin, with two-day flying coaches only in summer and three-day coaches throughout the year.[14]

The first regional coaches

THE FIRST HALF of the eighteenth century saw the tentative beginnings of regional services. The Bristol to Oxford coach was probably the first in the country.[15] In 1701 Thomas Eldridge was licensed by the Chancellor of the University of Oxford to provide both coaches and waggons on that route once a week between 25 March and 29 September. In 1735 Eldridge, who lived at Oxford, stated that he had kept the Bath and Bristol stage coach and waggon for 'near forty years', which would take the story back to the 1690s.[16]

Probably there were also local services between Bristol and Bath at an early date, though the first advertisement for these is not until 1727. In 1753 one of them was taking four hours for the 13 miles. Other services appeared only slowly: Bristol to Gloucester in 1721 and Bristol to Salisbury in 1730 (apparently reduced later to Bath to Salisbury). In 1733 the Gloucester coach was run by Nathaniel Underwood of Bristol and John Harris of Gloucester, who was also a Gloucester to London coachmaster. There was also a Bath to Exeter coach by 1716, taking a leisurely three days for 81 miles.[17] There were no other regional or local services from either city until 1759.

Operation

A TYPICAL COACH OF the late seventeenth century is shown in Fig. 8. The coach body was made of wood covered by leather, and was suspended on leather straps from poles at the front and back of the vehicle. Inside was seating for six people, facing forwards and backwards. The coachman sat on a raised seat at the front of the vehicle, on a bar or box between the two poles, and there was a boot or basket at the back for luggage, in which poorer passengers sometimes travelled. There is no evidence of outside passengers on the Bristol road in this period, apart from one reference to a boy travelling on the roof of a Bath coach in 1726. Stage coaches with glass windows existed by 1672, but leather flaps or curtains seem to have been common even in the 1750s, and must have made the coach extremely gloomy when closed.[18]

The horses used were the largest available, and were from 15 to 16 hands high. In 1672 stage coach horses were said to eat twice as much as saddle horses. As on other routes, teams are likely to have been of four horses in summer and six horses in winter. Unlike waggon horses, which drew in single file, stage coach horses were harnessed two abreast. This was possible because coachmen sat on the vehicle, whereas waggoners walked or rode beside their horses, which made drawing in pairs impossible in narrow roads. Stage coaches had smaller teams than waggons – four horses in summer rather than six or seven – and four horses could be driven from the vehicle. This had the advantage that more continuous attention could be given to each horse, ensuring that it did its share of the work and moved at the necessary speed, than if the coachman walked beside the team. The disadvantage was that in winter, with teams of six, a postilion was needed to drive the two leading horses (as shown in Fig. 8).[19]

The pattern of three-day coaches all year supplemented by two-day flying coaches in summer was unique to the Bristol road. Elsewhere there was often a relatively slow service in winter, with the same teams drawing the coach throughout the journey, and a faster one in summer, with at least one change of team each day. What was distinctive about the Bristol route was that the slower coaches continued through the summer, giving passengers a choice between two-day and three-day coaches. This must have reflected the desire by travellers to Bath, who were often old or unwell, for easier journeys, with departures several hours later than the flying coach, even at the cost of an extra day on the road. The same preference was evident much later: two-day coaches between London and Bath, halting overnight, continued until 1825/6, many decades after services stopping overnight had disappeared from other routes. In December 1725 what was probably a four-day coach was started, with 10 am departures instead of 6 am, so that 'we shall, for the future, drive no part of the road by night', but this experiment was quickly abandoned.[20]

Unlike most other coachmasters, the Bristol ones must have needed to purchase new horses for the flying coaches every spring and sell them again in the autumn, which would have been expensive. The flying coaches would have needed eight or nine teams of four horses in summer, requiring 32 to 36 horses. Two three-day coaches a week would have needed five or six teams in summer with 20 to 24 horses, bringing the total to around 56.[21] Whereas some firms elsewhere used the same number of horses per mile covered in winter as in summer (the effect of poorer roads being offset by the lower speed), others kept more horses in winter per mile covered (the higher number of miles per week possible at the lower speed with larger teams being more than offset by the use of six-horse teams), and the latter may have been what occurred in Bristol's case, which would have reduced the number of horses having to be bought and sold.[22]

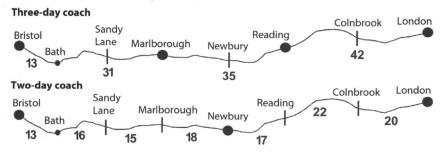

12 Plan of the three-day and two-day coaches between Bristol and London in the late seventeenth and early eighteenth centuries. The large black circles indicate overnight stops; lines indicate stops for breakfast or dinner; numbers indicate the length of the stages in miles for the two-day coach and the length of the day's journey and the separate stage to Bristol for the three-day coach. (Sources: see text)

Fig. 12 shows the route, with the stops for breakfast and dinner. The western part lay across the downs rather than following either of the later routes through Chippenham and Devizes. This had the advantage of being on chalk, which provided a relatively hard and well-drained surface. The disadvantages were steep hills and sometimes extreme cold, snow and strong winds on the downs.

Only one record survives of a journey in the three-day coach, from August 1696. It was from London to Bath only, with overnight stops at Reading and Marlborough, dividing the route into 42, 35 and 31 miles. Adding the Bath

13 *Sandy Lane, where both the two-day and three-day coaches dined between Bath and Marlborough. The further building was the Bear Inn, apparently of late seventeenth-century date. Bell Farm on the right probably incorporates much of the former Bell Inn.*

to Bristol road raises the distance on the last day to 44 miles. This was slow travelling for summer, when about 46 to 51 miles (two stages of 20-25 miles) was more typical, but the passengers in these coaches were opting for easy journeys with short days. By analogy with better-documented services elsewhere, there would have been one change of team each day, where the passengers dined. If the practice elsewhere was followed, there was a different arrangement in winter, with the teams (of six horses) not changed and the coaches running slower, though still completing their journeys in three days. Miles per day elsewhere in winter were typically 29 to 36, with anything more apparently requiring a change of team, so a change of team would have been needed on the first day out of London, and also a separate team between Bath and Bristol, where there was probably sufficient custom to keep it fully employed on extra trips between the two cities.[23]

The flying coaches, like those elsewhere, travelled no faster than ordinary coaches. The extra miles per day were covered instead by means of an extra change of team and longer hours on the road. Whereas more miles per hour would have resulted in extra cost, this was merely a reorganisation of the work of the teams, each of which could continue to cover the same number of miles per week, so there was little or no extra cost. Four records are available indicating the stops made by the flying coach – two in works of fiction (1700 and 1717), one in a diary (1718) and one in a traveller's description (1752).[24] These show that, just like on other routes, there was strong continuity in the way teams and stages were organised. The only change in lodging and eating places was that by 1717 Colnbrook had been replaced by Slough, four miles further from London, clearly because Thomas Baldwin was innkeeper there. In each case the overnight stop was at Newbury, and each day was divided into three parts by breakfast and dinner. These refreshment stops almost certainly indicate where the teams were changed. There could have been a simple arrangement, with two 61-mile days broken down into 20-mile stages, but instead the arrangement was more complicated, probably because of the importance of Bath. Many of the stages were much less than the usual 20-25 miles of coaches in summer, and Bath to Bristol apparently formed a separate fourth stage. One team could have handled all services there, covering the 13 miles down one day and up the next. In *A step to the Bath* of 1700, Ned Ward noted that, after the party's arrival at Bath, 'our merchant took his leave of us, in a fresh coach for Bristol'.[25] Short stages did not of course mean less work for the horses; they would simply have covered more stages per week.

There is no evidence of stage coaches anywhere increasing their travelling speed (i.e. their miles per hour when actually moving) until the 1750s, though some began to cover more miles per day through longer hours on the road. The few indications of speeds on the Bristol route up to 1755 are consistent with the national evidence. For the three-day coach, the timing between Bristol and Bath in December 1725 suggests 3.5 miles per hour and the times for the whole route in a guide of 1750 (10 am to 10 pm), assuming the same times each day, suggest 3.7 miles per hour, comparable with the average of 3.4

miles per hour in winter indicated by the evidence nationwide. For
the two-day coach in summer, guides of 1753 and 1755 state that
they set off at 2 am and reached their destination between 5 and 6
pm. Again assuming the same times on both days, that indicates 4.4
miles per hour, while the timing between Bristol and Bath in March
1733 suggests 4.7 miles per hour. This was close to the nationwide
average of 4.3 miles per hour, which seems to have been the speed at
which, for a relatively light vehicle such as a coach, conveyance was
cheapest. The one example of an actual journey, from summer 1752,
is 4.3 miles per hour between Marlborough and Sandy Lane and only
3.3 between Sandy Lane and Bath, but too much should not be made
of a single journey. These are all travelling speeds, not counting the
time taken by passengers eating and horses being changed; overall
speeds were about 3.8 and 3.1 miles per hour in summer and winter
respectively as opposed to travelling speeds of 4.3 and 3.4. By analogy
with services elsewhere, the Bristol coaches would have been highly
reliable in reaching their destinations within the two or three days
intended, even if hours on the road were sometimes lengthened
by breakdowns, accidents or bad roads.[26] However, this reliability
indicated a determination to keep to the scheduled times rather than
that the roads were satisfactory. On the contrary, the slow speeds
and the need to use six horses in winter indicate the poor state of the
roads.

Fares were reasonably stable, reflecting the absence of any
major fluctuations in provender prices in this period. From 1658
to 1753 all those recorded between Bristol and London were from
20s. to 25s. (1.97d to 2.46d per mile), compared with the national
average of about 2.34d per mile. As flying coaches cost no more to
run than ordinary ones, firms elsewhere usually charged the same
fares throughout the year for ordinary and flying coaches, but on
the Bristol road, uniquely, both were running at the same time and
the proprietors evidently thought a higher charge could be made for

the service which arrived sooner. The difference was not large – 25s. compared with 22s.6d in 1725 and 23s. compared with 21s. in 1752.[27]

Thomas Baldwin's advertisements indicate how he organised his coachmen (Fig. 11). Coachmen seem normally to have driven about 40 or 50 miles up and down on alternate days, but in April 1725 John Baldwin (presumably a relation) and John Pinfold were driving the flyers all the way between London and Bath and Anthony Summerhill and Robert Tiller were doing the same with the three-day coaches; Henry Gardener drove all the coaches between Bath and Bristol, which confirms that the Bristol leg was organised separately. The miles per week were unequal, but that was because a day's journey was different in each case. Pinfold and John Baldwin must have been on the road twelve hours a day six days a week in all weathers. Thomas Baldwin emphasised that he was the only coachmaster whose coachmen all went through from London to Bath, with the unstated benefit that passengers had to tip only one coachman instead of several.[28]

Passengers

L ONG-DISTANCE STAGE COACH passengers in the seventeenth and early eighteenth centuries were predominantly from the gentry and what may be called the 'middling sort', such as merchants, lawyers and clergymen. There is some evidence that more women than men used them, and they certainly increased the opportunities for well-to-do women to travel on their own. The very rich generally made their own transport arrangements and coach fares were too high for poorer people.[29] The Bristol coaches would have carried merchants, but they also conveyed gentry from along the route and from south Wales and people we would regard as leisure travellers making their way to Bath.

Diarists and other writers in this period tended to be more informative about their coach journeys than later ones were, because

14 Hogarth's engraving of a stage coach in an inn yard in 1747. Note the passengers in a basket at the back and perched precariously on the roof.

journeys were longer and coach travel was more unusual than it later became. The earliest account is a fictional one by Ned Ward, in *A step to the Bath* of 1700.[30] He 'gave earnest for a place' (usually half the fare) two days before, and went to stay at the coach's London inn, the Saracen's Head, Friday Street, the previous night. The other passengers were two gentlewomen, their maidservant and a merchant of Bristol. They 'were call'd upon to board our leathern-conveniency, and were pen'd up like the beasts in the Ark'. Breakfast was taken at Colnbrook, dinner at Reading and there was a stop at the Bell, Theale, 'noted for bottle-ale and plumb-cakes'. Before dinner there was 'but very indifferent company, for our masculine traveller, the married lady, and Mrs. Betty the chamber-maid, had a long game at noddy', but the party was more sociable thereafter: 'the ladies oblig'd us with several songs, which they perform'd with an excellent voice, and good judgment'.

At Newbury the party had supper and went to bed soon after because of the early start on the following day. On the rocky descent into Marlborough the coach was 'so damnably jolted' that the bottle in the merchant's pocket broke. Breakfast was at Marlborough and dinner at the Bear in Sandy Lane. On the downs they received information about a party of light horses nearby and feared highwaymen, but it proved to be a false alarm. After Sandy Lane the coach proceeded 'with a great deal of difficulty; for the road was so rocky, unlevel, and narrow in some places, that I am perswaded the Alps are to be passed with less danger'. Eventually 'we agreed to [a]light rather than endure it any longer', but by then the coach was nearly at Bath. The party then ate at the White Hart 'after our tedious mortifying-journey', and the merchant departed in a different coach for Bristol.

The anonymous author of a poem of 1717 set out from the Saracen's Head in London before the sun had cleared the morning mist. On the first day, spicy cakes and ale were consumed at Turnham Green, wine at Brentford, breakfast at Slough, a cold dinner with wine and brandy (eaten hurriedly) at Reading and a delicious supper at Newbury. The coach overturned on Hounslow Heath, causing indignity rather than injury. On the rough road leading to Marlborough which had troubled Ned Ward the coach axle broke and the passengers were flung all over the coach, but they rode into Marlborough and waited at an inn until the coach had been repaired. The rest of the journey was uneventful, and they were able to admire the view from the downs towards Devizes.[31]

Thomas Smith of Shaw House near Melksham recorded several stage coach journeys in his diary. In June 1718 he went to Sandy Lane 'and had a place in the two days coach in which I came to Newbury after nine, having but indifferent company, viz sick and unhealthy people, so after eating privately by my selfe retir'd to rest'. Sick people must have been a particular hazard in coaches serving Bath. On the next day the coach set off early, dined at Slough and reached London at about 8. The return journey later in June was 'in company with five persons unknown to me'. The coach arrived at Newbury 'through much heat and dust about nine'. It reached Sandy Lane the following day at 11 am, and Smith again mentions 'the fatigue of heat and dust'. In May 1721 he used the two-day coach again, reaching London at about 9 pm on the second day and returning a few days later. He 'fortun'd to have pretty agreeable company in both journeys'.[32]

The final account is by 'an Irish gentleman' in 1752. He and his three companions stayed overnight at the coach's inn, the One Bell in The Strand. They went to bed early, 'as we were told we must be up at two o'clock, at which hour the chamber-maid aroused us'. Three travelled inside and one on the coachman's box. They brought with them a bottle of white wine and a twopenny bun. The other three passengers, all women, were picked up at what was evidently their own house:

> I heard one of them cry out in a peevish, affected tone, "Lord, how many have you got in the coach?" to which I replied, putting my head out of the window, that we would endeavour to make room for the ladies. She made no answer but that it did not signify complaining, but that she was a fool for not taking another place in the coach. The ladies placed themselves with the profoundest silence, not even making an answer to the many compliments I made them. ... As we had no conversation to enliven us, most of us took a nod till we arrived at Slough to breakfast.

They went to sleep that night only at 1, and 'I hardly knew I was asleep when I was startled by the screaming of a maid at my chamber door, who bellowed forth the coach was ready', accompanied by the coachman shouting from the yard that he would not wait. Back in the coach, 'we passed the morning very agreeably. Phaedrus sung many witty airs, and took more than uncommon care of pleasing the lady; and he managed his part with so much dexterity that she began to practise over some of her hours'. On the Marlborough Downs the coachman stopped the coach to show them the famous stones called the grey wethers. The ladies shortly afterwards alighted, one saying 'she hoped she never would meet [again] with such a wild Irishman as Phaedrus'. The Irish party reached Marlborough for breakfast at about 9, Sandy Lane about 1, where they dined and had the famous Sandy Lane pudding, and Bath about 7. The Irishman observed that 'I very frequently regretted being so confined in these kind of vehicles, which afford no other prospect than what you have inside, as there is no glass in 'em', indicating that 'glass coaches', with windows instead of a leather flap, were not yet common.[33]

Some conclusions can be drawn as to what stage coach travel was like. Hours were very early and the days were long, especially in the flying coaches. It was vitally important who one's fellow travellers were, and relations within the coach were often frosty, despite (or because of) the close proximity. Passengers were thrown very much on their own resources during the long tedious journey, and responded by means of singing, games and conversation. Since the speed was so slow, passengers sometimes had the option of getting out and walking when bored or restless. There were many trials on the journey, such as rocky stretches of road, breakdowns and heat and dust in summer. The leather flaps must often have been down, preventing views, but travellers nevertheless did sometimes see fine views or interesting objects.

Highwaymen

WEALTHY PEOPLE GATHERED together without means of escape were a tempting prospect for highwaymen. Apart from one reference to a coach carrying a guard in 1738, no others anywhere are recorded doing so until 1764 and none on the Bristol road until 1776. However, if stage coaches had been robbed frequently it is

Robbery on Hounslow Heath, 22 October 1726

John Anstis, Esq, depos'd, That returning from Bath in a coach with a lady, a servant maid and some children, they had come but a little way on Hounslow Heath when he saw a person on horseback making towards them; a little before he came at the coach he made a stop, put on a mask, caused the coach to stop and demanded their money. Mr Anstis told him that he was just come from Bath, where he had spent all his money excepting a guinea and a little silver, which he would readily deliver him, provided he would not fright the lady and the children: That he gave him the silver first and the guinea afterwards, but by reason of the mask he could not swear to the person, though the horse answer'd the description that was given of the horse the prisoner was taken upon.

Source: Proceedings of the Old Bailey *website, t17261207. (The prisoner was acquitted.)*

doubtful that people would have used them, and the national evidence suggests that such robberies were rare: of 258 stage coach journeys recorded in diaries between 1654 and 1750, only one was interrupted by a robbery.[34] 29 robberies, or groups of robberies, of Bristol or Bath coaches are recorded in newspapers (mostly London ones) from 1724 to 1771, and there were a few later ones, or attempted robberies, up to 1792.[35] That was just over one every two years up to 1771. There is no reason to regard that as a complete record, but it is clear that highway robberies were unusual and newsworthy.

About two-thirds of these robberies were by a single highwayman, and the others by either two or three. A highwayman who robbed the Bath coach near Newbury in 1748 was described as 'a lusty man, dress'd

in a white surtout coat, with a cape over his head'. One at Maidenhead
Thicket in 1738 was described as an old man. In all but five cases an
approximate location is given, and these indicate that while eight were
on Hounslow Heath, which was famous for robberies, and three near
Hammersmith, the others were spread out along the route, the earliest
recorded being between Bristol and Bath. In nine cases the sum taken
is stated, and only once did it exceed £25 – the £50 taken from four
coaches robbed on Hounslow Heath in 1765. When the Bath coach
was robbed near Gunnersbury in 1771 the innkeeper at Newbury had
to give the passengers breakfast on credit.

Several robbers lived up to the image of the gentleman
highwayman. The old man at Maidenhead Thicket took 12 guineas
and returned 2 guineas. Another near Maidenhead in 1752 'behaved
very genteely', which description called forth the response that 'It
is but lately that robbing on the highway has been called behaving
genteely'. One who robbed three Bath coaches and an Exeter one
in 1764 'behaved very generously to one of the passengers ... by
returning him five shillings for travelling expenses'. Another, robbing
a Bath coach near Devizes in 1768 'had the generosity to give the
coachman half a guinea to drink his health'. In 1769 a highwayman
suffered for his chivalry when robbing a Bath flying machine with
four passengers near Devizes: 'Their happening to be a lady in the
coach, the highwayman was prevailed on to withdraw his pistol; on
which the three gentlemen instantly jumped out, resolutely declaring
they would not be robbed, and obliged the villain to decamp without
his booty'.[36]

Only in one other case is it recorded that the passengers fought
back. In 1762 a Bristol coach was attacked on its way to London by a
single highwayman,

> who presented a pistol, demanded money, and immediately put his
> head in the coach in order to rifle the passengers; but as soon as his

head was within the coach, a Welshman, an outside passenger, made a blow at him with his stick, and nearly dropt him; but the highwayman at length recovered his horse and rode off, but by the blow lost his hat, rattan, and crape.

On the other hand, when a single highwayman robbed the Bristol and Bath coaches on Hounslow Heath two years later, it was noted that this was despite there being 30 men travelling as inside or outside passengers.[37]

New coach firms

THE LONG-ESTABLISHED BATH and Bristol coach firm began to be challenged in the 1750s. The first new firm, Halliwell & Co, began by providing caravans from Bath to London in 1750, though a price was stated for Bristol to London as well. There were three proprietors in London and one in Bath, suggesting a London origin. Caravans were not common: they seem to have been intended largely for passengers, and to have travelled at not much less than stage coach speeds (in this case the same three days in winter and two in summer) but with lower fares (just 14s. from Bristol to London), perhaps achieved through a lower travelling speed and therefore more hours per day. In 1753 the caravans were replaced by coaches called machines, with just four inside passengers, and by the following year they were known as 'the old Bath machines'. Other new services were the post-chaises on steel springs of John Clark of Newbury and another firm from Bath to London in 1752 (both in two days).[38]

New firms often either disappeared quickly, as the two post-chaise ones did, or merged with an established firm, as Halliwell & Co's did by joining the old-established firm, now under Thomas King and Joseph Glasier of Bath and others, in February 1755. Nevertheless, two more new firms then appeared, and there continued to be two competing firms for almost all of the next 30 years. Timothy Thomas of Bath offered machines on steel springs from Bath to London from February 1755, perhaps prompting the merger just mentioned. In March they were taking 28 hours over two days, indicating an overall speed of 3.9 miles per hour, comparable to the overall speeds of the preceding century. Thomas's appears to have been a one-man business, whereas the next new service, Day & Co's, advertised in September 1756, was run by a partnership of innkeepers from Hounslow to Marlborough (Fig. 15). Their coaches were advertised as a Bath service, but 'There is likewise a machine sets out from Bath [to] Bristol.' Thomas's firm was taken over by King and Glasier in December 1756, but Day & Co's remained separate for 20 years.[39]

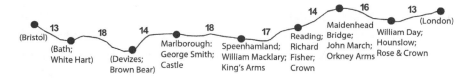

15 Plan of Day & Co's Bath machines in 1756, indicating the proprietors and (by the black circles) where the horses were changed. Although Day & Co advertised them as Bath machines, they also offered machines between Bath and Bristol. By 1768 Day & Co had added proprietors at Devizes and Bath, but otherwise had proprietors at the same places. (Source: London Evening-Post, *19 October 1756.)*

What is most notable about the new firms is their emphasis on Bath and the relative unimportance of Bristol. As its surviving buildings make obvious, Bath grew spectacularly in the eighteenth century: from perhaps 4,000 people in 1700 to 10,000 in 1743 and 33,000 in 1801.[40] Even in 1800 Bath was only about half the size of Bristol, but it had a constantly shifting population of prosperous visitors who needed to be conveyed to and from the city. It was undoubtedly the growth of Bath which gave rise to the setting up of the new coach firms.

Turnpikes and steel springs

BETWEEN THE 1680s and the early 1750s there was a decline in the number of coach services per week between Bristol and London, from eight in summer to five, reflecting the disappearance of one of the two firms. Elsewhere in the country the number of services covering over 120 miles did not decline, but nor did it grow, and the same applied to services covering over 40 miles. Moreover, speeds did not increase and fares did not fall, either on the Bristol-London road or elsewhere in the country. Why was there this period of stagnation, and when and why did it end? Part of the answer is that travel by stage coach was dearer and often slower than on horseback, and not much cheaper than using post-horses. It was faster than using private coaches without changes of teams but had the disadvantages of lack of flexibility and having to share the vehicle with strangers. John Byng complained somewhat later that to be 'box'd up in a stinking coach, dependant on the hours and guidance of others, submitting to miserable associates, and obliged to hear their nonsense, is great wretchedness!', putting in an extreme form a view that was probably shared by many. From the 1740s there was new competition from postmasters and innkeepers hiring out post-chaises and also horses to draw gentlemen's own carriages, the Bath to London road in 1742 being the first where this was done. Stage coaches could have been operated faster, but only at much increased cost, which coachmasters clearly did not believe travellers would be willing to pay.[41]

Improved horses might have changed this situation, and there is some not very firm evidence (discussed later) of coach horses requiring less feed in this period, but if there was such a change it apparently had little impact. Similarly, turnpike trusts should have made a difference. The trusts were new bodies set up to levy tolls on

16 *The dates of the establishment of turnpike trusts on the Bristol road (after B.J. Buchanan). The dotted line is the road through Sandy Lane abandoned by stage coaches in the 1750s. Key: A – 1714, B – 1726.*

road-users and spend the proceeds on maintaining and improving the roads in their charge. On these roads they replaced the old system of maintenance by individual parishes using 'statute labour' (the legal requirement placed on parishioners to work a number of days a year on the roads or provide carts and horses or oxen). The trusts themselves were entitled to draw on statute labour, but tolls provided them with substantial additional resources. The first trust on the Bristol road was established in 1707, at Bath, and by 1744 the main route was fully turnpiked (Fig. 16), with ten separate trusts responsible for it.[42]

The impact of the trusts should have been reflected in greater speed or lower fares, or both, but it was not, either on the Bristol road or elsewhere. The mere establishment of a trust made no difference in itself: it was what the trust did to its roads that mattered. A number of trusts on the Bristol road proved ineffective at first. Sometimes this was because violent opposition to tolls made it difficult or impossible to collect them, as in the case of the Bristol trust. The Kingswood colliers and later farmers destroyed the Bristol trust's gates in 1727, 1731, 1734 and 1749, and the Chippenham trust had gates destroyed in 1727 and 1732. The Bristol riots were ended by a regiment of dragoons, and subsequently opposition seems to have been defused by protecting local interests in turnpike Acts.[43] Another reason for ineffectiveness was that the line of road taken over was a poor one with steep hills. Indeed it was often the worst stretches of road with steep hills which were turnpiked soonest, precisely because they were bad roads needing improvement, as on the Sandy Lane route. Even moderate hills had a severe impact on horses drawing vehicles. A horse uses more than three times as much energy ascending a gradient of 1 in 9.3 at 3.1 miles per hour as in walking the same distance slightly faster on the level, and the cost of drawing a stage coach one mile at ten miles per hour was estimated in 1831 to rise from 33d on the level to 51d at 1 in 20 and 77d at 1 in 10.[44]

17 Beacon Hill, near Heddington, Wiltshire, looking towards Sandy Lane. This stretch of road was turnpiked in 1714, but it fell out of use as a coach route in the 1750s when better routes became available and eventually ceased to be a turnpike road.

Many trusts were slow to make improvements. For example the road from Hungerford to Marlborough, known as Ramsbury Narrow Way, was to have been replaced by a new road at a lower level under an Act of 1726, but the new road was not constructed until after a further Act in 1744, and even then the new road had a steep descent into Marlborough. Many steep hills continued in use, such as Beacon Hill on the Sandy Lane route (Fig. 17). While the trusts towards Bristol tended to have good access to stone, those near London had to rely largely on gravel for road repairs. Neither on the Bristol road nor elsewhere is there any sign of improved methods of road repair, and the method was often just to spread gravel on the road. There is some evidence elsewhere of trusts not repairing their roads in winter, though it is not known if this was common on the Bristol road.[45]

The trusts may have had limited ambitions at first, aiming to bring the standards of bad roads up to those of better ones. Indeed it has been suggested that the main motivation for the early turnpikes was less to improve transport facilities than to shift the burden of road repair from local people in general to road users (hence the hostile response from some of the latter). Limited ambition is suggested by the fact that sometimes only the worst stretches of road were turnpiked at first, the gaps between turnpiked sections were only very slowly filled and at least some of the early trusts were expected to be extinguished once the road had been put into repair. The trusts also at first had limited ability to raise money.

The combined effect of limited resources and ambition can be seen in the activities of the Colnbrook trust, set up in 1727 and one of the few on the Bristol road for which records have survived from

18 *Turnpike gate on the London road at Bath in 1826, with the toll collector looking out for traffic.*

this period. It was responsible for the 13 miles from Cranford Bridge to Maidenhead Bridge. On 4 November 1728 its surveyors were ordered to carry out no new work until the next meeting (4 January) other than employing six men to drain and level the road; mending of any 'holes' was to require the Treasurer's consent. A similar embargo applied from 12 October 1730 to 1 March 1731. The accounts of one of the surveyors were questioned in 1728 because work done at the end of October 'we conceive to be at a very unseasonable time of the year, when some days were so wet'; he was discharged. The strategy until at least 1740 (after which there is a gap in the records) was to repair specific stretches of road as determined by the trustees, and in 1731 there were still parts of the road which had not been repaired at all since the trust was established. Repairs were by means of gravel, except in the towns. Another example is the Chippenham trust, also of 1727. It had to re-erect gates which had been attacked and destroyed in 1727 and 1732, and in October 1736, noting 'the great complaints made against the turnpikes and being willing to ease the country of the burthen thereof', it ordered that its treasurer use the toll income up to 25 December in repairing 'the most founderous parts of the turnpike road' and thereafter use it to pay off the sums

19 Toll gates across the Bath and Bristol road (right) and the Exeter road (left) at Hounslow in about 1864. Tolls continued to be collected here until 1872.

borrowed, apparently amounting to only £400. In this case there was a quickening of activity in 1744, when a new Act added the road from Chippenham to Pickwick. £4,200 was borrowed in 1744-5, many labourers were employed (42 in September 1744) and there are many references to the 'new road' at Derry Hill and elsewhere.[46] The Chippenham and Marlborough examples suggest that it was only in the second half of the 1740s that the trusts began to make significant improvements.

What seems to have been the worst stretch of the Bristol-London road, through Lacock and Sandy Lane, was eventually supplanted by two other routes: a northern route through Calne and Chippenham, turnpiked between 1707 and 1744 (but until 1761 still approaching Bath over Kingsdown), and a southern one through Devizes and Melksham, turnpiked from 1706 to 1753. The main coach service transferred to the northern route in 1750, as did the 'Old Bath Machines' by 1754.[47] On its own that would have had only a minor impact, as it was only a small part of the Bristol-London route as a whole, but there were several developments in the mid-1750s which suggest that road improvements, combined with improved vehicles and perhaps improved horses, were at last starting to have a significant impact.

One was that the three-day coaches disappeared in 1754, in both summer and winter. As regards summer, this could just have reflected a change in passengers' preferences, since two-day coaches had long been available in summer. On the other hand, two-day services in winter, first advertised in February 1754, were an innovation. They left Bristol at 2 am and Bath at 6 am. It is unlikely that at this date they travelled overnight; instead they probably matched the long-established summer speed, which would have meant 14 hour days between Bath and London and 8 pm arrivals each day, and would have been consistent with what happened on several other roads in 1752-5. The announcement of two-day journeys in winter coincided with the introduction of new vehicles: the 'Bristol flying machine' was '(instead of the stage-coach) intirely new, and hangs on steel springs'. It also had slightly higher fares than previously – 26s. In the previous year Halliwell & Co had also adopted new vehicles – four-inside machines. Another change was that Day & Co in 1756 had shorter stages near London than the traditional ones, so that all its stages were from 13 to 18 miles long, and that the same stages were used throughout the year (Figs. 12 and 15). However, any speeding up seems to have been confined to winter.[48]

Both on the Bristol road and elsewhere, the situation changed radically in the early 1760s, as stage coach timings which had endured for a century were suddenly cut drastically, usually to half as many days as before.[49] One-day coaches were established between Bath and London in 1761[50] and Bristol and London in 1763 (Fig. 20), though 'one day' meant departures at 10 or 11 pm and travel throughout the night, and the one-day coaches at first ran only in summer. A reasonable estimate, assuming a journey of about 21 hours, is a travelling speed of about 6.3 miles per hour, or 5.8 overall, a massive increase from 3.8 overall. Two-day coaches continued in summer at first. Almost certainly the two-day coach as well as the one-day coach ran faster than its predecessors, which

BATH, BRISTOL and LONDON, FLYING MACHINE, in One Day,

BEGINS Flying To-morrow, from the Bell Savage on Ludgate-hill, London, and continues going every Sunday, Tuesday, and Thursday Night, at Eleven o'Clock, to Bath; and from Gerard's-Hall Inn, in Basing-Lane, near Bread-Street, every Monday, Wednesday, and Friday Night, at Ten o'Clock, for Bristol, and carries Passengers and Parcels as usual. To Bristol 30s. to Bath 28s.

The two Days Machine as usual, from the Saracen's Head in Friday-Street, the Bell-Savage on Ludgate-Hill, and the One Bell in the Strand; at Six o'Clock. The Fare as usual, to Bath 25 s. to Bristol 27s. Half to be paid at taking the Places, and the other Half at going into the Machine.

All the above Machines call at the White Bear, Black Bear, and the Old White-horse Cellar, Piccadilly. Performed by
T. BANNISTER, London,
W. CLARKE, Reading,
R. HOLLIWELL, Newbury,
T. HANCOCK, Marlborough, and
J. GLASIER, Bath.

20 *The first advertisement for a one-day Bristol coach, in 1763, albeit with departures at 10 or 11 pm. The two-day coach at first continued with a lower fare. (London Evening-Post, 14 April 1763.)*

would explain why there was only a small difference in fares – 30s. and 27s. for one-day and two-day coaches respectively.

That this speeding up occurred throughout the country within a few years indicates that it depended more on technical change than directly on the state of the roads, which must have varied from one route to another. The technical change was steel springs, which cut the draught power required, mainly because the horses no longer had to raise the entire vehicle to pass over protruding stones. In the nineteenth century coach springs were estimated to save the work of one horse in four or five.[51] They also made it possible to construct less sturdy coaches and increased the comfort of passengers. Coachmasters almost invariably took the benefit in the form of greater speed rather than lower fares; indeed, in a few cases they *increased* their fares in the 1760s in order to provide even faster services, sometimes travelling at more than seven miles per hour.[52] Bristol-London speeds did not increase to that level, but fares were higher from 1763.

Steel springs were first used on stage coaches in 1752, including services from London to Reading and Newbury with overall speeds of 6.0 and 4.9 miles per hour respectively, together with the two short-lived post-chaise services to Bath. There is some evidence that the first steel springs were an import from France. However, it seems that at first they could be used only for smaller vehicles, with just four inside passengers rather than the usual six, probably because they were not yet strong enough. That situation was changed by Richard Tredwell, a London blacksmith, who obtained four patents for improved coach springs between 1759 and 1766. In 1759 his patent springs were said to be 56 lb lighter per set than those previously used and less liable to break, but in 1759-60 many of them were in fact breaking, causing 'greatly decreased' demand for them. Tredwell blamed poor-quality steel supplied by his Walsall ironmonger, and it was perhaps for that reason that he was living at Rotherham when his next patent was taken out in 1763. By then he had apparently solved the problem, and coaches with six inside passengers were recorded as having steel springs in 1764. It was at about that time that coaches speeded up throughout the country. Tredwell went bankrupt in 1766, but by 1769 he had coach-spring manufactories in Bath and London, promising that his springs were 'above forty pounds a sett lighter than the common sort of springs' and more durable, and offering to keep them in repair for seven years for one guinea per year per set.[53] However, there is no further evidence of these manufactories, nor of Tredwell himself. Although Tredwell does not seem to have benefited much himself from his springs, he revolutionised road passenger transport, making much higher coach speeds possible.

In fact the speeding up of stage coaches resulted from the combination of Tredwell's springs and improved roads. The connection was that steel springs could not easily be used on very rough roads because they tended to break.[54] Better roads were therefore a precondition for use of steel springs on large coaches and faster stage coach journeys, but the precise timing was determined by Tredwell. The combination of improved roads and Tredwell's springs opened the way for further improvement and growth in coach services, as described in the next chapter.

Notes

1   *Publick Adviser*, 26 May, 22 June 1657; *Mercurius Politicus*, 13 May, 12 Aug 1658; R.C. Tombs, *The King's post* (1905), p. 24.
2   *Perfect Diurnall*, 11 Apr 1653; Gerhold, pp. 81, 84-5.
3   Gerhold, pp. 81, 93-7. The miles per hour here are travelling speeds rather than overall speeds.
4   Gerhold, pp. 81, 146.
5   Gerhold, pp. 89-90.
6   *London Gazette*, 11 Dec 1693 (a Bath coach). See also *Post Boy*, 15 Jan 1717.
7   *A list of the 400 hackney-coaches licensed in July and August, 1662* (1664), No. 207 and p. 12; *Mercurius Politicus*, 30 Sept 1658; TNA, PC 2/62, p. 188; TNA, SP 29/319, No. 200; Gerhold, pp. 86-7, 109-11; below, p. 60. There was a hackney

coachman called William Baldwin in 1662 (*A list*, No. 32).

8   Thomas Delaune, *The present state of London* (1681); Thomas Delaune, *Angliae metropolis: or, the present state of London* (1690); Gerhold, p. 88.

9   Above, p. 18; Maxwell Fraser, *The history of Slough* (1973), p. 55; Fig. 11; *London Topographical Record*, vol. 4 (1907), p. 98; Delaune, *Present state*; TNA, PROB 11/420, Robert Toobey; Bodleian Library, Bankes MS, 5/77.

10   TNA, PROB 4/9736.

11   On the basis of teams covering 80 to 90 miles per week (Gerhold, pp. 202-5; below, p. 177).

12   *Post Boy*, 21 & 23 Oct 1707.

13   *Post Man*, 19 Apr 1709, 12 May 1711; *Evening Post*, 19 Apr 1718, 1 Sept 1719, 6 Aug 1724; *Post Man*, 21 Jan 1718; *Daily Journal*, 14 May 1724; Fig. 11. In 1718-19 and 1724 the three-day coaches were one a week each to Bath and Bristol. All the advertisements are from 1709, 1711, 1718-20 and 1724-5.

14   *London Journal*, 3 July 1725; *Farley's Bristol News-Paper*, 11 Dec 1725, 30 Mar 1728; Charles Pickman, *The tradesman's guide; or the chapman's and traveller's best companion* (1727); *The intelligencer: or, merchants assistant* (1738); *The Bath and Bristol guide* (1750, 1753); TNA, PROB 11/800, John Pinfold; TNA, PROB 11/651, Henry Pratt.

15   The possible example between York and Hull in 1678 is very uncertain (Joseph Hunter (ed.), *The diary of Ralph Thoresby* (1830), vol. 1, p. 28).

16   Bodleian Library, University Archives, Chancellor's Court, 134/1/1; *London Evening-Post*, 29 Apr 1735.

17   *Farley's Bristol News-Paper*, 25 Feb 1727, 4 Apr 1730, 27 Jan 1733; *Evening Post*, 19 Oct 1721; *The Bath and Bristol guide* (1753), p. 47; *Exeter Mercury*, 24 Aug 1716. The Bristol and Bath coach advertised at Exeter in 1727 actually served Bath (Robert Newton, *Eighteenth century Exeter* (1984), p. 19).

18   Gerhold, pp. 112-14; *Proceedings of the Old Bailey* website, t17261207.

19   Gerhold, pp. 115-16.

20   Gerhold, pp. 119-35; *London Evening-Post*, 27 Mar 1733; Webb 2, p. 23; *Farley's Bristol News-Paper*, 11 & 24 Dec 1725.

21   Based on estimated numbers of horses per double mile and miles per team (below, p. 177).

22   Gerhold, pp. 149-50. There is no evidence of Bristol's three-day coaches running more frequently in winter (see e.g. *London Journal*, 21 Nov 1724; *Daily Advertiser*, 21 Jan 1752).

23   Charles E. Davis, *The mineral baths of Bath* (1883), p. 48n; Gerhold, pp. 119-25, 142-3. The lodging and dining places of the three-day coaches were conceivably different in winter, though they could not have been much different.

24   [Ned Ward], *A step to the Bath: with a character of the place* (1700), pp. 3-12; *A journey to Bath and Bristol: an heroi-comic-historic- and geographical poem* (1717) (copy in the library of Worcester College, Oxford); Wiltshire and Swindon RO, 161 bdl 170, 23-4 June 1718; Henry Huth (ed.), *Narrative of the*

journey of an Irish gentleman through England in the year 1752 (1869), pp. 126-39.

25 [Ward], *Step to the Bath*, p.12.

26 *Farley's Bristol News-Paper*, 24 Dec 1725; *The Bath and Bristol guide* (1750, 1753, 1755); Gerhold, pp. 141-2, 146-8, 224-6; *London Evening-Post*, 27 Mar 1733; Huth (ed.), *Narrative of the journey*, pp. 135-9. In the 1750-55 examples, times in directories are assumed to be the same on each of the two or three days; breakfast is assumed to take half an hour and dinner an hour. In the Bristol-Bath examples, 15 minutes is allowed for loading at Bath.

27 Gerhold, pp. 233-5; *London Journal*, 3 Apr 1725; Webb 1, p. 22; *Daily Advertiser*, 21 Jan 1752; FFBJ 17 Mar 1753. Between Bath and London fares were 25s. compared with 20s. in 1696 and 1748-9 (Davis, *Mineral baths*, p. 48n; *Bath Journal*, 21 Mar 1748, 27 Mar 1749).

28 Fig. 11; Gerhold, p. 118. In May 1724, one of the three-day coachmen was covering the whole distance between London and Bristol (*Daily Journal*, 14 May 1724).

29 Gerhold, pp. 91-3.

30 [Ward], *Step to the Bath*, pp. 3-12.

31 *Journey to Bath and Bristol*. The route in this case was via Chippenham. The writer refers to the refreshment at Turnham Green as breakfast and that at Slough as dinner.

32 Wiltshire RO, 161 bdl 170.

33 Huth (ed.), *Narrative of the journey*, pp. 60, 123-39.

34 Gerhold, p. 101; FFBJ 27 July 1776.

35 *British Journal*, 8 Aug 1724; *Daily Post*, 5 Nov 1725, 15 April 1726; *Daily Courant*, 17 Aug 1730; *Evening Post*, 15 Sept 1730; *London Evening-Post*, 20 Jan 1733, 2 Mar 1738, 19 May 1748, 7 Mar 1752; *Universal Spectator*, 14 May 1737; *Common Sense*, 25 Nov 1738; *Country Journal*, 7 May 1743; *Jacobite's Journal*, 25 June 1748; *Penny London Post*, 26 Aug 1748; *Whitehall Evening Post*, 27 July, 28 Nov 1749, 30 Oct 1750, 2 July 1751; *Old England*, 21 Dec 1751; *Covent Garden Journal*, 18 Feb 1752; *Read's Weekly Journal*, 3 Feb 1753; *Gazetteer and London Daily Advertiser*, 2 Aug 1762; *Lloyd's Evening Post*, 27 Oct 1762, 2 July 1764; *St James Chronicle*, 2 Nov 1762; *Gazetteer and National Daily Advertiser*, 5 July 1764; *Public Advertiser*, 12 July 1765, 11 June 1766; *Salisbury Journal*, 22 Aug 1768, quoted in Wiltshire Heritage Museum, MS 1289; *Middlesex Journal*, 22 July 1769; online index to *Bath Chronicle*, 14 June 1770, 18 July 1771; below, p. 151.

36 *London Evening-Post*, 2 Mar 1738, 7 Mar 1752; *Covent Garden Journal*, 10 Mar 1752; *Gazetteer and National Daily Advertiser*, 5 July 1764; *Salisbury Journal*, 22 Aug 1768, quoted in Wiltshire Heritage Museum, MS 1289; *Middlesex Journal*, 22 July 1769.

37 *Lloyd's Evening Post*, 27 Oct 1762, 2 July 1764.

38 Webb 1, pp. 21-4; Gerhold, p. 140; *The Bath and Bristol guide* (1753), p. 31; FFBJ

23 Feb 1754.

39 Webb 1, pp. 32, 36-7; *Bath Journal*, 3 Feb, 31 Mar 1755; below, p. 63. A Bristol service (via Chippenham) bypassing Bath was recorded only in 1756 (*London Evening-Post*, 27 Mar 1756).

40 R.S. Neale, *Bath 1680-1850: a social history* (1981), p. 44.

41 Above, pp. 21-2; Gerhold, pp. 151-2; C. Bruyn Andrews (ed.), *The Torrington diaries*, vol. 1 (1934), p. 330. Byng's observation is from 1787.

42 There may have been a mile or two of unturnpiked road separating the Bristol and Bath trusts until 1757 (O. Bryan Morland, *An introduction to the infrastructure of the Industrial Revolution in Somerset* (1982), pp. 7, 10).

43 John Latimer, *The annals of Bristol in the eighteenth century* (1893), pp. 156-8, 274-5; William Albert, 'The turnpike trusts', in Derek H. Aldcroft and Michael J. Freeman (eds.), *Transport in the Industrial Revolution* (1983), pp. 34-5; William Albert, *The turnpike road system in England 1663-1840* (1972), pp. 27-8.

44 Gerhold, pp. 154-5; Brenda J. Buchanan, 'The Great Bath Road, 1700-1830', *Bath History*, vol. 4 (1992), pp. 81-5; W.A. Henry and F.B. Morrison, *Feeds and feeding: a handbook for the student and stockman* (1917), p. 289; *Report from Select Committee on steam carriages*, PP 1831 (324), p. 102.

45 Buchanan, 'Great Bath Road', pp. 81, 85; Wiltshire and Swindon RO, G18/990/1; London Metropolitan Archives, Tp.Col/1; Eric Pawson, *Transport and economy: the turnpike roads of eighteenth century Britain* (1977), p. 189.

46 London Metropolitan Archives, Tp.Col/1; Wiltshire and Swindon RO, 1316/1, 9 Sept 1727, 18 Sept 1732, 20 Oct 1736, 31 May, 4, 12 & 29 June, 19 July, 31 Aug, 7 & 25 Sept, 13 Oct 1744, 27 Apr, 17 & 27 May, 24 June, 3 Sept 1745.

47 Buchanan, 'Great Bath Road', p. 82; Webb 1, pp. 20-1, 43; FFBJ 23 Feb 1754.

48 FFBJ 17 Mar 1753, 9 Feb 1754, 25 Sept 1756; Webb 1, pp. 29-32, 36; *The Bath and Bristol guide* (1753, 1755); Gerhold, pp. 143-4, 158; *London Evening-Post*, 1 Apr, 19 Oct, 9 Nov 1756, 3 Mar 1757.

49 Gerhold, pp. 156-7.

50 Webb 1, p. 40.

51 *Mail coach contracts*, PP 1835 (542), pp. 5-6; Harris, p. 91.

52 Gerhold, p. 161.

53 Gerhold, pp. 158-9, 162; *Whitehall Evening Post*, 12 Apr 1759; *Lloyd's Evening Post*, 27 Jan 1766; FFBJ 29 April 1769. In 1754 travellers in the four-inside machine transferred to a six-inside vehicle for Bath to Bristol (*London Evening-Post*, 22 Aug 1754).

54 Oliver W. Holmes and Peter T. Rohrbach, *Stagecoach east: stagecoach days in the East from the colonial period to the Civil War* (1983), pp. 105, 137.

3

London coaches
1763–1838

Growth, acceleration and
productivity

Growing numbers

THE STORY OF Bristol's London coaches from the 1760s to the
1830s is one of growing numbers, increasing speeds and only
moderately rising fares. This first section seeks to determine the
timing of those changes and thereby to prepare the way for explaining
why they happened. It also sets the scene for the discussion of
coachmasters and their companies and services which follows.

The evidence for the number of services is derived from
newspaper advertisements up to 1785 and thereafter mainly from
Bristol directories. There are many hazards in using directories to
determine numbers of services, usually resulting in substantial over-
estimates, and Appendix 1 explains how those hazards have been
avoided as far as possible. Fig. 21 shows the growth in the number of
services, from six per week in the early 1760s to 69 in 1838. The rate
of growth somewhat exceeded that of London services nationwide,[1]

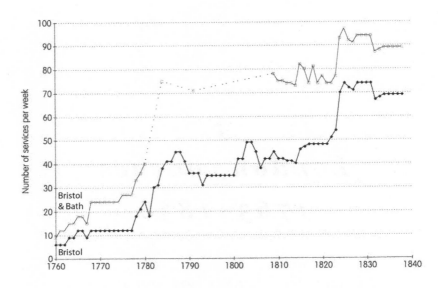

21 *Numbers of coaches per week, 1760-1838. The lower line is Bristol-London coaches only. The upper line is Bristol-London and Bath-London coaches together in those periods when there is adequate information on the latter. (Sources: Newspaper advertisements, Bristol and Bath directories,* Cary's new itinerary *(1810-28),* Robson's London directory *(1832-9).)*

and considerably exceeded the rise in the populations of Bristol, Bath and London. The timing is more interesting than the absolute numbers. Growth was concentrated in two periods – the late 1770s and 1780s and the early 1820s, the 1780s being the key decade in the whole period covered. In between the two periods of rapid growth was one of stagnation lasting about 30 years.

Three cautions are needed at this point. The first is that, since from the 1770s services were generally daily or six times a week, any new service or the disappearance of an old one has a major impact on the figures. The precise timing of changes, even if reflecting longer-term developments, depended on decisions by coachmasters.

The second is that, in practice, there was little difference between a coach advertised as a London to Bristol one and a London to Bath coach which forwarded passengers to Bristol by another conveyance. Even some Bristol to London firms treated Bath to Bristol as a separate part of the journey. Until about the mid-1810s there were generally as many Bath-London coaches as Bristol-London ones, but after that the proportion of Bath-London services declined (Fig. 21). In part this reflected the changing importance of the two cities. Bath's population grew from about 10,000 in 1743 to 33,000 in 1801 and 53,000 in 1841 and Bristol's from about 50,000 in 1750 to 61,000 in 1801 and 125,000 in 1841.[2] Bath therefore grew much faster than Bristol in 1750-1801 and much slower than Bristol in 1801-41. Even more significantly, while the estimated annual number of visitors to Bath rose from about 12,000 in 1749 to probably 40,000 by 1800, that growth ceased in the 1790s, thanks to the cost of treatment, the increasing preference for private rather than public entertainments and the fact that the city had grown too large for the company to be exclusive.[3] Also, as coach travel became faster and more routine, the relative importance to coachmasters of places to which people travelled for special and occasional reasons, such as Bath, was likely to diminish and the greater size and commercial importance of Bristol to assert itself. In part, however, the growing proportion of Bristol-London coaches may merely reflect change in the way coachmasters chose to organise and advertise the Bath to Bristol part of their service, thereby potentially distorting the picture. Bristol-London and Bath-London coaches therefore need to be considered together, as shown in Fig. 21. This reduces the rate of growth, with services multiplying by ten times instead of 11 to 12 times, but it does not substantially change the pattern of growth and stagnation at different periods.

The third caution is that the number of passengers per service varied from one period to another. The diligences of the late 1770s carried up to four, and some machines only four or five, whereas the coaches of the 1830s were usually licensed to carry 12 or 15. The most important change was the increased number of outside passengers. Taking that into account would scale down somewhat the growth in the 1770s and magnify it in the early nineteenth century, as well as almost doubling the rate of growth between 1760 and 1838. Again it would not transform the pattern of growth and stagnation shown in Fig. 21, other than by moderating the picture of stagnation in the 1800s.

Faster journeys

MILES PER HOUR help to explain the changing numbers. As elsewhere in this book (except where referred to as travelling speeds), the speeds given here are overall ones – miles per hour from end to end, making no allowance for stops for passengers to eat and horses to be changed; miles per hour while on the move, or travelling speeds, were always somewhat higher. The evidence on speeds becomes plentiful only from 1776, when some advertisements began to indicate journey times in hours rather than days. It is presented in Fig. 23, and the reliability of advertised timings is discussed in Appendix 2. The main risk is that the timings were simply unrealistic, even when coaches were not impeded by snow, fog or floods. Although there would have been little point

22 'I could have travelled much cheaper by the opposition coach.' Drawing by Rowlandson, providing a reminder that passengers were intensely interested in the basics such as fares, as opposed to the romantic aspects which have dominated much of the writing about stage coaches.

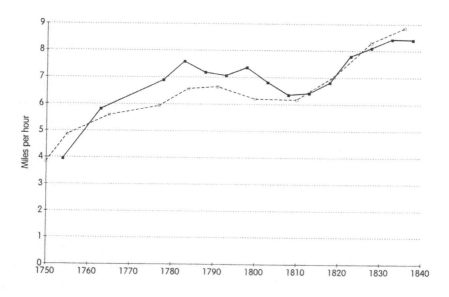

23 *Average Bristol-London coach speeds, 1753-1838 (the unbroken line). These are overall speeds from end to end, making no allowance for stops for refreshment or changing horses, rather than travelling speeds. No winter speeds were advertised until 1776, except that the 1753/5 figure was summer-only in 1753 and all-year in 1755. The 1763 figure is an estimate. From 1776 the figures are averages of all the speeds recorded for five-year periods. The dashed line, based on work in progress, shows average speeds of London coaches nationwide (excluding East Anglia), gathered from pairs of years about a decade apart. These are summer speeds up to and including 1776/7, after which there was little difference between the speeds advertised in summer and winter; the figure for 1750 is the summer average for 1653-1750. As in the Bristol-London case, inclusion of winter speeds in the early period would have resulted in the graph showing larger increases in speeds then, from a lower base. (Sources: Gerhold, pp. 224-6; newspaper advertisements, local directories.)*

in persistently advertising completely unrealistic timings, it is possible that the advertised timings were achieved only when everything went well, with reasonable weather, good roads, moderate loads and no problems with the horses. For example, Lewis Dillwyn lamented in February 1829 that the Company's coach had reached Bristol two hours later than usual because of 'the badness of the roads and a heavy load'. In 1837 a London coachmaster, William Chaplin, indicated that, while both mail coaches and ordinary stage coaches kept to time in summer, the stage coaches, unlike the mail coaches, did not do so in winter.[4] The limited evidence from actual journeys which can be compared with advertised timings (Appendix 3) suggests that coaches were sometimes on time or even early, but were often half an hour or an hour late, and not just in winter. Advertised times therefore need to be regarded with caution, but they were rarely far from actual timings, and they do therefore provide a reasonable guide to the times achieved in practice and how they changed.

A clear picture emerges from Fig. 23. Speeds rose to a peak in the early 1780s. A gentle decline followed to a trough in 1806-15. After that, average speeds rose again, reaching a new and higher peak in the 1830s. Advertised journey times between Bristol and London fell from 31 hours in the early 1750s to 18 hours by the fastest coaches in the mid-1770s and just under 12 hours by the mail coach in 1836 – the fastest coach recorded. As one would expect, it was when coaches were speeding up that their numbers increased most impressively, though the periods of growth were more concentrated than the periods of rising speeds. The Bristol evidence is consistent with that for London coaches in general (Fig. 23). Where the two diverge somewhat – the sharper decline in Bristol-London speeds during the period of stagnation – the reason seems to be that in the late eighteenth century passengers from Bristol who were not in a hurry went to Bath and took a two-day coach from there, whereas from 1801 Bristol increasingly had slow coaches of its own.[5] Fig. 23 provides the basis for dividing the period covered by this chapter into three: one of rising speeds, followed by one of stagnation and then one in which speeds rose again.

The evidence of coach fares (Fig. 24) is possibly less reliable than that of timings because fares varied over a wider range and also fluctuated more. Also, information is scarce in 1791-1815. The changes in fares can be related to the three periods already identified,

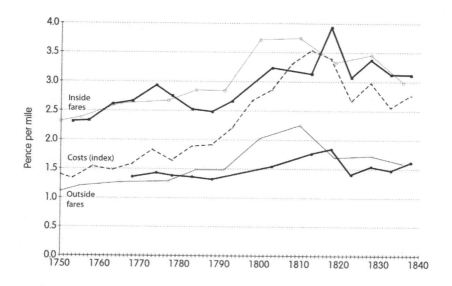

24 *Inside and outside fares of Bristol-London coaches, 1750-1840 (the two thick lines). These are averages of the fares recorded for five-year periods (with gaps in 1796-1800 and 1806-10). The high average for 1816-20 is probably the accidental result of an unrepresentative sample. Average fares of London coaches nationwide (excluding East Anglia), based on work in progress, are given for comparison (the two thin lines). The dashed line is the index of coachmasters' costs, compiled as explained in Appendix 2, showing how costs rose faster than fares up to 1813 (average costs in 1653-1750 equal 1.4 on the left-hand scale). All the figures for 1750 are averages for 1653-1750. (Sources: Gerhold, pp. 233-5; newspaper advertisements, local directories.)*

though not always in straightforward ways. From about 1750 to 1790, fares varied within a fairly narrow band despite rising speeds and costs. There was then a period of significantly higher fares, reflecting higher costs and starting at the time when the number of services ceased to grow and speeds began to decline. That was followed by a final period of moderate decline or stability in fares despite rising speeds, partly reflecting reduced costs. Again, the Bristol evidence is reasonably consistent with the somewhat fuller evidence for London services in general, though again the comparison is affected by the development of slow services from Bristol from 1801.

Increasing productivity

IN THE SHORT term fares reflected the cost of horse provender and other costs, together with the intensity of competition, but there was also a longer-term process whereby stage coaching became more efficient, reflecting, for example, better roads. If that was happening, fares might decline even if costs were rising, or speeds might increase without any rise in fares. Conversely, if costs were falling, services might become faster or cheaper without any increase in productivity. Therefore, in order to explain how stage coaching developed, we need a way of discounting short-term changes such as rising and falling provender prices in order to identify the extent to which productivity increased and when that happened.

For this, the evidence of speeds and fares is used, together with evidence on changes in the coachmaster's costs, as explained in Appendix 2. Speeds and fares are used only when both are available for the same coach at the same date – 108 examples in total, only really numerous in 1786-91 and 1824-34. The method is, for each example, to take the average fare of the period up to 1750 as the baseline, multiply it according to the increased cost of inputs such as horse provender in the year concerned, multiply it again according to the estimated increase in costs for the higher speed, and then compare the result with what the fare actually was. The outcome is what was actually paid as a percentage of what the journey at the same speed would have cost had there been no improvements in roads, vehicles, horses or organisation since 1750. The results are shown in Fig. 25. Considerable variation in the percentage can be expected in any particular period, not least because fares might be strongly influenced by the intensity of competition, because a coachmaster might be able to charge more for a more reliable or prestigious (but no faster) service, and because it is hard to relate fares to provender

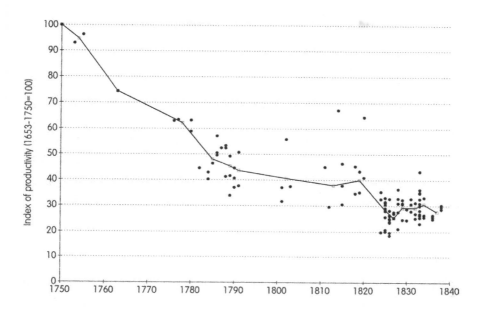

25 *The increasing productivity of Bristol-London coaches, 1750-1838, compiled as explained in Appendix 2. The index figure is fares as a percentage of what they would have been without the increase in productivity. Black dots are individual examples where both fare and speed are known for the same coach at the same time. The line links the averages for groups of years, each from 1776 onwards relating to at least four examples. The figure for 1750 is the average for stage coaches nationwide in 1653-1750; that of 1763 is based on estimated timings. Two outlying examples from 1814 and 1820 are omitted from the averages.*

prices when they were fluctuating strongly (as in 1799-1814), so the figures can only be a rough guide.

What Fig. 25 shows is in some ways surprising, though less so in the light of the evidence presented here about speeds and fares. The period of the most rapid and sustained increase in productivity was not the golden age of the 1820s and 1830s but the 1760s to 1780s. By 1790-1 the figure was about 44%. Then there was little change until a sharp increase in productivity in the early 1820s, after which the figure was around 30%, with a dip to 28% in the late 1830s.

Rapid growth, c.1763-90

IN THIS PERIOD, the number of services per week increased from nine to a peak of 45; speeds rose from a probable five to six miles per hour to about seven to eight miles per hour; fares rose only slightly, despite the increase in speed; there were several new types of vehicle; and near the end of the period mail coaches were introduced.

Coachmasters

DESPITE NEW CHALLENGERS, mergers and closures resulted in the number of London coach firms remaining at two almost throughout this period. In 1763-5 the two established firms, Glasier & Co and Day & Co, provided nine Bristol-London services a week, and by 1768 twelve a week,[6] having seen off two newcomers in 1765. Both firms consisted of innkeepers along the route, not usually including any at London or Bristol (Figs. 15 and 26), and their timings and fares in 1768 were identical, suggesting collusion (Fig. 27).

One of the newcomers of 1765, Hanforth, Season & Co, offered post-coaches with timings the same as those of the established firms (two days in winter, one in summer). George Season was the first proprietor of a London coach based at Bristol, and John Hanforth was

26 *Plan of Glasier & Co's machines in 1763, indicating where the proprietors lived. The stages are not recorded, but the proprietors' residences suggest that they were the same as Day & Co's in 1757 (Fig. 15). By 1768, Glasier & Co no longer had a London proprietor. (Source:* Felix Farley's Bristol Journal, *9 April 1763.)*

London, Briftol, and Bath

MACHINES,

In ONE DAY, as ufual,

(To begin on SUNDAY the 10th Inftant, April,)

FROM the White Hart, Briftol, every Sunday, Tuefday, and Thurfday Evenings, and the White Lion, every Monday, Wednefday, and Friday Evenings, at Half after Nine o'Clock ; and from the White Lion, Bath, every Monday, Wednefday, and Friday Evenings, at Eleven o'Clock ; and from London every Night (Saturday excepted) from Gerrard's-Hall, Inn, Bafing-Lane; Saracen's-Head, Friday-ftreet; and Bell-Savage, Ludgate-Hill.

MACHINE in TWO DAYS, as ufual, from the Chriftopher-Inn, Bath, to the One Bell in the Strand, London.

POST-COACH in TWO DAYS as ufual, from the White Lion, Bath, and the Bell-Savage, Ludgate-Hill, London.

Prices for Infide Paffengers, as follow :

	l.	s.	d.
To and from Briftol, in One Day,	1	10	0
To and from Bath, in One Day	1	8	0
To Briftol, in Two Days	1	7	0
To Bath, in Two Days	1	5	0

POST-COACH Three-pence per Mile.

Children in Lap and Outfide Paffengers, Half Price. Each Infide Paffenger to be allowed 14lbs. Oufides or Children in Lap, 7lbs. of Luggage, ; all above to pay in the Flyers or Poft-Coach, One Penny Halfpenny, and in the Two Days Coaches, One Penny per Pound. —— Half the above Fares to be paid on taking Places ; the other Half on entering the Machine.

The Machines all call at the Old White Horfe Cellar, and the Black and White Bear Inns, in Piccadilly, both going in and coming out of Town.

Perform'd by
- JOSEPH GLAZIER, *Bath.*
- THOMAS HANCOCK, *Marlborough.*
- JOSEPH COOKMAN, } *Newbury.*
- ROBERT HALLIWELL, }
- ANNE BANNISTER, } *Reading.*
- WILLIAM CLARKE, }

☞ The Proprietors will not be accountable for any Plate, Money, Jewels, Writings, or Things of Value, unlefs entered and paid for as fuch.

The London, Bath, and Briftol,

MACHINE,

In ONE DAY,

WILL fet out Sunday the 10th of April, 1768, from the Rummer-Tavern, Briftol, and every Night (Saturdays excepted) precifely at Half an Hour after Nine o'Clock, for the Three-Cups in Bread-ftreet, London ; and from the Greyhound Inn in the Market-Place, Bath, every Monday, Wednefday, and Friday Evening, at Half an Hour after Eleven, for the Swan-Inn, Holbourn-Bridge ; and return every Sunday, Tuefday and Thurfday Night, at Ten o'Clock, from the Swan-Inn, Holbourn-Bridge ; and every Monday, Wednefday, and Friday (at the fame Hour) from the Three-Cups, in Bread-ftreet, for Bath and Briftol. All breakfaft at the George and Pelican-Inn, Speenhamland.

The POST-COACHES in Two Days, as ufual, from the Rofe-Inn, Holbourn-Bridge, London, and from the White-Hart-Inn, Bath.

And the MACHINE in Two Days, from the Golden Crofs, Charing-Crofs, London, and the White-Hart-Inn, Bath, every Monday, Wednefday and Friday Morning, the fame Hours as ufual.

All lie the firft Night at the George and Pelican-Inn, Speenhamland.

Prices of the above Machines as follows, viz.

	l.	s.	d.
Infide to and from Briftol in One Day	1	10	0
To and from Bath in One ditto	1	8	0
To and from Briftol in Two ditto	1	7	0
To and from Bath in Two ditto	1	5	0

The Poft-Coaches Three-pence per Mile.

Children and Outfides in the above Machines, Half-price.

Half the Money to be paid on taking the Places, the other Half on entering the Machines : Infide Paffengers to be allowed 14lb. and Children and Outfides 7lb. Weight of Luggage ; all above to pay in the One Day Machine and Poft-Coaches Three-Halfpence per Pound, and in the Two Days Machine One Penny per Pound.

The all call at the Black-Bear and New-White-Horfe Cellar, Piccadilly, both going in and out of Town. The Proprietors will not be accountable for any Jewels, Plate, Money, Writings, &c. unlefs enter'd as fuch.

Perform'd by
- THOMAS KING, Bath,
- GEORGE WHATLEY, Bear-Inn, Devizes.
- JAMES WHITE, Caftle-Inn, Marlborough.
- RD. FISHER, King's-Arms-Inn, Reading.
- JOHN MARCH, Maidenhead-Bridge.
- WILLIAM DAY, Hounflow. And
- THOMAS TIBAY, Speenhamland.

27 Advertisement for the machines and post-coaches of Glasier & Co and Day & Co, 1768. There was little difference between them in services and fares. (Felix Farley's Bristol Journal, 9 April 1768.)

a major London innkeeper; the other proprietors were innkeepers at Devizes, Hungerford, Newbury and Colnbrook. Hanforth had established the first stage coaches from London to Manchester, Leeds and Sheffield in 1760, and in 1761-6 became the first London innkeeper to take shares in a number of coaches on different roads and retain them for any length of time. However, his Bristol service, like many of the others, was not a success, and is not heard of after February 1765. The other new firm, offering post-coaches via Andover with the same timings, belonged to a Bristol innkeeper (Thomas Jones of the Greyhound), a Bath coachmaker and innkeepers at Melksham, Andover, Staines and London. But again there are no references after June 1765. Glasier & Co's temporary reduction of their fares from 27s. and 30s. to 21s. by April 1765 undoubtedly contributed to this outcome.[7]

The next challenge came in 1774, when Lewis Gevaux of London and partners put on fast post-chaises or diligences carrying only

THE Original Briftol and London DILIGENCE; or, FLYING POST-CHAISE, with a Guard, in One Day, (through Bath) fets out from the Lamb-Inn, Broad-Mead, Briftol, every Morning (except Sunday) at Two o'Clock, and from the Swan with Two Necks, in Carter-Lane, Doctors-Commons, at Four o'Clock and arrives at Briftol, at Ten; and at London, at Eight o'Clock the fame Evening.——Carries Three Paffengers at 1l. 11s. 6d. each, 10lb. Luggage allowed.——Small Parcels 1s. large in Proportion, if weighable at Three Halfpence per lb. The Proprietors difcharge the Turnpikes and Drivers.

Perform'd by   LEWIS GEVAUX, London.
WILLIAM HANKS, Brentford.
D. GURGIFIELD, Colnbrook.
M. CUMINGS and Co. Reading.
—— BROWN, Marlborough.
—— SAVERY, Caln.
JOHN HULBERT, Corfham.
MATT. ROOD, Bath.
FRANCIS SAWYER, Briftol.

N. B. The Proprietors will not be accountable for any Money, Plate, or Jewels, to a greater Amount than FIVE POUNDS.

28 *Advertisement for Gevaux & Co's diligences, carrying only three passengers, 1776. (Felix Farley's Bristol Journal, 27 July 1776.)*

Samuel Curwen in the diligence from Bristol to London, 8 March 1777

Entered the diligence for London at one o'clock at night, the frost was so intense that our breaths formed a hard cake of ice on the glass, scarce to be taken off by the nails. At the city of Bath we arrived, a distance of 12 miles, almost stiffened with cold; here I attempted to thaw myself, but this expedient, I fancy, only rendered my body and feet more susceptible of the cold; suffering, till the sun rose and chased away the frost, inconceivable pain. At Calne we changed horses again, and attempted a second thaw with better success than the first, being aided by the sun, then beginning to bless the upper hemisphere, showing in a cloudless sky. From hence to Marlborough the road lies over a place called the Down ... [At Colnbrook] we again shifted horses, and again at Hounslow; between those two places lies the noted heath, called by the name of the latter, which we passed over with a slow, solemn pace in the dark, being more than an hour in crossing it. We arrived safe at eight o'clock, evening, at the Swan-with-Two-Necks Inn, Doctors' Commons.

Source: George Atkinson Ward (ed.), The journals and letters of Samuel Curwen *(4th edn., 1864), pp. 111-12.*

three inside passengers (Fig. 28). Like Hanforth, Gevaux established services to numerous towns from his London base. Established coachmasters usually felt it necessary to emulate them, providing both fast diligences and slower coaches over the same routes. Gevaux' diligences seem to have prompted the two established Bristol-London firms to unite, and by February 1775 the merged firm had responded with its own post-chaises, though they were advertised only in that month.[8]

Gevaux' diligence service had fallen into the hands of Glasier & Co by April 1778, but in November 1777 Gevaux had launched a new flying coach service in partnership with John Snell of the Greyhound, Bristol. Gevaux himself soon left the new firm (and went bankrupt in 1779, spending two years in the Fleet Prison), and it may not have continued much beyond April 1780, but by October 1781 Snell was back, with new partners and engaged in fierce competition with Glasier & Co. The latter reduced their inside fares to 18s. and 21s., 18s. being the lowest ever recorded for Bristol to London coaches. Snell & Co made much of having challenged a monopoly, stating that 'for a long time past, passengers travelling to and from London, have been imposed upon in many respects, and the greatest impositions made in the charge of parcels, &c. which is principally owing to the stage-coaches travelling on the London-road being ingrossed into one concern, to the great prejudice of the public'.[9]

William Dillwyn from Bath to London, 7–8 May 1782

7 May. About 10 o clock set out in the stage coach for London.

8 May. Coachman in a drunken fit fell off his box in the night at Melksham. Left him behind. Got with difficulty to Devises. Dined at Slough and reached home [in London] about 9 o clock in the evening. On the whole a disagreeable journey.

Source: NLW, transcript of the diary of William Dillwyn, 1774-90.

Both firms seem to have prospered in what were especially favourable conditions for coachmasters. From 1784 to 1792 the number of Glasier & Co's weekly services ranged from 21 to 25, always at least half of all Bristol to London services. Glasier & Co also ran many of the Bath to London coaches. In 1784 what had been Snell's firm secured the contract for the first mail coach, while continuing its existing service, as discussed below. Two new firms both using the Andover road, and with partners mainly from Andover eastwards, are recorded in 1779 and 1782-4 but failed to become established,[10] so there continued to be just two firms.

In this period the Bristol-London coaches started to have proprietors in Bristol, though the Bath proprietors remained at least as important. Other than Season and Jones in 1765, neither of whose firms lasted, the first were Francis Sawyer in 1776 and John Snell of the Greyhound in 1777-82, both in firms

29 Monument to John Weeks in the cloister of Bristol Cathedral. The effigy was reckoned to be a good likeness by one who had known him.

founded by Gevaux.[11] A much more important figure was John Weeks (Fig. 29). In 1773 he took over the Bush Tavern in Bristol from his father-in-law (Fig. 30). His first coach ventures were regional ones, starting with diligences to Birmingham, but by 1779 he had services to London as part of Glasier & Co. Weeks remained a coachmaster until his death in 1819, as well as innkeeper at the

30 The Bush Inn, Corn Street, Bristol (painting by John Charles Maggs). The painting undoubtedly exaggerates the activity in the street outside.

Bush (except in 1804-12). Under him the Bush became one of the most important Bristol coaching inns, alongside the White Hart, White Lion and Rummer. He was long remembered for the annual dinner he gave at the Bush at Christmas to anyone who wished to come, 'and no nobler sight was there in Bristol, amidst all its wealth and hospitality, than that of honest John Weeks at the head of his table, lustily carving and pressing his guests to "Eat, drink, and be merry"'. By 1812 he was describing himself as a gentleman of Shirehampton. He left a fortune of £5,000 or more.[12]

Two other families became established as Bristol coachmasters in this period, closely associated with each other and with Weeks, though initially as Bristol to Birmingham proprietors. George Poston is first recorded as a coachmaster in 1782, and was also innkeeper at the White Hart from 1789 to 1797. He died in about 1815, leaving a fortune of about £6,000. His son Samuel took over the Rummer in 1802, being succeeded there in about 1809 by Sarah

31 The Belle Sauvage, Ludgate Hill, one of the major London inns used by Bristol coaches (drawing by George Shepherd, 1809).

Poston (possibly his sister), who remained there until about 1836.[13] George Coupland is first recorded as a coachmaster in 1787, and was from at least 1796 until his death in 1813 innkeeper at the White Hart, Horsefair, where some of the London coaches picked up passengers, as well as owning the Greyhound. He may have been the most successful of the Bristol coachmasters, as he left a fortune of about £11,000, including coach assets valued at £1,066. The coach business passed to his son Richard, innkeeper at the White Hart, Broad Street, from 1815, who left less than £200 on his death in 1829.[14] The name Coupland then disappeared from Bristol coaching, but for several decades around the turn of the century Weeks, Poston and Coupland had dominated the trade.

Another change from the 1770s onwards was the increasing involvement of London innkeepers as coachmasters. Gevaux' firm

*32 The Cross Keys, Wood Street, a London coaching inn used by Bristol coaches
from at least 1765 to 1829 (drawing by T.H. Shepherd, 1856).*

and Snell's always had one, but Glasier's and Day's usually did not, until John Whalley, innkeeper at the Three Cups, Bread Street, became a proprietor of the merged firm in 1780. Thereafter both firms always had a London partner. By 1791 some of the London coach businesses were large, including those of Wilson, Boulton, Mountain and Ibberson, all of whom had shares in Bristol coaches.[15]

Vehicles and services

S PEEDS INCREASED UP to the mid-1780s, by which time the fastest coaches (the mail coaches) were achieving up to 8.1 miles per hour. The increased speeds were often linked with new types of vehicle, as Table 1 shows. Advertisements provide little direct information about the differences between the vehicles, but they do

Table 1. Increasing speed in summer, Bristol-London, 1753-90

Date	Vehicle	Hours Bristol-London	Miles per hour overall
1753-5		31	3.9
1763	Machines in 1 day (n1)	21?	5.8
1776-80	Diligences (n2)	18	6.8
1780-2	Post-coaches	17-18	6.8-7.2
1784	Mail coaches	15-16	7.6-8.1
1788-90	Post-coaches (n3)	15½-18	6.8-7.9

Sources: *The Bath and Bristol guide* (1753, 1755); Fig. 20; FFBJ 27 July 1776, 5 July, 11 Oct 1777, 4 Mar 1780 (with *The new Bath guide* (1780), pp. 60-3), 15 June 1782, 28 Aug 1784, 12 Apr 1788, 1 Aug 1789, 10 Apr 1790; *St James's Chronicle*, 20 June 1780; *English Chronicle*, 25 July 1782; POST 10/366, pp. 19-23; *World*, 8 Oct 1789; *The Times*, 6 Mar, 9 Sept 1790.

Notes:
1. Departing at 10 pm, so cannot have taken more than about 24 hours at the most; 21 hours (i.e. 10 pm to 7 pm) would be consistent with the national data.
2. Initially advertised (in 1775) as taking 16 hours.
3. Seven examples of post-coaches or light-coaches, plus one 'flying coach'.

provide two valuable clues, by stating the capacity (often the inside capacity only) and by contrasting vehicles which had different speeds and fares. They indicate a trend towards smaller vehicles from the 1750s and then a gradual reversal of that trend from the 1780s.

As indicated earlier, new types of small vehicle were appearing in the 1750s. These were the 'post chaises' with steel springs carrying four passengers in 1752 (evidently larger than the later post-chaises) and the machines on steel springs carrying four passengers in 1754 (probably similar to the vehicles of two years earlier);[16] they coincided with the first speeding up in winter (but not summer) after a century of stability. Machines were evidently regarded as superior to stage coaches, and the term was almost invariably used for Bristol services from 1754 to 1773, remaining common until 1781, after which there is just one isolated reference in 1790. In 1770 ordinary machines were contrasted with 'large machines' carrying six inside passengers (they cost 23s. and 19s. respectively).[17] In 1774 machines were contrasted with faster and more expensive post-chaises, then from 1775 with diligences, which carried only three inside passengers, and from 1779 with post-coaches, which carried four inside. The first mail coaches in 1784 were described as diligences but were in fact post-coaches, as discussed later. In the early 1780s the post-coach ousted the diligence, which is not heard of again between Bristol and London, indicating that the trend was now towards vehicles with greater capacity. Thereafter vehicles were referred to either as post-coaches or just as coaches. These changes were broadly the same as on other London routes.[18]

Diligences, the first mail coaches and some post-coaches were drawn by only two horses, so in the 1770s and 1780s the fastest coaches had the smallest teams. These included the 'Balloon coaches' put on by two coach firms in 1784 – the name referring to their rapid progress, comparable to the newly-popular balloons, rather than to the shape of the vehicles. James Woodforde travelled in one of these in June 1786 from London to Bath:

> We had four of us in the coach and guard on top. It carries but 4 inside, and is called the Baloon Coach on account of its travelling so fast, making it a point to be before the Mail Coach. We trimmed it of[f] indeed [*sic*], tho' only a pair of horses.[19]

The Balloon coaches carried no outside passengers, and cost 27s., as opposed to 22s. for the (probably slower) four-horse coaches. Their advertisements indicate 18-hour journeys throughout the year, slower than the mail coach, though William Dillwyn's two journeys by the Balloon coach in summer 1786 took only 16½ and 17½ hours.[20]

The evidence in Table 1 is for the faster services, and there were also slower ones. Indeed the 1760s saw the start of a differentiation between faster and slower services which was to continue to the end of stage coaching. The slower services used larger vehicles, usually with six inside seats and an unknown number of outsiders. For example, Glasier & Co in March 1780 offered both a four-inside post-coach taking 17 hours at 28s. and a six-inside machine, evidently taking longer, at 24s.[21] How much slower the slower coaches were is not known.

Whereas faster coaches often carried no outside passengers, or just one on the box beside the coachman, slower coaches increasingly did so, carrying larger loads at the same time as the fast coaches were carrying smaller loads. Outside passengers are first encountered, on an Ipswich and Beccles coach, in 1734, and for a time were rare outside East Anglia. Outside fares were advertised on the Bristol road in 1754 and were common from 1766. Legislation restricted the number of outside passengers to eight in 1788 and five in 1790,[22] indicating that more than those numbers were sometimes carried. Outsiders usually paid 50 to 60% of the inside fare, and even five outsiders paying 50% of the inside fare would have increased the revenue of a fully-loaded six-inside coach by 42%. The horses had to draw the extra weight of the outsiders, but there was little or no increase in the weight of the vehicle. From the point of view of potential passengers, the low outside fares opened up coach travel to many who could not otherwise have afforded it. At first no special provision, such as something to hold on to, was made for outside passengers, and they were occasionally killed falling off, as happened to James Brown on Kingsdown Hill in 1771.[23] It may well have been steel springs and smoother roads, making it safer to travel on coach roofs, which determined when outside passengers became common, and the importance of road quality would explain why outside passengers are first heard of in East Anglia.

Smaller vehicles and teams examined

THE CHARACTERISTICS AND merits of the different sorts of vehicle at first sight appear baffling. Indeed the names were sometimes intended to bamboozle passengers into believing that something up-to-date and attractive was on offer when that was not the case. The explanation given here starts from the premise that, apart from the benefits of steel springs, the contest was essentially between larger and smaller vehicles rather than between vehicles of differing design and technology. That contest will have turned mainly on the impact of larger and smaller vehicles on the number of horses required. The best starting point for comparing the merits of large and small vehicles would be the numbers of horses required for services of particular capacity and speed, which was usually expressed in terms of horses per double mile (i.e. the number required to provide a daily service both ways over a mile of road). Unfortunately there is scarcely any evidence of the numbers of horses kept by coachmasters anywhere in the country between 1761 and 1823. Therefore, the comparison here will begin with some general principles, focusing on the horses, and then make deductions from what coachmasters chose to do.

Obviously the cost of drivers was higher per passenger when the vehicle carried fewer passengers, but drivers were a relatively small cost even if doubled in number. The weights of the vehicles may have varied per passenger carried, and nothing is known about this, but there is no reason to believe the variation was substantial. More significantly, the faster a horse moves, the less power is available for hauling a vehicle, so if the coachmaster wanted faster services he might have to reduce the load drawn, which would mean fewer passengers and a smaller vehicle.

Other considerations came into play when the size of teams was varied. Smaller teams did not mean fewer horses were needed in proportion, because the smaller teams would do fewer miles per week to compensate for the extra exertion. However, horses draw more effectively the closer they are to the load being drawn, and the more horses there are to a team the harder it is to induce all of them to pull their weight,[24] so smaller teams are more efficient, provided of course that they are capable of drawing the load. In other words, reducing the number of horses means less power, but each horse is then more effective. If coachmasters were seeking to provide faster coaches up to the limit of what passengers were willing to pay for, two-horse teams could be the best option, provided they could cope with the loads, and in the 1770s and 1780s that meant light vehicles carrying few passengers. In fact it could mean something close to a post-chaise. Four-horse teams could have drawn larger loads at the required speeds, but would have been less efficient and therefore more expensive per passenger. Two-horse teams did of course have the disadvantage that if one horse faltered the coach had to stop, whereas a coach could continue if it lost one horse out of four, and that is probably why advertisements of the 1790s began to emphasise the use of four-horse teams (Fig. 39). The shortness of the period during which two-horse teams were used, ending around 1790, suggests that the advantage of two-horse teams was small and very sensitive to the quality of the roads. In particular, before the 1770s two-horse teams may well have been incapable of drawing even three-seater vehicles fast enough, though they certainly drew two-seater post-chaises.

Now we can examine the various types of vehicle. The distinguishing feature of machines at first seems to have been that they held only four inside passengers instead of the usual six of stage coaches. The term apparently replaced 'stage chaise' in 1754. Not all machines then had steel springs, but, being smaller and lighter, the machine was able to use them, whereas heavier vehicles could not at that date, so there was an association between machines and steel springs. It was the improved steel springs of the early 1760s, which could be used on large vehicles and were probably better in general, rather than machines as such, which made possible one-day coaches to Bristol in 1763.[25] Once machines had become the superior vehicle, the temptation was apparently irresistible, at least at Bristol, to apply the same term to other vehicles, and this apparently explains the references in 1770 and later to 'large machines' carrying six inside passengers, which sound much like the old six-inside stage coaches with steel springs added.

A new wave of even smaller vehicles appeared in 1774, apparently in response to post-chaises (Fig. 33). From the 1740s the hiring out by innkeepers and postmasters of post-chaises and horses to draw gentlemen's own carriages remedied the difficulty of providing changes of team for private coaches. They also provided the example of small carriages which could be worked with only a pair of horses at high speed. They could apparently travel at nine or ten miles per

33 *Rowlandson's drawing of post-chaises at Bagshot in 1784. They could be drawn by either two or four horses, and were driven by a postilion on one of the horses rather than from the vehicle.*

hour by 1761, much faster than the stage coaches, though in 1808 ten miles per hour was reckoned to be the average speed of a four-horse post-chaise while two-horse post-chaises could manage just seven to eight miles per hour. There is even a hint, from 1771, that stage coach travellers were beginning to be looked down upon by innkeepers. The diarist Sylas Neville, travelling from Brighton to London in that year, noted that he had 'found on several occasions that little respect is paid to those who travel in stage-coaches, even if they are really gentlemen & ladies in dress and behaviour.'[26]

The vehicles which spread widely in the mid-1770s were known at first as post-chaises but later as diligences. In 1774 Gevaux advertised 'the London and Bristol post-chaise', carrying three passengers, whereas the following year he was calling it 'the original Bristol diligence, or flying post-chaise'.[27] He never stated that two-horse teams were used, but with so few passengers that was undoubtedly the case. The most unusual feature of the diligences was their uniformity. Throughout the country there were always three inside passengers (and often one outside), and fares were almost invariably 3d per mile (slightly more on the Bristol road). Also surprising is the frequent statement that drivers and turnpikes were paid for by the proprietors, which had always been the case with stage coaches, unlike post-chaises. These features confirm that the diligences were an adaptation of the post-chaises let out by innkeepers and postmasters, but, unlike those, running on scheduled routes at specified times. This certainly seems to have been true of the vehicles themselves. Three inside passengers and one outside suggests a post-chaise slightly widened to seat three rather than two inside and driven from the box, on which the outside passenger sat beside the coachman, instead of by a postilion riding one of the horses. In fact Rowlandson drew exactly such a vehicle, which was evidently the Salisbury diligence (Fig. 34). Two-horse teams meant that the stages had to be shorter than those of machines and post-coaches with four-horse teams, and the stages

34 Rowlandson's drawing of the Salisbury diligence at the Spread Eagle, Hook, in 1784 (detail). This is the only known view of a diligence. It was somewhat wider than a post-chaise, so as to hold three, and was driven from the box, which was often wide enough to take an outside passenger.

were probably comparable to those of post-chaises. On the Bristol road they averaged 11 miles, almost identical to those of three out of the four other examples available for diligences (Fig. 35).[28] The exception was Glasier & Co, who used the same stages for their diligences in 1775 as for their machines, averaging 15 miles (Fig. 36).

Gevaux had a foreign name, but he seems to have borrowed only a French word rather than any French expertise for his vehicles, presumably to make them more distinctive and exotic. The use of diligences greatly increased in France in 1775, but Gevaux' diligences had little in common with them, and still less with the lumbering vehicles later known as diligences in France.[29] The use of three-seater vehicles does seem to have been an innovation. But perhaps what was

35 Plan of Gevaux & Co's diligences in 1776, indicating the proprietors. On the assumption that the 35 and 22 miles break down into three and two stages respectively, the stages averaged 11 miles. (Source: Felix Farley's Bristol Journal, 27 July 1776.)

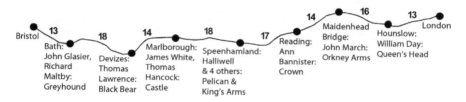

36 Plan of Glasier & Co's post-chaises (or diligences) in 1775, indicating the stages as stated in that year (marked by black circles) and the proprietors. The stages were exactly the same as those of Day & Co in 1757 (Fig. 19). (Source: Felix Farley's Bristol Journal, 4 Feb 1775.)

really new was a coachmaster determined to spread the use of small, fast vehicles to new routes.

How much more diligences cost to run than other coaches is not known. The one scrap of evidence is a payment by John Weeks relating to the Bristol to Exeter diligence, which he began to horse from Bristol to Bridgwater three times a week in 1777. It was for 'the keeping of a pair of horses at the White Hart at Cross and four pair of horses which went with the Dilly to Bridgewater at the beginning'.[30] Those ten horses were equivalent to 0.67 per double mile, probably comparable to or even somewhat less than other coaches (and certainly comparable to the stage coaches of 1654-1750)[31] but for only three passengers instead of six. Other evidence also suggests that diligences were expensive to run, especially their short life. Snell & Co last referred to 'flying dili.-coaches' in 1780, and the diligences Glasier & Co took over from Gevaux are not recorded after 1782. None of Bristol's regional coaches used diligences after 1783, apart

37 *Blewitt's Abingdon to London coach in the late eighteenth century, an example of a post-coach or machine (painting probably by John Cordrey). It is conveying six outside passengers and probably four inside ones. The coach body benefits from the springs but the box and the basket at the back do not.*

from short-lived ventures in 1788 and 1795-7. The Worcester to London diligence was abandoned even sooner, in 1777, with the proprietor's apology to its passengers that 'the expences attending it are so great, that it would be very imprudent to continue it'.[32]

On routes where both diligences and post-coaches had been in use there was usually no difference in fare and speed.[33] However, given that the post-coach continued and the diligence disappeared, the post-coach evidently proved the superior vehicle, providing one more inside seat for little increase in the weight of the vehicle (Figs. 37 and 38). Henceforth, all reasonably fast coaches were called post-coaches and described as having four inside passengers and sometimes no outsiders or just one outsider,

38 *A coach of 1796, with passengers on the roof and in the basket (drawn by George Woodward).*

who undoubtedly sat on the box beside the coachman. Whether the post-coach differed much from the machine as a vehicle is uncertain; the difference may just have been the greater speed, as implied by the word 'post'.

For a short time there were both two-horse and four-horse post-coaches, but the mail coach abandoned two-horse teams in 1788 and the Balloon coaches are last recorded in 1789. Hardly any other Bristol-London coaches were using two-horse teams in 1790 and none by 1792.[34] Apparently the contribution two-horse teams made to keeping down the cost of high speed had become less important as the roads improved, and was now outweighed by the inconvenience.

LONDON COACHES.

THE PROPRIETORS of the OLD LONDON COACHES, respectfully inform their Friends and the Public, that the COACHES from BRISTOL to LONDON, in their connection, are arranged in the following manner: Determined to render travelling in their Coaches expeditious, regular, and comfortable, they humbly hope to merit approbation.

A LIGHT POST-COACH, in ONE DAY, from the WHITE HART INN, *Broad-street* carrying FOUR INSIDE PASSENGERS, and work'd with FOUR HORSES all the way, every morning, (except Sundays) at Four o'clock.

Fare Inside, - - £1 5 0
Outside, - - 0 14 0

A LIGHT POST-COACH, in TWO DAYS, from the WHITE LION INN, *Broad-street*, TUESDAY, THURSDAY and SATURDAY mornings, at Seven o'clock; to sleep at the *George and Pelican Inn, Newbury*.

Fare Inside, - - £1 7 0
Outside, - - 0 14 0

A LIGHT POST-COACH, from the BUSH-TAVERN, *Corn-street*, every AFTERNOON, except *Saturday*, at Two o'clock, carrying FOUR INSIDE PASSENGERS; and worked with FOUR HORSES all the way.—Arrives at the THREE CUPS, *Bread street, London*, early in the morning. Sets out from *London* every evening at Five o'clock, and will arrive in BRISTOL earlier than any other Coach.

Fare Inside, - - £1 3 0
Outside, - - 0 12 0

A PAIR HORSE COACH from the BUSH TAVERN, *Corn-street*, SATURDAY afternoon, at Two o'clock.

A POST-COACH, from the WHITE LION INN, *Broad-street*, MONDAY, WEDNESDAY, and FRIDAY evenings, at Eight o'clock.

Fare Inside, - - £1 5 0
Outside, - - 0 14 0

A FOUR HORSE COACH, from the WHITE HART INN, *Broad-street*, TUESDAY, THURSDAY, and SUNDAY evenings at Eight o'clock.

Fare Inside, - - £1 0 0
Outside, - - 0 14 0

☞ The utmost care will be taken of all parcels and packages, which shall be delivered immediately on their arrival; but the proprietors will not be accountable, for any parcel, package or passengers luggage, above the value of *Five Pounds*, except the value shall be ascertained at the time of delivery.
Performed by

MOODY,	PO STON.
PICKWICK,	COUPLAND,
WEEKS,	And Co.
CARR,	

39 Advertisement by the main Bristol to London firm in 1790, offering a range of services, explicitly with four horses in most cases but also one 'pair horse coach'. (Felix Farley's Bristol Journal, 10 April 1790.)

Reduced variation by season

O NE OF THE most important changes in this period was the declining influence of the seasons. In the first century of stage coaching the organisation of services was very different in winter: speeds were lower, teams were larger, teams were not changed *en route* and the hours on the road each day were shorter. Fares remained the same throughout the year, but in terms of days the journeys were usually 50% longer in winter. Two changes are likely to have occurred on the Bristol road in the mid-1750s: changing teams in winter, to make two-day journeys possible, and (in consequence) dividing the route into districts horsed by individual proprietors in winter as well as summer. By the 1780s the other adjustments to winter had largely disappeared. Two-day journeys in summer (other than from Bath) ceased shortly after the first one-day coach ran, but Glasier & Co's two-day coaches in winter continued until 1776-7. In winter 1777-8 there were one-day coaches instead, at first setting off at 7 pm and travelling overnight.[35] This partly reflected an increased willingness among passengers to travel at night, and it became much rarer for coaches to stop overnight. That in turn reflected the fact that night travel had become less dangerous and the fact that a quicker journey made it more worthwhile to complete the journey in one stretch. There were still some two-day Bristol-London coaches in winter until at least 1793, probably because some passengers still preferred to stop overnight; the important point was that winter journeys were now possible in one day.

The gap in speed between summer and winter coaches was certainly narrowing. Five post-coach services advertised by three different Bristol-London firms in winter months in 1786-90 averaged 6.8 miles per hour, which was not much slower than average summer speeds of about 7.4 miles per hour and was far from the typical 3.1

miles per hour in winter up to the 1750s. Neither the diligences nor the Balloon coaches varied their advertised times by season. The narrowing of seasonal differences reflected what was happening nationwide: overall speeds were about 18% lower in winter in 1653-1750 and 5% lower in 1776-7, whereas the difference in advertised speeds was negligible from 1783-4 onwards.[36]

Another change at around the time of the introduction of one-day coaches in winter was the disappearance of the six-horse teams used in winter. There is no direct evidence from the Bristol road or anywhere else of exactly when it happened, but there is one strong pointer to the 1770s. In 1771 teams of six were still being used on the Norwich road, despite that road being one of the best and least hilly in the country, which indicates that they were still in general use elsewhere.[37] There is no subsequent evidence of routine use of six-horse teams, and the other changes of the 1770s make it likely that that was when they disappeared. Six-horse teams were occasionally still used even in the 1830s both on the Bristol road and elsewhere for particularly bad or steep stretches of road, such as Marlborough Hill,[38] but not routinely or for long distances. The end of six-horse teams is likely to have had a major impact on coachmasters' finances. In the first century of stage coaching, some coachmasters kept the same stock for a similar frequency of service in winter, but in general the figures for horses kept per double mile suggest that about a third more horses were required per mile covered in winter, despite the lower speeds.[39] Now the same stock was probably being kept in winter for services of similar speed.

The difference between summer and winter services did not disappear completely. Many coaches continued to vary their schedules by season. Bristol to London mail coaches continued to have different time bills for summer and winter until winter 1819/20, with winter services 5% slower. Other coach firms might advertise the same timings throughout the year, but their coaches were undoubtedly less reliable in winter, as Chaplin acknowledged in 1837.[40] Nevertheless, much of the difference between summer and winter services had gone by the 1780s.

Productivity, roads and growth

FIG. 25 CONFIRMS what change in coach speeds and lack of change in fares would lead one to expect: that there was a significant increase in productivity in stage coaching in the second half of the eighteenth century, from the 1750s to the late 1780s. Greater speed cannot be explained away as having been made possible by lower provender costs or higher fares. What did make it possible?

One possibility which can be dismissed is economies of scale. There was little if any economy of scale to be had from larger vehicles or teams – often the reverse. If there were any economies of scale they were likely to be the result of larger firms. For example, as their firms became larger, carriers of goods by long-distance waggons obtained significant economies of scale by purchasing provender directly instead of through innkeepers and by directly employing smiths and wheelers.[41] However, coachmasters were usually innkeepers and therefore bought provender directly anyway, and there is no evidence of them employing their own smiths and wheelers in this period.

A major change in the 1760s which did have an impact has been identified already – the use of steel springs – though this was only partly the result of technological innovation and partly the result of better roads making the use of steel springs feasible. Probably coach springs improved further later in the century, but little is known about this. Other changes in vehicles were probably also dependent on improved roads, including different sizes of vehicle.

There was almost certainly improvement in coach horses. This did not involve them becoming larger. As indicated above, in 1650-1750 coach horses in England were almost invariably between 15 and 16 hands high. In six sales of stage coach horses on the Bristol route or at Bristol in 1821 and 1841 for which sizes are recorded, involving 335 horses from most parts of the route, all were from 15 hands 1 inch to 16 hands high. This lack of change contrasted with the increase in the size of waggon horses, which had been slightly smaller than coach horses in 1650-1750 but in 1831 were said to weigh an average of 15 cwt compared with about 10 cwt for coach horses.[42] Rather than an increase in size, we should expect a change in coach horses from horses bred for strength to horses more suitable for faster coaches and requiring less feed in relation to the work done. There is a little evidence from other routes about the feed required. The feed for horses conveying the subscription coach between Exeter and Plymouth from 1812 to 1823 was said to be equivalent to half a bushel of oats per horse per day, reckoning each bushel of beans as equivalent to two of oats. On the same basis, horses working the Henley and Wallingford coach at Maidenhead and Colnbrook in 1699 consumed 0.875 bushels per day, and horses working a Warwick coach out of London in 1743-5 from 0.625 to 0.7 (depending on the work they were doing).[43] The reduction from 1699 to 1812-23 was therefore 43%, and from 1743-5 to 1812-23 was 20-29%. Too much should not be made of so few examples, and feeding evidently varied according to the horses' workload, but the scanty evidence does suggest that the benefit from horses needing less feed may have been substantial.

Moreover, the main source of coach horses changed between the seventeenth and nineteenth centuries from places where what had been exceptionally large horses could be bred, such as Leicestershire, to Yorkshire, County Durham and other northern counties. The breed of horse changed from the shire type to lighter breeds, notably the Cleveland Bay (hence perhaps the reduced feed).[44] According to Youatt, writing in 1831, the coach horse

> is as different from what he was fifty years ago as it is possible to conceive. The clumsy-barrelled, cloddy-shouldered, round-legged,

black family horse, neither a coach nor a dray-horse, but something between both, as fat as an ox, and, with all his pride and prancing at first starting, not equal to more than six miles an hour, and knocking-up with one hard day's work, is no more seen; and we have, instead of him, an animal as tall, deep-chested, rising in the withers, slanting in the shoulders, flat in the legs, with even more strength, and with treble the speed.[45]

Youatt's reference to 'fifty years ago' should not perhaps be taken too literally, as the strongest indication of when the transformation took place puts it slightly earlier. In the 1830s stage coach horses were generally known as 'machiners' or 'machine horses', long after vehicles known as machines had become a distant memory.[46] That the term became so firmly attached to stage coach horses suggests that a recognisably new type of horse began to be used for stage coaches in the period when machines flourished, from the 1750s to 1780s, and therefore that they contributed to the increasing productivity of that period.

However, like steel springs, improved horses were not an entirely independent development. A different type of horse was required, and was made available, because the nature of the coach horse's task had changed, from dragging a coach along low-quality roads at a low speed, for which strength was the main requirement, to walking or trotting at higher speeds along much smoother roads. In fact it would be hard to avoid the conclusion that improved roads were crucial to the increased productivity of the period from the 1750s to 1780s. The decline of seasonal variation points especially strongly to this conclusion, as it was only the roads, and not horses or the available vehicles, which varied by season. That period has not previously been regarded as one when turnpike trusts were especially effective, and there were no obvious innovations in road repair. What caused the improvement in the effectiveness of turnpike trusts from the 1750s onwards, and what did they do that increased productivity in coach services?

Trusts devoted much effort to widening roads in this period, but that was much less important to coachmasters than to carriers, whom it allowed to use waggon teams with horses two abreast instead of in single file. The turnpiking from Corsham through Box to Batheaston Bridge, which provided for the first time a low-level turnpike road into Bath instead of crossing Kingsdown, involved a new stretch of road, completed in 1761, but there seem to have been no other wholly new stretches of road of any length. What there was instead, and what apparently made the difference, was a process of piecemeal improvement, together with more intensive use of existing repair methods and probably greater activity in winter. For example, when the records of the Calne trust, covering nine miles of the Bristol road and several branches, begin in 1773, they record a continuous small-scale process of widening, straightening and levelling the roads, together with several short stretches of new road to reduce gradients at Cherhill in 1774 and 1790-1 and at Nockett's Hill in 1789. The Seend-Box trust similarly diverted its road to reduce the gradient at Seend Hill in 1781. The Colnbrook trust demonstrated a more systematic attitude towards its road than previously by commissioning a survey in 1780 of 'the narrow and dangerous parts of the road', following which it immediately ordered the repair of several stretches.[47]

This may have reflected more ambitious ideas of what constituted a good road and perhaps some emulation of other trusts, especially where different routes were in competition, as in the Chippenham and Devizes area. Ability to raise funds increased from about 1750 through the tapping of large numbers of relatively small sums by means of subscriptions or low-denomination mortgages secured upon the tolls, as opposed to the earlier method of obtaining just a few large loans. The Bath trust made considerable use of tradeable small-denomination mortgages, though many others, including the Calne, Seend-Box and Colnbrook trusts, continued to use the old method; indeed the Colnbrook trust had only a single creditor from 1728 to 1825.[48] The trusts' more important source of income, tolls, increased as traffic grew. Above all, while some of the trusts' work was quickly undone by weather and traffic and had to be regularly repeated, improvements such as reduced gradients and improved drainage remained and were cumulative. In the end, though, the best evidence of the effectiveness of the trusts in this period is not to be found in their own patchy records but in the greater speeds and increased productivity of the stage coaches.

Mail coaches

JOHN PALMER (FIG. 40), a theatre manager from Bath, put his plan for improving the postal service and increasing its revenue to William Pitt in 1782. Pointing out that the post was not only the slowest form of conveyance (39 hours between Bath and London) but also unsafe, he argued that the Post Office should contract for coaches taking just 16 hours between Bath and London. They would carry only four inside passengers, a driver and a guard. The Post Office would make a payment per mile to have letters carried and would specify timings, provide a guard and impose other requirements, but the service would be run by the contractors and supported mainly by revenue from passengers. Palmer's plan roused the intense hostility of the Post Office, but had the support of Pitt, who won an election in March 1784. Pitt was therefore able to insist that Palmer's experiment go ahead. The experiment was to take place, at Palmer's expense, on the Bristol to London road, starting on 2 August. The Bristol route was probably chosen because of its importance, but it was also reckoned one of the best roads in the country.[49]

40 *John Palmer (1742-1818), founder of the mail coach system (painting by Gainsborough).*

Palmer's first contract, unlike later ones, was with a single individual, John Williams, and was for two years. Williams had been an innkeeper at Beckhampton for ten years, and moved to the Three Tuns at Bath in January 1784, perhaps with the possibility of mail coaches in mind, but how it came about that he obtained the first mail coach contract is not known. Williams then himself contracted with the partners in what had been Snell & Co's coach to provide the mail service: John Dover of Bath, James Porter of Marlborough, Edward Fromont of Thatcham, James Slarck, coffee-house keeper of London, and Thomas Wilson, innkeeper at the Swan with Two Necks, London. Williams had perhaps expected the main Bristol and Bath coach firm to regard the mail coach as a competitor, or at least to have less interest in its success, and therefore turned to its smaller rival. He horsed the mail coach part of the way himself, using 11 horses, most likely between Bath and Bristol.[50]

Post Office officials tried to frighten off the contractors, telling them it would run for only two or three weeks and that anyone horsing it would be watched rigorously and prosecuted for carrying letters. Palmer's assistant had to reassure Wilson, who had previously assumed the Post Office supported the enterprise and now found it did not – 'This frightened the man out of his senses'. The first mail coach set off from the Rummer at Bristol at 4 pm on 2 August 1784 and reached the General Post Office in London at 8 am the next morning, achieving exactly the 16 hours intended. The result was that letters were delivered 12 to 18 hours earlier than before. A national network was established in the following year, together with the first cross-country route (Bristol to Portsmouth). The Bristol coach was sufficiently successful that in 1785 Williams sought to sell a share in it to two of the main Bath coachmasters for £500 and cut out his existing partners, but Palmer, evidently fearing ruinous competition as a result, prevented this.[51]

Not everything went smoothly at first. Williams went bankrupt in 1787. In 1788 Palmer complained that 'The manner in which the Bath & Bristol coach is continued to be work'd is such that it is impossible for me longer to suffer' and referred to 'the continued complaints of the coaches overturning, delays &c.'. He ordered that from 5 April 'Mr Bezant's coach will be put on the ground & no stops or baiting allow'd for passengers at any place whatever but during the time absolutely necessary for doing the duty of the Post Office at Marlboro' '.[52]

When the contract was re-tendered in 1793, without Williams but still with Wilson, Dover, Fromont and others, the contractors agreed to use the vehicles specified by the Post Office at a charge to them of 1¼d per mile each way, to adhere to the time bill and prevent stops at alehouses except in cases of accidents, impassable roads, floods or snow, to carry no more than one outside passenger and to receive 1d per mile from the Post Office as payment for conveying the letters. [53] The advantages of the mails to the contractors were the payment for conveying letters, the guard provided at the Post Office's expense and the exemption from tolls, together with the prestige of the mail coaches. The disadvantages were the limited number of outside passengers and the lack of flexibility or control over timings and vehicles.

Operation

THE FIRST MAIL coaches were very different from the later ones. Palmer's plan was to convey the mail by diligences, and the first mail coaches were described as 'mail diligences'. By 1784, of course, four-inside post-coaches had largely replaced three-inside diligences, and the mail diligence was in fact a post-coach (Fig. 41). Nevertheless, like the diligences, it was drawn by only two horses, and consequently had very short stages, said to be of only six to eight miles.[54] However, from April 1788 Besant's patent coaches were used on the Bristol route and from January 1789 on the Exeter

BY AUTHORITY.

PERSONS AND PROPERTY PROTECTED.

Published by S.W. Fores, Caricature Warehouse, Nᵒ 3 Piccadilly London — Novᵣ 26ᵗʰ 1785

41 Rowlandson's satirical view of the mail coach, 1785. Unlike the better-known, non-satirical view said to be of the first mail coach, Rowlandson correctly shows a two-horse team. The coach is evidently made as light as possible, without a box or basket at the back. The post is carried in the box at the front, on which both the coachman and the guard sit.

*42 Pyne's view of a mail coach, 1803. This is one of Besant's patent coaches,
introduced in the late 1780s. The mail is now carried in a box at the back, on
which the guard sits, and the team is of four horses.*

via Bath route.[55] These were heavier coaches, with a box for the
letters at the back, and it must have been then that teams changed
from two horses to four and that mail coaches assumed the form
familiar from later views (Fig. 42). Stages then became longer, all
but one between Bristol and London being from nine to 14 miles
(Fig. 43). Fares were at first little if at all dearer than other coaches.[56]

The 16-hour timing advertised was not entirely straightforward
in practice. In 1797 the time bills were in fact made out for 15 hours
in summer and 15¾ hours in winter, and this required extensive
explanation by Thomas Hasker, Superintendent of the Mail Coaches.
As regards down journeys:

> In winter the time bill is made to arrive at Bristol at ¾ past 11, but the
> contractors never agreed to be there before 12 [16 hours]. In summer
> they agreed to be there by eleven [15 hours] (great work) and which
> they generally are, allowing for a few minutes out of the London
> Office, and 20 minutes difference in the clocks – and sometimes they

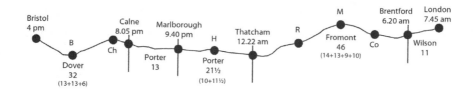

43 Plan of the mail coach in 1794-7, showing the contractors, the miles they shared for, the stages (starting and finishing at the black circles) and the timings of the up coach in summer. The stages are as in 1794; the other information is from 1797. Stages averaged 12 miles (counting Chippenham to Calne as a 'there and back' stage of 12 miles). Key: B – Bath; Ch – Chippenham; H – Hungerford; R – Reading; M – Maidenhead; Co – Colnbrook. (Sources: POST 10/366, p. 23; Proceedings of the Old Bailey website, t17941208, t17950416.)

even arrive before 11, which was the case this day, March 23rd, 1797 [when they] arrived at Bristol 10.50.

As for the up journeys:

> In winter the bill is made to arrive at ¾ past 7, but we do not expect it till 8, for their agreement is to work it up in 16 hours which, as the clocks are slowest at Bristol, will not bring it to London till about a ¼ or 20 mins after eight, and in summer about as much after seven, though we generally contrive to get them in by seven. Very great exertion – 122 miles in 14 hours and ¾, and not less than 1 hour & ½ lost in changing horses and supping exclusive of any trifling delay such as losing shoes, breaking a trace &c, some of which happen every journey.[57]

In other words, despite the advertised time of 16 hours, the intended time was 16 hours in winter and 15 in summer, and the time bills in winter were in fact made out for 15¾ hours. Hasker's observations indicate that the intended times normally were achieved – 7.6 and 8.1 miles per hour respectively. In October 1793 Hasker observed, apparently of up journeys in summer, that 'we always consider the Bristol at its time if 18 minutes after 7 tho it is not so said, for if that was known to coachmen guards &c. we should never have it in earlier.'[58]

Several lists of arrival times also indicate how reliable the mail coaches were in practice. Between 15 September and 16 October 1792 they arrived in London later than 7.18 nine times (once at 8.12 but otherwise never later than 7.40) and in the same period in 1793 also nine times (none later than 7.33). A more comprehensive set of figures relates to arrivals at Bristol in December in each year from 1790 to 1793, when Hasker expected arrivals to be at 12. Most arrivals were between 12 and 1 pm, but there were a few earlier ones and a number of later ones: five in 1790 (one at 2.55), seven in 1791 (two at 2.30), 11 in 1792 (four from 2.40 to 3.20) and five in 1793 (none later than 2.06).[59] In this period, a traveller in the mail coach could expect to arrive within reasonable range of the advertised time, but it was certainly not possible to set one's watch by the mail coach.

The mail coaches were unusual in carrying guards. As indicated earlier, guards were rare on any route in the first century of stage coaching. No Bristol coach claimed to have one until Gevaux' diligence in 1776 and some of Glasier & Co's machines in 1778.[60] Guards were clearly a comfort to passengers, and so would have been advertised if they had existed. The well-guarded mail coaches seem to have had an impact, and guards became more common on the faster coaches, though not the slower ones. Some coachmasters in the 1830s employed guards only at night and near London during the day.[61]

Mail coaches brought about a huge increase in the speed of postal services, with immense ramifications for economic, social and political life. They are often described as having revolutionised road passenger transport too, and they did indeed set new standards of reliability and security. However, it is easy to exaggerate their impact on passenger transport. They have been aptly described as 'a force for evolution rather than revolution in passenger road transport'.[62] They followed the example set by the diligences and, although their 15-16 hours was faster than the 17-18 hours of diligences and post-coaches in 1780-2, it was not a step change. Equally significant is the fact that the setting up of mail coaches was swiftly followed by the long period of stagnation already referred to. That was not the fault of the mail coaches, but they did not escape it themselves. Mail coach timings of the 1790s and 1830s are sometimes compared as if there was a continuous increase in speeds between those dates, but in fact the timings set for the Bristol mail coach in 1784 remained unchanged until 1819, and that made it typical of mail coaches in general.[63]

Stagnation, c.1790-1815

THE HEADLONG GROWTH in the number of Bristol's coach services ended abruptly in the late 1780s, and sustained growth did not resume until about 1815. There were slightly fewer services in 1814 than in 1789, though they probably had somewhat greater capacity. Speeds between Bristol and London in 1811-15 were lower than those of 1781-5, averaging 6.4 miles per hour compared with 7.6, despite higher fares. One coach (the Express) was advertised in 1809 as taking 24 hours, the slowest ever recorded in terms of hours and indicating only 5.1 miles per hour.[64] Of the down timings listed in Cary's *New itinerary* of 1812 for the six daily services, one was 16 hours (the mail coach), one 17 hours, three 20 hours and one 24 hours (the Express). The malaise affected coaching everywhere in a similar way (Fig. 23).[65] Not surprisingly, coach advertisements became scarcer in this period, as there was rarely anything new to offer.

What happened in the 1790s to curtail the growth of the industry? The answer is provided by examining the coachmaster's costs, as shown in Fig. 24, and especially the cost of horse provender. The cost of provender rose substantially in the 1790s, and remained high for about 25 years. The average price of a quarter of oats in England and Wales, never over 20s.6d before 1795, peaked at 39s.4d in 1800 and 44s.6d in 1812.[66] In part, the coach trade was a victim of the long wars with France, which disrupted both the coastal trade and imports. Other costs also increased, including the duties on stage coaches (first imposed in 1779), but none of these were nearly as important as provender costs.

Rising costs meant higher fares, unless speeds were reduced. Some passengers cared more about the speed than the fare, but others would go by a cheaper, slower coach if fares rose. Even many mail coach passengers did so, as Hasker stated in 1811: 'many passengers that are of a superior description, will go by the mail coaches let the price be what it will; others go for cheapness, and very likely they may be half the number of passengers that travel by the mail; of course, those would go where they could travel the cheapest, and would descend to other coaches'.[67] In fact the mail coaches probably did relatively well because of their reliability and prestige, and Hasker observed in 1793 that their earnings were holding up better than those of other coaches.[68] In general, there is likely to have been a pattern of trading down or 'descending', from post-chaises to stage coaches, from faster coaches to slower ones and even from coaches to waggons, [69] with coachmasters sometimes following the trend by slowing down their services. That adaptation by coachmasters is why average fares did not rise in proportion to provender prices.

The posting trade, being the dearest form of road passenger transport, probably suffered most. The lessee of the duties on post-horses complained in 1800 that he was especially hard-hit by the 35% increase in the price of posting, which had caused 'a very considerable diminution in travelling by chaises', reducing the duties by about a quarter; unlike himself, coachmasters who also let out post-horses 'indemnify themselves' by their coaches for the loss on post-horses.[70] He apparently meant that the coach trade held up better because some who would have used post-chaises now used coaches instead. That helps to explain why there was little decline in the number of Bristol-London coach services. There were even some new coach services, though none in the 1790s, and those set up from 1801 onwards tended to be slow and cheap ones. Hasker summed up the situation as early as 1793: 'corn is so dreadfully dear and travelling by no means so brisk as heretofore'.[71]

Coachmasters and coach firms

WHEN THE MAIN Bristol firm advertised in 1790, the Bristol proprietors were listed as Weeks, Poston, Coupland and Carr (of the White Lion), in alliance with Moody and Pickwick of Bath. But from late 1792 the three Bristol inns (Bush, White Hart and White Lion) advertised their services separately, suggesting that the coach firm which had dominated Bristol coaching for more than half a century had broken up. Whether it was an amicable separation is not known, but there is no obvious sign of intense competition. Given the background, and the continuing co-operation of Weeks, Poston and Coupland in Birmingham and Exeter coaches, a fair amount of collusion could be expected, especially over fares. From 1797 to 1800 the three main inns had four of the six daily services, including the mail. The others were at the London Inn and Talbot Tavern (apparently the Royal Blue, belonging to Snell's successors) and at the Rummer (a shadowy venture apparently set up when the Rummer lost the mail coach). Two new coaches were started in 1801 and 1802, but two of the older ones disappeared a few years later, so the number of services per week changed little. Another new service, the Trafalgar of 1806, foundered in 1807.[72]

A peculiarity in 1810 was a Bristol to London coach via Oxford, advertised by Boulton of London and others. The route was longer (141 miles compared with 122), and the time was 21 hours (it was

Rev James Woodforde from London to Bath, 28 June 1793

We got up about 4 o'clock this morning and at 5 got into the Bath coach from the Angel and set off for Bath. Briton on top of the coach. The coach carries only 4 inside passengers. We had a very fat woman with a dog and many band boxes, which much incommoded us, and also a poor sickly good kind of a man that went with us. We breakfasted at Maidenhead on coffee & tea. For strawberries at Maidenhead pd 1s.0d. For our breakfasts pd 2s.0d. We were very near meeting with an accident in Reading, passing a waggon, but thank God we got by safe and well. It was owing to the coachman. ... At Reading there were two young gentlemen by name Jolliffe that got up on the top of the coach, being going home from school for the vacation. I remembered their father at Winchester School. We dined at the Pelican Inn, Speanham Land. The young gentlemen dined with us, I franked [paid for] them. ... For our dinners, coachman &c. pd abt. 14s.0d. Paid at Speenham Land for extra luggage abt. 4s.0d. About 10 o'clock this evening, thank God, we got safe and well to Bath, to the White Hart Inn where we supped & slept – a very noble inn.

Source: John Beresford (ed.), The diary of a country parson: the Reverend James Woodforde *(1924), vol. 4, p. 39.*

aptly named the Perseverance), but probably few passengers were expected to travel the whole distance.[73] That was the only attempt ever made to serve Bristol via Oxford.

A glimpse of how one of the Bristol companies operated and how it adapted to hard times is provided by a Chancery suit relating

Rev James Woodforde from Bath to London, 28-9 October 1795

28 Oct. Paid at the Coach Office at Pickwicks for two inside places and one outside to London £4.0s.0d viz: inside each £1.11s.6d outside 17s.0d. The coach carries only four insides and goes from Pickwicks at the White Hart. ... At four we got into the London coach, and had two gentlemen with us, one of them was a Counsellor Bragge Member for Monmouth & a cotemporary of mine at New-College, as he did not acknowledge me, I did not him. It turned out a very fine afternoon & evening.

29 Oct. I thank God we had fine weather and a good moon all last night, and about 10 o'clock this morning we got safe & well to London to the Angel Inn at the back of St. Clements Church in the Strand, where we breakfasted, dined, supped & slept. We were not much fatigued with our journey or otherwise indisposed, tho' travelling all night. Paid for refreshment on the road abt. 2s.0d. To coachmen on the road, gave 4s.0d. To guard near London, gave 1s.0d. To extra luggage, 50 lb. at 1½d. pd. 6s.0d.

Source: John Beresford (ed.), The diary of a country parson: the Reverend James Woodforde (1924), vol. 4, pp. 239-40.

to 1801-2.[74] The Bristol partners were Poston and Coupland but not Weeks, confirming that the main Bristol firm had split in the 1790s. The suit was initiated by Edward Edwards of Reading, coachmaster, and others. Edwards and two partners had until 1802 worked a Bristol coach between London and Speenhamland (in

Rev Francis Witts from Bath to London, 7-8 January 1802

Thursday was fine; Friday, sleet & rain. ... Made an excellent luncheon on mock turtle soup previous to our departure from the White Lion in Broad St. at two. The vehicle was an opposition coach the places at £1.1s. each, we took in one passenger at Chippenham & arrived in London at 8 o'clock the next morning having completed without difficulty the 108 miles. Of the road I can say but little, darkness commencing soon after our departure nor did the light appear till we arrived in the well known vicinity of London. The snow being well beaten rather accelerated than impeded our progress; tho' from the drift upon Marlborough Downs we there took with us a guide. The chief places we passed thro' were Chippenham, where we got some excellent mulled wine, Calne, Marlborough, Spinham Lands, where we supped, Newbury, Reading, Maidenhead &c. We found George well on our arrival in Friday St. where we breakfasted.

Source: Alan Sutton (ed.), The complete diary of a Cotswold parson: the diaries of the Revd. Francis Edward Witts 1783-1854 *(2008), vol. 1, p. 497.*

Newbury). It was one of four Bristol-London coaches advertised together in August 1801, along with a Bath-London and a Frome-London coach.[75] The earnings of each coach were submitted to the bookkeeper at Speenhamland, and the proprietors each received weekly from him a share of the clear profits (after the payment of joint costs) in proportion to the miles their horses worked. The system was the same as that of other coach partnerships, except that earnings were being pooled for several coaches, apparently

Rev Francis Witts from London to Bath in Pickwick's coach, 26-7 February 1808

After an early dinner at Lady Lyttelton's repaired to Hatchett's; took my place in the Bath (Pickwick's) post coach with three other gents: an Irishman, a conversible lawyer, & a Swiss: ... conversed a great deal, slept a little; took refreshment at Colebrooke, tea at Speenhamland, beer &c. at Kennet: breakfasted at Devizes with the Bustons: reached home by 10 o'clock; the day very fine.

Source: Alan Sutton (ed.), The complete diary of a Cotswold parson: the diaries of the Revd. Francis Edward Witts 1783-1854 *(2008), vol. 2, p. 150.*

including some on different routes, and collective decisions were being made about a group of services.

In July 1801 there was a general meeting at Speenhamland at which a majority of the partners decided that the service horsed by Edwards should use six-inside coaches instead of four-inside ones, its fares should be lowered, and those horsing it should receive an allowance in compensation. The new fare was 24s. inside and 16s. outside, compared with 35s. and 21s. for the other coaches. Putting on a six-inside coach to operate more slowly at a lower fare is exactly how one would expect coachmasters to respond to rising provender prices. A fully-loaded six-inside coach at a lower fare could generate more revenue (depending on the number of outside passengers carried) than a fully-loaded four-inside coach with higher fares, and in the circumstances of 1801 there was also more chance of filling it. Edwards later claimed that his coach had earned more from February to October 1802 than any of the others. The increased revenue of course went to the partnership as a whole, and the allowance must have been intended to compensate those horsing that coach for higher operating costs, presumably because greater weight outweighed the effect of reduced speed. The allowance was an eighth of the coach's earnings, and amounted to £578.13s.0d for the first 26 weeks.[76]

During 1801 Edwards' partners had sold their shares to Richard Taylor of London, Esquire, and John Calley of Langley near Newbury, coachmaster, who apparently expected the allowance to be permanent. Instead they were told in 1802 that it had been just for the 26 weeks. Edwards, Calley and Taylor thereupon left the partnership and started their own Bristol-London coach. It was advertised in 1803-4 as the Royal Sailor double post-coach, with two compartments each holding four passengers, taking 20 hours. By September 1804 the Royal Sailor was an ordinary four-inside post-coach, now run by Taylor alone and using the Bush Inn in Bristol. Taylor is not heard of again, but the coach continued until 1842 to run from the Bush, with numerous changes of name until it became The Age in the 1830s.[77]

Double post-coaches such as Edwards & Co's are not recorded for any other Bristol-London service, but may have been used by the Royal Blue, which by 1811 was carefully describing itself as 'single bodied'. Bath directories record several 'double-bodied' services to

44 *A double-bodied coach, c.1805. This example is a Norwich to London coach.*

London in 1809 and 1812, and there were several regional ones too. Other large vehicles were Fromont's 'long coach' from Bath to London in 1800 and a Bristol to Birmingham one in about 1807.[78]

One other feature of this period is that coaches began to be named. Apart from the Balloon coaches in 1784, the first named Bristol to London coaches seem to have been the Royal Blue and the Mercury in 1788 and 1789.[79] There followed the Royal Charlotte and Royal Sailor (both 1790), the Duke of York and Duke of Clarence (1792), and the Express, the Defiance and the Immortal General Abercrombie (1801). From about 1810-15 it was unusual for a coach not to be named.

Edward Fromont

THE MOST SUCCESSFUL newcomer in this period was Edward Fromont of Thatcham, who had a significant impact on Bristol's coach services. In 1781 he described himself as a shopkeeper of Thatcham, and in that year he was first recorded as a coachmaster, in Snell & Co's firm, which served not only Bristol but also Exeter via Bath. As a result he became a contractor for both the Bristol mail coach and the Exeter mail coach via Bath. In 1797 Fromont had 46 of the Bristol mail coach's 123½ miles, from Brentford to Thatcham, which was more than any other contractor (Fig. 43). He had even more of the Exeter mail coach, horsing 122 of the 197½ miles, from Brentford to Wells, as well as benefiting from the 20 minute refreshment break both coaches had at Thatcham.[80]

From 1793 or earlier until he sold his carrying business in 1805 Fromont was also a carrier between Bristol and London, and from 1796 until at least 1801 he conveyed goods by barge from London to Froxfield in Wiltshire. He continued to live at Thatcham, basing his business at the King's Head there, which he seems to have obtained as a result of it being mortgaged to his wife's previous husband (Fig. 45). He also leased at least one farm near Thatcham, an inn and land at Hounslow from 1794 and Gerrard's Hall (an important London inn) from 1799, installing his stepson Henry Dibben at the latter (Fig. 46).[81]

Given Fromont's large stake, the initial success of Bristol's mail coach was as much due to him as to anyone. However, his attentiveness evidently declined. Whereas Wilson in London was highly regarded for his reliability and good timekeeping, Fromont was increasingly regarded as an exasperating problem. In 1788

45 *The King's Head, Thatcham, headquarters of Fromont's coach business, seen in about 1930, when the building still combined the hospitality and transport functions of an inn. It still stands, but has lost its porch.*

46 Gerrard's Hall, Basing Lane, a London coaching and carrying inn leased by Fromont and run by his stepson, Henry Dibben.

Palmer hoped Fromont would continue, but added that 'I expect he will by no means undertake it, unless he is determin'd to conduct it with spirit & good humour'. In July 1793 Hasker noted that in the previous winter he had allowed Fromont to carry both mails in a single coach for 40 or 50 miles and to use an additional pair of horses for it: 'this I thought was necessary and accelerated the deliveries, and had not such indulgence been given, and exertion used, I do not think he would have got through the winter, that road was so heavy'. Now, however, Fromont was saying 'that he will not run his horses so fast another winter to the ruin of himself and family', though Hasker added that 'during this quarter he has done the business very well'. In November 1796 Hasker was criticising the time lost through the 'obstinate idleness' of Fromont's coachmen and told Fromont that 'the people below [i.e. the contractors further from London] say (as they did last year) if Mr Fromont is suffered to take so much time on his ground we will take it on our own also ... I am nearly tired of writing to you for every winter your two coaches give me more trouble than all the rest of the mails. ... It is not only that your coaches are the worst and detain the delivery for they will soon make the other coaches as bad as themselves.'[82]

In 1801 the Post Office finally lost patience with Fromont's poor timekeeping and he was expelled from the mail coaches. He immediately retaliated by establishing the 'Express Opposition-Coach' and Defiance coach, one to Bristol and one to Bath, using his mail coach horses (Fig. 47). It was a difficult time to start new coaches, but Fromont succeeded in establishing himself, probably for two reasons: he had sufficient resources to avoid being forced off the road by price-cutting, and he eventually found a niche by running relatively slow and cheap coaches, which were to be his distinctive contribution to Bristol stage coaching. This was despite his experience as a mail coach contractor, but perhaps reflected his role as a carrier. His Express coaches were advertised as taking 17 or 18 hours in 1801, but 24 hours in 1809. By then the gap between Bristol's fastest and slowest coaches was as large as it was ever to be. The Express continued until about 1824, when it was replaced by a faster coach. The slowness and cheapness of Fromont's coaches must have limited their impact on his competitors, and perhaps therefore the ferocity of their response. By 1806 he also had part-shares in Taunton, Southampton and Windsor coaches, and in 1809/10 he added a network of new coaches, also slow and cheap, linking Bristol and Barnstaple and Exeter. That was set up in association with George Coupland of Bristol, and Fromont and Richard Coupland later co-operated over London coaches, with Fromont horsing some stages of Coupland's Regulator, a fast coach, and Coupland doing the same for the Express and Defiance. By 1809, therefore, Fromont was accepted by the Bristol coachmasters as someone they could do business with.[83]

EDWARD FROMONT respectfully begs leave to inform his Friends and the Public, that on and after the 5th of July, a new Poft-Coach, called THE EXPRESS OPPOSITION-COACH

(To be performed by the Stock now employed in the Bath Mail) will fet out for London every day at Twelve o'clock, from his Warehoufe, BROADMEAD, *Briftol*, and at Two o'clock in the Afternoon from the THREE TUNS INN, STALL-STREET, *Bath*; and will arrive in London, at Six o'clock the fucceeding Morning. It will return from GERRARD's HALL, BASING-LANE, BREAD-STREET, London, at Five o'clock in the Afternoon, and will arrive at the above Inn at Bath at half paft Eight, and at the Warehoufe at Briftol, at Ten o'clock the next morning.

Parcels taken in, at the above-mentioned places, WITHOUT ANY DEMAND FOR BOOKING and delivered, to the extent of a mile from them, WITHOUT ANY CHARGE FOR PORTERAGE.

WAGGONS every day, and BARGES by the *Kennet* and *Avon* Canal, every week as ufual.

☞ No Paffenger's luggage, parcel or package, of any denomination whatever, above the value of 5l. will be paid for, if loft or injured, unlefs infured as fuch at the time of entry.

Fare from Briftol, infide - l. 15s.
Ditto from Bath, ditto - l. 12s.
Ditto ditto outfide - l. 1s.

47 Edward Fromont announces his Express coach, 1801. (Felix Farley's Bristol Journal, 4 July 1801.)

In 1821, when Fromont retired from stage coaching, he had over 200 horses, working the Regulator, Express and Defiance coaches to Bristol and coaches to Marlborough and Swindon. 100 of his coach horses were then sold, but his daughter, Maria Fromont, took over part of the business and continued to work the New Company's day and night coaches at Thatcham until 1841, apparently from Hungerford to Twyford. Fromont himself died in 1831.[84]

Vehicles and productivity

IF COSTS ARE rising, increasing fares and stable or declining speeds do not necessarily mean that productivity has stopped growing. Nevertheless, Fig. 25 indicates that there was at best only very slight productivity growth from about 1790 to 1820. There was probably less incentive to improve the roads if the speed of travel was no longer increasing, but both on the Bristol road and elsewhere turnpike trusts continued to make improvements such as reduced gradients, as the Chippenham trust did with new roads avoiding Monkton Hill in 1792 and Derry Hill in 1802-5 and as the Beckhampton trust did at Silbury Hill in 1793.[85] The apparent lack of impact of the trusts in this period may indicate simply that they were close to the limit of what could be achieved by traditional methods of road repair and improvement, and that a step change in repair methods and ambition would be needed for them to give rise to substantial further productivity growth. There may have been some increase in the reliability of coaches, at least in summer, as in 1811 it was argued by William Waterhouse that the mail coaches had lost passengers because 'in the summer season our post coaches are so much better done than they were formerly'.[86]

What did change significantly, and therefore needs to be considered here, was the stage coach as a vehicle and its capacity. That change has been attributed to a technological innovation, once again in the form of improved springs. Obadiah Elliot's elliptical spring, invented in 1804 and patented the following year, was a horizontal spring in the shape of an elongated eye between the coach body and the axle, making a perch (the coach's equivalent of a ship's keel) unnecessary. It has been argued that, once the elliptical spring was used, coach body, coachman's box and back boot were all connected and benefited from the spring, and the coach's centre of gravity was lower, reducing the risk of the coach overturning. As the coach roof was lower, instead of passengers sitting on the edge of the roof with their legs dangling over the edge, they could rest their feet on one of the boots, and were increasingly provided with a seat back (Figs. 54 and 55). Such coaches could therefore carry a larger number of outside passengers in safely and comfort, and the increased safety apparently resulted in the legislation of 1806 which allowed ten outside passengers to be carried in winter and 12 in summer (amended to ten including any guard in 1810, plus two more if certain limits on luggage were observed). However, the connecting of body, box and boot (but not the lowering) pre-dated Elliot, as it is shown in a painting of 1801, and similar benefits could apparently be obtained by means of the telegraph spring, which had appeared by 1804. It was used for coaches which retained a perch and consisted of four semi-elliptical or 'grasshopper' springs forming four sides of a square. Fromont used 'telegraph coaches' from 1809.[87]

More fundamentally, the fact that it was legal and safe to carry more outside passengers did not necessarily mean that coachmasters would do so. More passengers meant more weight to draw, and for that reason fast post-coaches in the late eighteenth century had often carried no outsiders or only one or two. Yet in the 1830s fast coaches were usually licensed to carry eight or 11 outsiders, and there was much less difference in capacity between fast and slow coaches. That change has received far less attention than it deserves. When did it take place, and was it caused by elliptical and telegraph springs or by something else? As regards the timing, statements by several London coachmasters in 1811 indicate that it was by then normal for four-inside coaches to carry ten outside passengers, the same number that six-inside coaches carried, making the four-inside coaches of 1811 comparable to those of the 1830s but very different from those of the 1790s.[88] That being so, it is reasonable to assume that the change took place not long after Elliot's patent of 1805 and the Act of 1806. It probably coincided broadly with the disappearance of double-bodied coaches, which were no longer needed when so many more passengers could be carried on a single-bodied coach.

As for the reasons, one possible explanation would be that, whereas in the late eighteenth century a high speed at reasonable cost meant keeping the weight down to what four horses could draw at that speed, improved roads made it possible for greater weight and therefore more passengers to be drawn at the same speed and cost. However, in that case, the fare for any given speed ought to have declined and productivity ought to have risen, which did not happen. In fact the view that Elliot's spring was important is based mainly on the assumption that carrying twice as many passengers was an unalloyed benefit, but that would be the case only if coachmasters kept the same number of horses for those greater loads. Moreover, there was no consensus even in the 1830s on which sort of spring – elliptical, telegraph, 'C' or whip – was best for draught, and coachmakers tended to favour the telegraph spring.[89] What may well have happened is that, in order to draw the extra weight, the number of horses kept did in fact rise to the one horse per double mile or thereabouts which was normal by the 1820s.[90] There must have been some benefit from elliptical springs or they would not have been used at all, and from carrying larger numbers of outside passengers or they would not have been carried, but the benefits were apparently marginal, and were perhaps confined to fewer drivers and slightly less vehicle weight per passenger. It is not possible to be certain in the absence of information about the numbers of horses kept by coachmasters in this period, but that seems likely to be the reason why significantly larger numbers of outside passengers did not result in a substantial rise in productivity.

Renewed growth and acceleration, c.1815-38

BY ABOUT 1815 the coachmasters had survived the hard times. Provender prices fell and growth resumed. The number of Bristol to London services rose from 40 a week in 1814 to peaks of 74 a week in 1825 and 1828-31, following which it stabilised at 69 in 1834-8. Average speeds rose from 6.4 miles per hour in 1811-15 to 8.4 in 1831-5. Fares remained stable or declined slightly from the previous high level.

Coachmasters and coach firms

R ENEWED GROWTH INVOLVED both the expansion of existing businesses and the founding of new ones. In 1815 there were five separate businesses or alliances at Bristol and evidently a competitive situation. Of the seven services each day, Weeks had two at the Bush, Coupland and Fromont had two at the White Hart and the Bell, Thomas Luce had one at the White Lion, Charles Bessell had one at the Swan and Sarah Poston had one at the Rummer. The latter was the Triumph, first recorded in 1815, which seems to have been set up by middle-ground men excluded when Coupland re-established the White Hart coach as the Regulator.[91] Four of the seven services were slow and cheap ones – Weeks's Regent (formerly the Royal Sailor), Fromont's Express, Bessell's Royal Blue and Sarah Poston's Triumph – so there was competition on price as well as speed.

Colonel Richard Starke from London to Bath, 21 August 1815

Very fine day – determined to go by midday Bath coach ... had an early dinner at Hatchetts & at ½ past 5 left Town ... Our coach was terribly full – 6 inside – 16 or 17 out – terribly hot – went outside great part of the way – met at [on the way to?] Bath a German born at Spa with whom I had much conversation in French – and an odd would-be very knowing lady, 2 merchants ... , & a very old man from Putney – journey very hot, crowded and disagreeable – got to Bath at ½ past 2 [?].

Source: Carmarthenshire RO, CDX/734 (typescript).

Three of Bristol's most important coachmasters entered the trade in this period. Isaac Niblett, the greatest of them, was a servant at the White Lion from 1804, at the age of about 11, and was innkeeper there (succeeding Thomas Luce) from 1820 to 1859, an association with the White Lion lasting 54 years. John Townsend took over the Bush in 1807 and eventually acquired its coaching business too after Weeks's death in 1819. He was then aged about 52 and remained a coachmaster there for 22 years, latterly in partnership with his son William Henry Townsend. William Clift was innkeeper at the Plume of Feathers by 1816, aged about 25, and became a coachmaster two years later, continuing until his bankruptcy in 1837. Clift's most important characteristic was his unwillingness to collude with other coachmasters.[92]

There were two wholly new ventures in 1824-5, one successful and one not. The unsuccessful one was Stephen Rogers of Bristol's two coaches of April and May 1824, the Magnet and the Economist, day and night coaches respectively (Fig. 48). Rogers' London partners were, for the Magnet, William Gilbert, a relatively minor London coach proprietor at Blossoms Inn, and, for the Economist, Algernon Wallington, an energetic but often unsuccessful coach and waggon proprietor at the Castle and Falcon. The Magnet also had partners at Bath, Chippenham, Newbury and Hounslow. It apparently ceased to run when the Newbury partner, Abner Clarkson, unilaterally increased the fares and then refused to provide horses any longer. Neither coach is recorded after January 1825.[93]

Two established coachmasters had set up new coaches, so after the failure of the Magnet and Economist there were nine services a day. There were still five groupings, as there had been ten years before. Three of the nine daily services were Coupland's (the Regulator, the Shamrock which had replaced the Express, and the newly-established Chronometer); Niblett had two (the Night Regulator and the newly-established Emerald); Townsend had two (the Mail and the Sovereign, formerly the Regent); Clift had the Triumph; the other was the Royal Blue.

The successful new venture of 1825 was the 'General Stage-Coach Company', which provided fast day coaches and night coaches taking 14 or 15 hours. It was intended as a new type of coach firm, providing a superior service 'upon all the principal roads', with capital of £500,000. According to its prospectus:

The levies which coachmen and guards are allowed to make, with the sanction of the coach proprietors, upon passengers, to supply the inefficiency of their wages, – and the numerous changes of them, even in short journeys, has become a tax of very

Cheap and Expeditious Travelling, by DAY, to
LONDON.
BEWARE OF DECEPTION:
The ORIGINAL, CHEAP, and INDEPENDENT
MAGNET COACH.

AFTER many manœuvres to suppress the MAGNET Coach, its Opponents have endeavoured to delude the Public by putting a Coach on the Road also called the MAGNET, and imitating the Original Magnet Coach-Bills in the Bills which they have posted at their counterfeit Magnet Offices : —
The Public are therefore respectfully requested to observe, that the ORIGINAL MAGNET COACH will Start in future (only) from *Rogers's Opposition Coach-Office, corner of Wine-Street*, at Ten Minutes before Seven, and the *Talbot Inn, Bath-Street*, BRISTOL, precisely at Seven in the Morning ; the *Three Cups Inn, Northgate-Street*, BATH, at Half-past Eight ; and arrive at the *Old White Horse Cellar, Piccadilly*, at Nine ; and the *Blossoms Inn, Lawrence Lane, Cheapside*, at Half-past Nine the same Evening.
It will leave the *Blossoms Inn, Lawrence Lane*, LONDON, at a Quarter before Six : and the *Old White Horse Cellar, Piccadilly*, at Half-past Six in the Morning ; and arrive at BATH at Seven, and at BRISTOL at Half-past Eight in the Evening—*Certain.*
Performed by
S. ROGERS, W. GILBERT, & Co.

THE CHEAPEST NIGHT COACH TO LONDON.
THE Public are respectfully informed, that a New
NIGHT COACH,
THE ECONOMIST,
will leave ROGER's Opposition Coach-Office, corner of *Wine-Street, Bristol*, at Half-past Ten in the Morning, the Three Cups Inn. *Market Place, Bath*, at Half-past Twelve, through BRADFORD, TROWBRIDGE, and DEVIZES, and will arrive at the OLD WHITE HORSE CELLAR, *Piccadilly*, at Half-past Six, and the CASTLE and FALCON, *Aldersgate Street, London*, at Seven in the Morning; leaves the Castle and Falcon at Twelve in the Day, the Old White Horse Cellar, Piccadilly, at a Quarter before One, arrives at Bath at Six and Bristol at Eight o'clock on the following morning.
All Parcels to and from London, not exceeding 14lb. at 1s.
Heavy Luggage, Three Farthings per lb. Passengers taken equally cheap.
Performed by
S. ROGERS, A. WALLINGTON & Co.
Who will not be accountable for any Parcel or Package, above the value of £5 unless entered as such, and paid for accordingly.
A Coach to CHELTENHAM, at Half-past Eight in the morning, at Reduced Fares.

48 *Advertisements for the short-lived Magnet and*
Economist coaches, 1824.
(Bristol Gazette, *24 June 1824.*)

considerable magnitude ... The shameful imposition[s], also, at the road inns, where the coaches stop for refreshments, are intolerable; – the charge is usually heavy, – the fare bad, – the attendance deficient, – punctuality seldom observed, – and, as to comfort, it has almost become proverbial 'that a man must not expect comfort in travelling'. Yet he pays *more than sufficient* to ensure it.

The Company promised to pay coachmen and guards full wages and not allow them to demand fees, and to fix the price of refreshments (including waiters), 'so that any person travelling by the Company's coaches may know to a fraction what money it will cost him to the journey's end'. It also undertook 'to avoid delays on the road, by observing one regular pace, equal to the present rate of travelling, and to prevent the necessity of *galloping* when time is lost; from which latter circumstance much and serious danger is always to be apprehended'.[94]

The Company's formation prompted a furious letter in the *Bristol Gazette* from 'a coach proprietor', arguing that 'the system which has been spreading so rapidly of late, of thus taking from individuals the trade by which they obtain their livelihood, is one which calls, not only for general reprobation, but a general determination and exertion to put it down; I say *general* because there is no knowing whose turn it may be next.' The Company was 'set on foot for the purpose of filling the pockets of a few restless or pennyless individuals, from the purses of the public'.[95]

Nothing more is heard of the Company on the Brighton road, its other main target, nor on any other road except the Bristol one, where its coaches did become established. The proprietors boasted in 1827 that they had been able 'to withstand the measures adopted for the suppression of their establishment'. The principle of 'No fees' for coachmen and guards became firmly established, and was copied by Niblett's and Coupland's coaches (but not Townsend's), evidently proving popular with passengers. Thomas Cooper, innkeeper at the Castle, Marlborough (the most opulent inn on the Bristol road), stated in 1825 that he had contracted to horse the Company's coaches, presumably for a stage or two, and the Company was probably organised like the subscription coaches of 1812 from London to Exeter and Plymouth, which were horsed by contractors paid fixed rates per mile. The subscribers paid the other costs and kept the revenue. In that case the subscribers lost interest within four years, once it became clear that the expected large profits

No Fees to Coachmen, Guards, or Waiters on the Road.

COOPER'S OLD COMPANY

London Day Light Post Coach,

Carrying FOUR INSIDE. leaves the ROYAL GLOUCESTER HO-TEL, CLIFTON HOTWELLS, every Morning at a quarter past SEVEN, COOPER'S Old Company Coach Office, NO. 6, HIGH STREET, BRISTOL, at a quarter before EIGHT, and CHRISTOPHER INN. BATH, at NINE o'clock precisely; arrives at the OLD *White Horse Cellar*, Piccadilly, at a quarter before NINE, and *George Inn*. Aldermanbury, at a quarter past NINE. On its return leaves the *George Inn*, Aldermanbury, at SEVEN, and the OLD *White Horse Cellar*, Piccadilly, at a quarter before EIGHT precisely.

ROUT—Chippenham, Calne, Marlborough, Newbury & Reading.

FARES.—Inside, £2. 5s.; Outside, £1. 1s.

Dine at COOPER'S COTTAGE, *Thatcham*, 3s. each.

COOPER's
Four Inside London Night Coach

The Old Company Light Post Coach, carrying FOUR IN-SIDE, leaves the ROYAL GLOUCESTER HOTEL, CLIFTON HOTWELLS, at FIVE, COOPER'S Old Company Coach Office, NO. 6, HIGH STREET, BRISTOL, at HALF-PAST FIVE, and the CHRISTOPHER INN, BATH, at SEVEN, and arrives at Piccadilly at HALF-PAST SEVEN o'Clock. On its return leaves the GEORGE INN, ALDERMANBURY at FIVE o'clock, and OLD WHITE HORSE CELLAR, Piccadilly, at a quarter before SIX.

ROUT—Melksham, Devizes. Marlborough, Newbury, & Reading.

FARES—Inside, £1. 18s.; Outside, 18s.

Sup at Cooper's Cottage, Thatcham, at 2s. 6d. each, including Waiters.

In case of any incivility being experienced by the passengers travelling by the Old Company's Coaches, from the servants, it is particularly requested that a prompt notification will be given at the George, Aldermanbury, as it is the anxious desire of the Proprietor to render all the convenience to the Public in his power, he will therefore feel obliged by any communication or suggestion, which, on any occasion, may be considered deserving of report.

☞ T. Cooper begs to observe, that the time stated will be strictly kept, and racing with other Coaches not allowed.

THOMAS COOPER, Proprietor.

The Old Company Coaches book only at the *Royal Glouces-ter Hotel, Clifton Hotwells*; in BRISTOL, at *Cooper's Office*, No. 6, *High Street*; in BATH, at the *Christopher Inn, Market Place*; and in LONDON, at the *George Inn, Aldermanbury*, and *Old White Horse Cellar. Piccadilly*, adjoining the Bath Hotel.

49 Advertisement for Cooper's day and night coaches, 1834. (Matthews's annual Bristol directory, 1834.)

were an illusion, and probably something similar happened quickly on the Bristol road.[96]

The coachmasters horsing the Company's coaches separated in 1828, perhaps because of disagreement over whether to keep to the original plan of running fast coaches. Henceforth there were the Old Company and the New Company, each with a day coach and a night coach daily. 'Cooper's Old Company coaches' were under the sole control of Thomas Cooper, who had moved to what became known as Cooper's Cottage at Thatcham by 1827. His coaches were fast ones: it was later recorded that 'As Cooper was particular about time being kept, no coaches being allowed to pass his, in answer to any complaints by the coachmen as to the horses, his answer was sometimes: "You find whipcord and I'll find horses." ' In contrast, the New Company's day coach had a middling speed and its night coach became the slowest on the road. The Bristol proprietor was William Clift, but probably the key figure was Maria Fromont at Thatcham.[97]

The new coaches replaced the Triumph (a slow coach), and the slow Chronometer coach also disappeared, followed in 1831 by the slow Royal Blue coach.[98] After that the same coaches continued until 1838 – ten coaches a day, including just two slow ones, which were The Age (formerly the Regent) and the New Company's night coach. The story of the last years of stage coaching on the Bristol road is less about changing numbers and types of services than about the increasing dominance of Isaac Niblett. On taking over the White Lion in 1820 he had just one London coach each day – the Night Regulator. In 1824 he established the Emerald, a fast day coach. In 1827 or 1828 he took over the Regulator, the Shamrock (renamed the Monarch) and the Chronometer (soon discontinued) following Coupland's departure from the coach trade, together with the White Hart Inn. When Cooper went bankrupt in 1833 Niblett became the Bristol proprietor of Cooper's Old Company. That gave him six of the ten daily services, leaving only the Mail and The Age at the Bush and the New Company coaches. At some point he became partner with the Townsends in the coaching business at the Bush, until the partnership was dissolved at the end of 1841, but the partnership may have been a recent one prompted by the railways' impact on the Townsends' business.[99] Of course Niblett's coaches did not necessarily have the same proprietors throughout the route, and several different London coachmasters were involved in them.

WHITE LION FAMILY HOTEL,

BROAD STREET, BRISTOL.

50 Isaac Niblett's trade card for the White Lion. The date must be between 1838 and 1841, as a coach is shown but a sign proclaims 'Railway Coach Office'.

As for services between Bath and London, these declined from 33 a week in 1809-14 to 20 in 1826-38. Evidently travellers to and from Bath were increasingly served by the Bristol-London coaches. After the disappearance of Fromont's Defiance in about 1823 and the two-day coach in 1825/6, the three survivors at Bath were the mail coach, the York House coach and the White Hart coach.[100]

Coachmasters between Bristol and London, unlike those near the east and south coasts, did not face the threat of steamships providing fast, reliable and cheap passenger transport from the 1820s, but they would have experienced the threat of steam in another form had it not been for political action. In 1827, Goldsworthy Gurney agreed a contract with two men who were to operate eight of his steam-powered road vehicles between Bristol and London. Contracts were also agreed with William Hanning for Bristol to Exeter and other roads and with Sir Charles Dance for Bristol to Birmingham and other roads in 1830. In 1831 Dance actually began regular services over the eight miles from Gloucester to Cheltenham three times a day. He was said to have exceeded coach speeds while charging only half the coach fare and making a profit. A parliamentary committee concluded in that year that steam vehicles could convey 14 or more passengers at an average of 10 miles per hour in perfect safety. As Gurney pointed out, the vehicles would have continued to be improved as experience was gained. However, many turnpike trusts were hostile to the new vehicles, believing they would damage the roads, and they began to obtain parliamentary approval for prohibitive tolls. Dance abandoned his service after three months when it became clear that Parliament favoured such tolls, and the other contracts were stillborn.[101] Experiments with steam road vehicles continued, but nothing came of them until decades later.

Services

COACH SPEEDS HAD begun to increase by 1818 (Fig. 51). This seems to have affected the slower coaches first, such as the Regent and Triumph. After 1824, no coach ever advertised a time exceeding 18½ hours. 18 hours or thereabouts became the standard for slow coaches, and until the arrival of railways there continued to be coaches taking about that time. As for the faster coaches, the only one other than the mail coach for which there is a series of timings before 1825 is the Regulator, whose advertised timing fell from 17 hours in 1815-18 to 13 hours in 1831, never bettered by any coach except the mail coach. Whereas timings in 1812 ranged from 16 to 24 hours, in 1833 they were from 13 to 18 hours, all but the two slow coaches taking just 13 to 15 hours (Table 2).

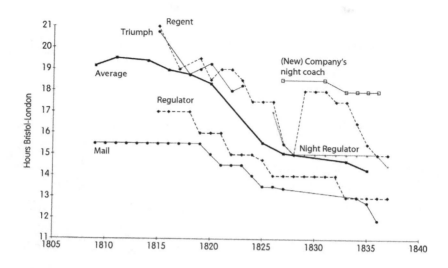

51 Coach timings, 1809-37. The thick line showing average Bristol-London speeds is largely based on Cary's *new itinerary, but with some corrections and filling of omissions from other sources. Information from Cary and directories is assumed to relate to the year before publication. (Sources:* Cary's *new itinerary (1810/12/15/17/19/21/26/28); Table 2; Alan Bates,* Directory of stage coach services 1836 *(1969), pp. 11-12; Bristol directories; newspaper advertisements.)*

This speeding up posed problems for the mail coaches, which were in danger of losing their position as the fastest coaches. Christopher Johnson, Superintendent of Mail Coaches from 1817 in succession to Hasker, began to accelerate the mails in the late 1810s, usually meeting complaints from the contractors that the mails were not worth working and that more money would need to be paid. His reply was that 'You must put yourselves first in the position in which you originally were of being the fastest carriages upon the road' and extra payment could then be considered. It was Johnson as much as Palmer or Hasker who created the mail coach system that was so much admired in the 1820s and 1830s. As in the 1780s, the mail coaches responded to the speeding up of other services rather than initiating the process. In 1819-20 separate time bills for the Bristol mail coach in summer and winter were abolished and the summer schedule of

Rev John Skinner from London to Bath, 8-9 December 1826

[Evening] The inside was full, and the outside covered with live stock and luggage; however we left Town with the velocity of a Mail; and indeed this mode of driving was kept up, with little intermission, till one poor horse dropped down, and was with difficulty got again on his legs. I had some tea at Reading; the rest of the party procured supper at the same rate, namely, half a crown a head. I forgot to mention when speaking of the fare, it was £1.18s., which includes every thing, besides the supper, no fees being expected by the coachmen or guards, and no charge made for luggage over weight. Nothing of consequence occurred till we were descending the hill to Bath Ford, when another horse fell, and on the course of a minute, after three loud groans, breathed his last. ... The three remaining horses however conveyed us in safety to the Christopher Inn, where we arrived about a quarter before 8.

Source: British Library, Add 33,695, pp. 187-8.

15 hours was applied to the winter. It was later observed that for the first 35 of the 40 years before 1821 the coach 'never kept the time in winter', suggesting that it became more reliable in winter from about 1816. Otherwise the timings established in 1784 remained in effect until April 1821. The new time then was advertised as 14½ hours, and fell further to 13 hours in 1825 and 12¾ hours in 1835 (9.6 miles per hour). In 1836, in order to deliver the mail sooner to South Wales and southern Ireland, the mail coach's speed was increased further to 10.3 miles per hour, saving 58 minutes and cutting the journey time to an unprecedented 11.9 hours. The reliability of the Bristol mail

C.J. Thomas from London to Bristol in the Company's night coach, 16-17 October 1828

Called at several of the western coach offices to ascertain the fares, made up to return by the Mail although they asked 6s. more to book me down than I paid coming up … bought some fancy neck hdkfs [handkercheifs], found when I came to pay for them that I had laid out 10s. or so more than I should have done and had not sufficient by a few shillings to bear my expenses per Mail. I therefore instantly resolved to go by way of Bristol and took a place by the Company's No Fee Coach and started by it at ½ after 4 from the White Bear Basinghall Street … It was a fine night but dark and I travelled very pleasantly, got to Thatcham in Berkshire about 11 and got a stylish kind of tea supper therefore [*sic*], passed soon through Reading [Hungerford?] and in the course of the morning of Friday 17th through Marlborough, Devizes, Melksham & several smaller places, reached Bath about 7 and Bristol before 9.

Source: Bristol RO, 39951(1).

coach was high, at least in December 1826, when a record of arrivals at Bath indicates that, of 25 arrivals on weekdays, 13 were at 8.10, the intended time, and only three were later than 8.20, the latest being at 8.39.[102]

The mail coaches nevertheless struggled to maintain their competitive edge. They generally remained the fastest coaches, and certainly the most reliable, but they were tied to particular times, often inconvenient for passengers, and were restricted to four outsiders at most, whereas other coaches could carry ten. Lewis Dillwyn, who lived near Swansea, invariably used the mail coach between Bristol

52 *The mail coach arriving at Bristol, 1826.*

and London from 1818 to 1825, but thereafter a variety of fast coaches, including the mail, Emerald, Monarch and Regulator. Probably the mail coaches were never again as profitable as they had been during the period of stagnation, but Chaplin's judgment in 1837 was that they were on average more remunerative than other coaches, even if less beneficial to innkeepers along the route because of not being allowed to stop for refreshments. The Bristol mail coach certainly seems to have been profitable: in four weeks in December 1839 it earned £5.4s. per mile, somewhat above the £5 regarded in 1827 (when costs were higher) as the minimum making it worthwhile to horse a mail coach, and well above the £4 then regarded by Johnson as the minimum 'remunerating price'.[103]

The speeding up of stage coaches appears to have attracted some who would otherwise have posted at higher cost. National figures indicate that post-chaises lost ground: there were 3.9 times as many post-chaises as stage coaches in 1810-14, but only 2.1 times as many in 1825-8. A similar comparison for the Bristol road is not possible, but post-chaises had become a small aspect of passenger transport there by 1834, when there were estimated to be 1,472 passengers a week by stage coach between London and Bath and Bristol but only 168 by post-chaise.[104] Travel on horseback and by private carriage probably also declined.

Coach speeds increased much less after 1825 than before, and from about 1833 there is little sign of any coaches becoming faster, except the mail and the Regent. This is similar to other routes, and may reflect the fact that the fastest coaches were approaching the maximum speed that horses drawing vehicles could achieve. Average speeds nevertheless rose, mainly because the slower coaches such as the Royal Blue tended to disappear. The only coach other than the mail which accelerated significantly was the Regent, timed at 17½ hours in 1826. The next year it was re-launched as the Sovereign, taking 15-15½ hours, but this was evidently a failure, as it reverted to being the Regent taking 18 hours in 1828. It was again re-launched in 1833, as The Age, taking only 15 hours by 1836.[105] The two increases in speed

53 A busy scene in the yard of the Swan with Two Necks, London, from which most of the mail coaches set off. Detail from drawing by Pollard.

Rev John Skinner in the Regulator from Bath to London, 14 May 1833

We were delayed ... nearly half an hour as one of the horses fell on the stones and was disabled from proceeding. As the coach drove to the door Miss Sophia Warner and her friend Miss De la Pont who were to go under my escort having taken their stations Anna and myself occupied ours, and we started about ten minutes after eight and drove nearly at the rate of ten miles an hour all the way to London so that allowing for stoppages, changing of horses &c we were only twelve hours on the road. The coach called the Regulator is moreover convenient for travellers on another account namely no fees are to be paid coachmen &c. The fare for each is £2.5s.0d including every thing but dinner. Having seen the young ladies safe we proceeded on a hackney coach to Portland Place, a little before nine o'clock and after tea I was not sorry to retire to rest having been much fatigued.

Source: British Library, Eg 3100.

were accompanied by higher fares, so the speeding up was a purely commercial decision rather than a reflection of improved roads or some other gain in productivity. The successive attempts to re-launch the Regent indicate that the profit was now to be made from fast coaches rather than slow ones. On the other hand, the Bristol road was not notable for the very highest speeds. Apart from the mail in 1836 and Bath's York House coach in 1838 (10.3 and 10.9 miles per hour respectively), no others exceeded 9.4 miles per hour overall, whereas the Birmingham, Brighton, Oxford, Cambridge and Windsor roads in 1835-6 all had coaches which were not mail coaches whose advertised speeds exceeded ten miles per hour.[106]

Henry Ellis from Bath to London, 17 July 1836

Took an early morning breakfast with Mr H. and left Bath at ½ past 8 of the clock for London by one of the Company's coaches. The morning was beautiful beyond description, and the whole country seemed one vast garden. ... We sat on the front seat of the coach in company with a young man from Exeter, who turned out to be a relative of the Wilcocks's, and whom we found an agreeable compayon du voyage. Dined at Newbury, passed through the pretty town of Reading, and saw Windsor Castle in the distance ... About 25 miles from Town we took up Major Hennis ... [We] were much amused by the familiar style in which he was accosted on getting on the coach by a cockney tailor. "Well, s'pose you came down this morning; hey? Had a fine day haven't ye?" evidently taking the gallant Major for a brother artiste from Cockayne who, like himself had come out for a day's spree ... The roads were more than ordinarily dusty, which was accounted for, from its being Sunday, when we were told, the pumps and water carts were not in use. ... We reached the Bull and Mouth at ½ past 8 o'clock having spent just 12 hours in performing the journey from Bath.

Source: Devon RO, 76/20/5, pp. 65-7.

Advertisements and directories make it possible to compile a complete record of fares, speeds and vehicles for late 1833 (Table 2). There were four day coaches, setting off from 6 am to 7.45 am and timed to reach London from 8 pm to 9.15 pm. The six night coaches set off from 1 pm to 6 pm and were timed to reach London from 7 am to 8 am; evidently the favoured arrival time in London determined the time of departure from Bristol. Five coaches took the

Table 2. Times and fares of Bristol-London coaches, 1833-4

Name, owner, Bristol inn	Day or Night	Hours	Overall speed	Fare in (s.)	Fare out (s.)	Seats (in-out)	Income (full load, s.)	Index of costs
Mail, Townsend, Bush	Night	13	9.4	38	18	4-3	206	352
Emerald, Niblett, WH & WL	Day	13	9.4	42	18	4-8	366	391
Regulator, Niblett, WH & WL	Day	13	9.4	35	15	4-11	305	391
Old Company's, Cooper's	Day	13.5	9.0	45	21	4-8	411	352
Old Company's, Cooper's	Night	14.5	8.4	38	18	4-11	350	298
Monarch, Niblett, WH & WL	Night	14.5	8.4	38	14	4-11	306	298
New Company's, Swan & Rummer	Day	14.5	8.4	30	14	4-8	274	298
Night Regulator, Niblett, WH & WL	Night	15	8.1	30	12	4-8	252	280
Age, Townsend, Bush	Night	17.5	7.0	24	10.5	4-8	235.5	227
New Company's, Swan & Rummer	Night	18	6.8	21	10.5	6-9	252	219
Average		**14.7**	**8.4**	**34.1**	**15.1**		**306***	**306***

Sources: *Bristol Gazette*, 14 Nov 1833, 5 Dec 1833, 28 Aug 1834; *Matthews's annual Bristol directory* (1834), including advertisement for Cooper's Old Company; *Robson's London directory* (1834).

Note: All information is from November-December 1833, except that for the mail coach (August 1834). The *Age's* outside fare was cut from 12s. to 10s.6d in December 1833 (*Bristol Gazette*, 5 Dec 1833). 'WH & WL' indicates White Hart and White Lion. Passengers in Townsend's two coaches were expected to pay fees to drivers and guards; the others were 'no fees' coaches. The number of seats is the number declared for tax purposes and reflects the tax bands; some coachmasters declared four and 11 in summer and four and eight in winter; the income column, for passengers only, is based on the higher figure (but 12 outsiders in the case of the a six-inside coach and just three for the mail coach). The index of costs makes average costs for all the coaches (except the mail coach) the same as average income (again except the mail coach) and then adjusts the costs for each coach in accordance with its speed, as explained in Appendix 2. It takes account of varying lengths of stops for meals (short in the mail coach's case), but not of varying loads (light for the mail coach, heavy for the New Company's six-inside night coach). The productivity index for these coaches varied from 23 for the Regulator to 35 for Cooper's two coaches, averaging 30. The asterisks indicate that average income and costs exclude the mail coach

54 A stage coach of the golden age: the Emerald in the 1830s (painting by Charles Cooper Henderson).

Chippenham road and five the Devizes road. There was a reasonable correspondence between high speeds and fares on the one hand and low speeds and fares on the other. The main exceptions were Cooper's coaches, both more expensive than their speeds would seem to have justified. On the other hand Cooper's were no fees coaches, unlike the mail coaches, so the latter's passengers incurred higher costs than the fare suggests. The night coaches were generally cheaper, but that was because they were usually slower, not because it was cheaper to run coaches at night. What is most impressive is the range of fares. The dearest coaches were twice the cost of the cheapest. The time taken by the journey varied much less than the fares.

To deliver on the promise that passengers should know exactly what the whole journey would cost, both Old and New Companies advertised the price of their meals at Thatcham ('supper, with tea and coffee' for the New Company's night coaches). In fact, passengers in the New Company's night coaches sometimes found their journey unexpectedly expensive. When the coach reached Thatcham, their luggage, which was not weighed on starting, was weighed there instead and the excess was charged for, by which time they had no alternative to paying. When they complained that they would not use her coach again, Maria Fromont was accustomed to say that 'she didn't care if she could only see them once', reflecting the fact that the coach lacked an established connection of frequent travellers.[107]

Vehicles

THE MAIN CHANGE in vehicles in this period was the virtual disappearance of the six-inside coach. At least in the nineteenth century six-inside coaches and 'heavy coaches' were evidently the same thing. Examples include Coupland's Chronometer, carrying ten outside passengers in the mid-1820s, and later the New Company's night coach carrying 12 outside, both taking 18 hours. Colonel Starke recorded a journey in a six-inside coach with 16 or 17 passengers on top (exceeding the legal limit) in 1815. Six-insides were probably always unpopular with passengers, especially those who ended up in the middle seats. According to figures given in 1811 and 1819 the weights of six-inside and four-inside coaches were not very different (19-20 cwt compared with 17-18 cwt), but the six-insides carried more passengers. In fact, depending on the quantity of passengers and luggage, the total loaded weight of either could be 50 cwt or more, consisting of perhaps 18 cwt of coach, 15 passengers at 1½ cwt each and 10 cwt of luggage.[108]

The connection between heavy, six-inside coaches and slow and cheap services is clear, for example from the decision in 1801 to change the coach horsed by Edwards to a six-inside one and lower the fare, and from the decision in 1833 to change the Regent to a four-inside one when it was speeded up under a new name. Presumably working a six-inside coach fast would have incurred disproportionate expense, whereas working a four-inside coach slow would have sacrificed revenue unnecessarily. The reason for the decline of six-inside coaches was therefore the decline of slow services. Whereas the London coachmaster, John Willan, stated in 1811 that nothing was more lucrative than a six-inside coach, another London coachmaster, William Horne, said in 1819 that only two of his 40 coaches were heavy ones. From 1833 Bristol's only remaining six-inside coaches were the New Company's night coaches. By 1836 six-inside coach services were rare on long-distance routes anywhere: apart from the Bristol road, the Exeter, Yoxford (for Halesworth), Salisbury, Portsmouth and Hastings roads each had one.[109]

Average coach weights may therefore have declined, but it is less clear that the weight of four-inside coaches declined. The evidence is most plentiful for mail coaches. The London ones were all patent coaches supplied by Besant and later Vidler under a single contract. One of Palmer's employees complained in 1788 that they were too heavy. He had weighed five, which averaged 17 cwt, and some later arrivals had weighed 18 or 19 cwt. According to Hasker, in about 1806 there had been a clamour about the weight, which had been reduced to 17¼ cwt. In 1808 Hasker said they were generally 17-18 cwt, though the coachmaker stated 16¾-17 cwt. Later references are to 17 cwt in 1811, 17 cwt (formerly 18-19 cwt) in 1827, 17-17½ cwt in 1832, 17-18 cwt or, according to the coachmaker, 17¾ cwt (formerly 18 cwt) in 1835 and 18 cwt in 1837.[110] In other words there was little change in the weight of the mail coach in almost 50 years, despite persistent claims that they had become lighter. The probable reason for the lack of change is that, while improved roads reduced wear and tear, potentially making it possible to build lighter, less sturdy coaches, raised speed increased the wear and tear, offsetting the effect of the improved roads.[111]

The evidence for other coaches is less clear, and often contradictory, but suggests that they were usually around the same

55 A surviving coach from the final years of stage coaching. The seats for outside passengers and the coachman are clearly visible. The coach body is lower than in earlier times, and firmly attached to the boot and box, making it possible to carry outside passengers with somewhat more comfort and safety. There is no record of a Comet coach between Bristol and London, nor of a coach from the Bush in Bristol to the Golden Cross, Charing Cross, and those details were probably painted on later.

weight as the mail coaches or slightly lighter. The coachmaker Waude stated in 1835 that coaches had been much heavier 25 years before, being not less than 23-24 cwt, because 'we were obliged to have such strength of timber', but he was probably making a contrast with six-inside, heavy coaches. The London coachmaster, Butler William Mountain, who built his own coaches, stated in 1811 that his four-inside coaches were 1-2 cwt lighter than the mail, and in 1827 Horne considered there was not much difference in weight between a mail coach and an ordinary stage coach. In 1831 the engineer John Macneill put the weight of four-horse coaches at 15¾-18 cwt, and in 1835 16-17 cwt seems to have been a typical weight for a fast coach.[112] The weight of ordinary four-inside stage coaches, like that of mail coaches, may therefore have changed little, again reflecting the contrasting impact of better roads and higher speed.

Roads and productivity

HOW WERE THE Bristol coachmasters of the 1820s and 1830s able to provide increased speed without a rise in fares? Part of the answer is that provender prices declined (Fig. 24), but Fig. 25 shows that there were significant gains in productivity as well, reducing fares to about three-quarters of what they would otherwise have been. The gains were apparently concentrated in the first half of the 1820s, though the precise timing may partly reflect the strong competition of the mid-1820s. One possible contributor to quicker journeys was cracking down on unauthorised stops and reducing the time taken for changes of team and refreshment stops. By 1828-36 the latter were typically 15 to 20 minutes for breakfast and 20 to 30 minutes for dinner. The Monarch was stated in 1836 to have saved an hour 'by making no unnecessary stoppages', but the new time of 14 hours had in fact been advertised for several years previously and the claim was probably intended to demonstrate that its speed was not achieved by 'racing or galloping'. The extent to which there was further improvement in horses is not known. There was certainly further improvement in coach springs, but apparently mainly in response to better roads. According to John Macneill in 1835, 'a much lighter spring is found to answer, now that the roads are so much improved'.[113]

In fact in this period there is no reason to doubt that improved roads were the main reason for increased productivity. That was certainly the view of the Bristol coachmasters themselves. The most important aspect was the better road repair associated with J.L. McAdam (Fig. 56). McAdam emphasised the method of applying the road material rather than the foundations. His method was to use small, angular stones (none more than an inch across) which were bound together rather than pushed aside by heavy weights passing over them, together with an insistence on good drainage. Measurements made in 1831 showed the force of traction exerted by horses in drawing a 21 cwt waggon to be 33 lb on a well-made pavement, 46 lb on a broken stone road such as McAdam provided,

56 John Loudon McAdam, the 'Colossus of Roads' (1756-1836).

65 lb on a broken stone surface laid on an old flint road and 147 lb on a gravel road. McAdam became the Bristol trust's surveyor in 1816, and by the end of 1818 his son William was surveyor of the Melksham, Devizes, Newbury and Reading trusts, among others. Numerous other trusts had sought McAdam's advice on their roads.[114]

McAdam was not of course the only surveyor using new repair methods. The Bath, Chippenham and Calne trusts appointed his rival, Benjamin Wingrove, in 1817, 1820 and 1821 respectively. Wingrove's methods differed mainly in a greater emphasis on costly foundations, the expense of which caused the Bath trust to replace him by McAdam in 1826. And McAdam was not involved in the Brentford trust, which by 1819 had considerably improved the road from Hounslow to London through better construction and materials (chalk and flints brought by canal from Kent instead of gravel). In the late 1820s and 1830s only about three-quarters as many horses were required on the Brentford trust's road per double mile as for the same coaches further from London.[115] Nevertheless, McAdam's impact was profound. Fromont stated in 1819 that 'nearly one-third less labour is required to work a fast coach over part of the road between Reading and London, where Mr. McAdam's plan has been adopted, than there is over other parts of the road where they still continue the old plan', reducing the expense by nearly a third as well as increasing the ease and safety of travelling. The coachmasters William Horne and George Botham also praised McAdam's work on the Bristol road. Chaplin reckoned in 1827 that, thanks to the breaking of stones, there was not a third as much wear and tear on coaches as seven years before.[116] The timing of the increase in speeds and growth in productivity supports their views.

The other important aspect of the trusts' work in this period was the construction of new stretches of road to reduce gradients. This was not a new activity, but throughout the country it was carried out with new determination from the late 1810s to the early 1830s. The evidence from the Bristol road is limited, but the Chippenham Trust improved Black Dog Hill in 1818-20 and McAdam stated in 1823 that as surveyor of the Bristol trust he had 'lowered a great number of hills' and made 12 to 14 miles of new road. The one example of a major new route was that from Blue Vein to Box, authorised in 1829 and enabling users of the Devizes road to avoid the steep hill into Bath at Kingsdown.[117]

The stage coaches of the 1830s presented a strong contrast to those of the 1760s and earlier. There were vehicles carrying many more passengers at much greater speeds, and fares were little more than a quarter of what they would have been but for road improvements and improvements in horses since the 1750s and 1760s. By the 1830s there was little scope for further increases in speed, as coach speeds were approaching the limit of the horse's capabilities. Continuing road improvements might have resulted in some further reductions in fares, but that was not to be, as Bristol to London coaches were rapidly and completely swept away by the Great Western Railway.

Notes

1   Gerhold, p. 152; RLD 1838.
2   R.S. Neale, *Bath 1680-1850: a social history* (1981), p. 44; C.M. Law, 'Some notes on the urban population of England and Wales in the eighteenth century', *Local Historian*, vol. 10 (1972), p. 23; *Census of Great Britain, 1851*, PP 1852-53 (1631), pp. cxxvi-cxxvii.
3   Neale, *Bath 1680-1850*, pp. 46, 263.
4   NLW, transcript of diary of Lewis Weston Dillwyn, 6 Feb 1829; *The seventh report of the Commissioners appointed to inquire into the management of the Post Office Department*, PP 1837 (70), pp. 71, 107.
5   The nationwide evidence is least plentiful in 1754-5 and 1764-5.
6   FFBJ 9 Apr 1763; *Boddely's Bath Journal*, 8 Oct 1764, 25 Feb, 29 Apr 1765; Webb 1, pp. 40-1; Fig. 27. The apparent increase may only have been because three London-Bath services per week were extended to Bristol.
7   FFBJ 19 Jan, 2 Feb 1765, 13 Apr, 1 June 1765; Dorian Gerhold, 'John Hanforth and Manchester's first stage-coaches', *Transactions of the Historic Society of Lancashire and Cheshire*, vol. 156 (2007), pp. 158, 164-5; *Public Advertiser*, 9 Jan 1765; *Boddely's Bath Journal*, 29 Apr 1765.
8   FFBJ 1 Oct 1774, 4 Feb, 22 Apr 1775; *Gazetteer & New Daily Advertiser*, 27 Apr 1776.
9   *Daily Advertiser*, 7 Apr 1778; FFBJ 29 Nov 1777, 24 Jan, 18 Apr, 13 June 1778, 7 Aug 1779, 1 Apr 1780, 27 Oct, 3 Nov 1781; Corporation of London RO, DS 15/38; *London Gazette*, 13 Nov 1781.
10 FFBJ 4 Sept, 25 Dec 1779, 15 June 1782, 6 Mar 1784. Four of the 11 proprietors of 1784 had been proprietors in 1779.
11 FFBJ 27 July 1776, 29 Nov 1777, 5 Jan 1782.
12 FFBJ 1 May 1773, 20 Aug 1774, 2 Jan, 1 May 1779, 8 Sept, 3 Nov 1781; BG 14 & 28 June 1804; below, pp. 206-7, 214; BD; R.C. Tombs, *The King's post* (1905), pp. 94-5; TNA, PROB 11/1630, John Weeks; TNA, IR 26/846, No. 349. Weeks later claimed to have taken the Bush in 1772 (FFBJ 14 May 1814). Weeks's estate was initially sworn as under £8,000 and later as under £5,000; the items listed total £7,358.
13 FFBJ 13 Apr 1782, 28 Mar 1789, 1 Apr 1797; BG 25 Nov 1802; BD; TNA, PROB 11/1577, George Poston; TNA, IR 26/684, No. 84.

14 FFBJ 7 July 1787; BD; TNA, PROB 11/1545, George Coupland; TNA, IR 26/572, No. 368; Bristol RO, FCW/1826/3, frames 5-6; TNA, IR 26/1191, No. 714.

15 FFBJ 15 July 1780; *Universal British directory* (1791).

16 Two routes elsewhere had 'stage-chaises' from 1750 and 'berlins' from 1752 (Gerhold, pp. 114, 159).

17 FFBJ 20 Oct 1770.

18 On some routes machines continued to be contrasted with slower stage coaches in the 1760s (e.g. *Ipswich Journal*, 3 Mar, 8 Sept 1764).

19 John Beresford (ed.), *The diary of a country parson* (1924), vol. 2, p. 255. 'Trimming off' seems to mean arriving in less than the mail-coach time.

20 FFBJ 16 Dec 1786, 28 Apr 1787, 5 Jan 1788; NLW, transcript of diary of William Dillwyn, 11-12, 19-20 May 1786. A time of only 15¼ hours was indicated in 1784 (FFBJ 6 Nov 1784).

21 FFBJ 4 Mar 1780, with *The new Bath guide* (1780).

22 Gerhold, p. 155; FFBJ 9 Feb 1754; 28 Geo III, c. 57; 30 Geo III, c. 36.

23 R.F. Hunnisett (ed.), *Wiltshire coroners' bills 1752-1796*, Wiltshire Record Society, vol. 36 (1981), p. 43. See also *ibid.*, p. 118; online index to *Bath Chronicle*, 14 Aug 1788.

24 *First report from Committee on the highways of the kingdom*, PP 1808 (225), pp. 79-81, 84-5, 88; William Youatt, *The horse; with a treatise on draught* (1831), p. 414.

25 Gerhold, pp. 158-9, 162.

26 Count Frederick Kielmansegge, *Diary of a journey to England in the years 1761-1762* (1902), pp. 135-6; W.H. Pyne, *Microcosm, or, a picturesque delineation of the arts, agriculture, manufactures, &c of Great Britain* (1808 edn.), text for post-chaises; Basil Cozens-Hardy (ed.), *The diary of Sylas Neville 1767-1788* (1950), p. 118.

27 FFBJ 1 Oct 1774, 20 May 1775. The early claim of 16 hour journeys (*ibid.*) was soon adjusted to 18 hours (Fig. 28).

28 *Hampshire Chronicle*, 8 May 1775 (London-Southampton, 11.4 miles); *ibid.*, 25 Nov 1776 (Winchester-Oxford, 11.4 miles); *Norfolk Chronicle*, 25 Jan 1777 (London-King's Lynn, 12.0 miles).

29 G. Arbellot, 'Les routes de France au XVIIIe siècle', *Annales – Économies Sociétés Civilisations*, Année 28 (1973), p. 789; Paul Charbon, *Au temps des malles-poste et des diligences* (1979), *passim*.

30 C 104/140, Ross *v.* Weeks, receipts book 1775, p. 34, 20 March 1777, with FFBJ 22 Feb 1777; below, p. 214. The overall speed was 6.4 miles per hour, compared with Gevaux' 6.8 between Bristol and London.

31 See p. 177 below.

32 FFBJ 1 Apr 1780, 2 Nov 1782, 1 Nov 1783; below, pp. 215-16, 230; *Berrow's Worcester Journal*, 3 April 1777.

33 e.g. *Daily Advertiser*, 29 Apr 1783 (London-Carlisle); *Gazetteer and New Daily Advertiser*, 14 May 1784 (London-Leeds); *The Norwich directory* (1783), p. 73

(London-Norwich).

34 Below, pp. 89-90; FFBJ 8 Aug 1789, 10 Apr 1790, 6 Oct 1792. For the two-day Bath-London coach, see *Oracle*, 28 April 1791.

35 Gerhold, pp. 115, 119, 137, 142-4, 147, 208-20; Fig. 27; FFBJ 2 Nov 1776, 6 Dec 1777.

36 Based on work in progress on stage coach speeds and fares nationwide.

37 *Norwich Mercury*, 16 Feb 1771.

38 *Report from Select Committee on Mr Goldsworthy Gurney's case*, PP 1834 (483), p. 81.

39 Below, p. 177.

40 POST 1/34/308; POST 10/366, pp. 19, 23; PP 1837 (70), pp. 71, 107.

41 Dorian Gerhold, 'Productivity change in road transport before and after turnpiking, 1690-1840', *Economic History Review*, vol. 49 (1996), pp. 502-3.

42 Gerhold, pp. 48-9, 115; *The Times*, 20 Nov, 5 Dec 1821, 29 May, 7 & 21 July, 24 Aug 1841; *Report from Select Committee on steam carriages*, PP 1831 (324), pp. 19, 27. Only the London area is not covered by the 1821/41 sales. Some horses used by regional coaches are included.

43 TNA, E 112/2159, No. 57; Gerhold, p. 195.

44 Gerhold, p. 115; W. Marshall, *The rural economy of Yorkshire* (1796), vol. 2, pp. 156-8; Youatt, *Horse*, pp. 35-6; George Culley, *Observations on live stock* (1807), pp. 26-7; R.W. Dickson, *An improved system of management of live stock and cattle* [1822-4], part 2, pp. 120-1, 124; Nicholas Russell, *Like engend'ring like: heredity and animal breeding in early modern England* (1986), p. 111. See EFP 24 Mar 1769 (col. 4d) for a coach horse 'of a remarkable good Yorkshire breed'.

45 Youatt, *Horse*, pp. 35-6.

46 See sources cited in Appendix 4. Also, earlier, *Morning Post*, 24 Mar 1794, 23 Mar 1807.

47 Wiltshire and Swindon RO, G18/990/1, 3 May 1774, 14 April 1783, 18 April 1786, 14 April 1787, 13 Oct 1789, 7 & 28 Sept, 9 Nov 1790, 14 April, 16 Aug, 18 Oct 1791; *ibid.*, 519/1, 13 Aug 1779, 5 Jan, 20 Mar 1781; London Metropolitan Archives, Tp.Col/1, pp. 494-8.

48 William Albert, *The turnpike road system in England 1663-1840* (1972), pp. 93-102; Eric Pawson, *Transport and economy: the turnpike roads of eighteenth century Britain* (1977), pp. 211-13; B.J. Buchanan, 'The evolution of the English turnpike trusts', *Economic History Review*, 2nd ser., vol. 39 (1986), pp. 228-30, 238; Wiltshire and Swindon RO, G18/990/1; *ibid.*, 519/1.

49 *Report from the Committee, who were appointed to consider of the agreement made with Mr. Palmer*, PP 1807 (1), pp. 102, 106, 117; Edmund Vale, *The mail-coach men of the late eighteenth century* (1960), pp. 15-21; FFBJ 28 Aug 1784.

50 TNA, E 112/1935, No. 506; *Bath Chronicle*, 8 Jan 1784; online index of *Bath Chronicle*, 15 Feb 1787.

51 POST 96/21, 30 July, 14 Aug 1784; Webb 1, p. 50; FFBJ 7 May 1785; Vale, *Mail-coach men*, p. 19; TNA, E 112/1935, No. 506.

52 Online index to *Bath Chronicle*, 8 Feb 1787; POST 96/21, f. 18.

53 POST 10/251.

54 PP 1807 (1), p. 102; FFBJ 28 Aug 1784; Webb 1, p. 50; POST 96/21, f. 18; online index to *Bath Chronicle*, 17 Apr 1788. During bad weather in December 1784 it was recorded that four-horse teams had been used part of the way instead of the usual two-horse ones to save time (Online index to *Bath Chronicle*, 16 Dec 1784).

55 Online index to *Bath Chronicle*, 17 Apr 1788; *Bath Chronicle*, 8 Jan 1789.

56 28s. in 1784; 32s. in 1785.

57 POST 10/366, pp. 20, 22.

58 POST 10/24, p. 125.

59 POST 10/24, pp. 125-7, 140. Similar figures indicate two out of 18 later than 1 o'clock in November 1792, 12 out of 31 in December 1792 (the times differing from the other list), 14 out of 30 in January 1793 (one day being missing), 7 out of 31 in January 1794 and 5 out of 28 in February 1794 (POST 96/21, f. 58).

60 FFBJ 27 July 1776, 24 Jan 1778.

61 *Mail coach contracts*, PP 1835 (313), p. 40.

62 Brian Austen, 'The impact of the mail coach on public coach services in England and Wales, 1784-1840', *Journal of Transport History*, 3rd series, vol. 2 (1981), p. 218.

63 Below, pp. 117-18. See also Brian Austen, *British mail-coach services 1784-1850* (1986), p. 159.

64 BG 7 Sept 1809.

65 The period of stagnation and its cause was identified by M.J. Freeman in 'The stage-coach system of South Hampshire, 1775-1851', *Journal of Historical Geography*, vol. 1 (1975), pp. 264, 266, but has otherwise received little attention.

66 *Corn*, PP 1843 (177), p. 18; PP 1821 (201), p. 11.

67 *Report from the Select Committee on mail coach exemption*, PP 1810-11 (212), p. 39.

68 POST 10/24, p. 139.

69 *Third Report from Committee on the highways of the Kingdom*, PP 1808 (315), p. 206; Dorian Gerhold, *Road transport before the railways* (1993), pp. 115-16.

70 *Western Flying Post*, 31 Mar 1800.

71 POST 10/24, p. 139.

72 FFBJ 13 Feb, 10 Apr 1790, 6 Oct 1792; BD; BG 11 Sept 1806; *Morning Post*, 23 Mar 1807. The White Lion's London services are recorded by directories only in 1793 and 1797 onwards

73 BG 27 Sept 1810.

74 TNA, C 11/489/40.

75 FFBJ 15 Aug 1801.

76 Using the figures in the lawsuit and the fares in the advertisement, and assuming a capacity of 12 outside passengers on the six-inside coaches (admittedly exceeding the legal limit) and five on the four-inside, the load factors of the six-

inch coaches were 76% in August 1801 to January 1802 and 60% in February to October 1802, and that of the other coaches in the latter period was 64%.

77 TNA, C 11/489/40; BG 14 Oct 1802, 22 Dec 1803, 27 Sept 1804; BD.

78 BG 22 Aug 1811; *The new and improved Bath directory* (1809); *The new Bath directory* (1812); online index to *Bath Chronicle*, 23 May 1799; *Robbins's Bath directory* (1800); below, pp. 211-12.

79 *Bath Chronicle*, 7 Aug 1788; BG 27 Dec 1788, 1 Aug 1789.

80 TNA, C 12/119/10; FFBJ 27 Oct 1781; POST 10/366, pp. 13, 19.

81 TNA, C 12/205/21; BG 22 Aug 1805; Fig. 47; TNA, C 13/89/36; TNA, C 12/119/10; *Morning Chronicle*, 19 Apr 1809 (farm at Wargrave); TNA, C 13/2078/10.

82 POST 96/21, f. 18; POST 10/24, pp. 89-90; POST 10/27, pp. 195, 305-6, 333, 349, 362-3.

83 Fig. 47; PP 1810-11 (212), p. 35; BG 8 July 1802, 7 Sept 1809, 4 May, 27 July 1815, 20 June 1816; BD; TNA, C 13/89/36; below, pp. 216-17.

84 *The Times*, 20 & 23 Nov, 4, 5 & 14 Dec 1821, 19 July 1841; *Morning Post*, 8 Feb 1822; BM, 21 Jan 1828; Harris, p. 171; Berkshire RO, transcripts of monumental inscriptions, Thatcham.

85 Richard Baines, *A history of Chippenham from Alfred to Brunel* (2009), p. 149; Wiltshire and Swindon RO, 1316/2, 23 May, 24 Aug 1802, 6 & 18 Nov 1804, 15 Jan 1805; *ibid.*, 1371/1, 10 July, 25 Sept 1793. For an example elsewhere (the Exeter road via Ilminster and Honiton), see *Taunton Courier*, 6 June 1811, pp. 1132-3.

86 PP 1810-11 (212), p. 36.

87 Philip S. Bagwell, *The transport revolution from 1770* (1974), pp. 48-9; 46 Geo III, c. 136; 50 Geo III, c. 48; PP 1808 (315), pp. 204-5, 210; Science Museum, London, painting of Birmingham coach in 1801 by Cordrey; *Morning Post*, 23 Apr 1804; *Mail coach contracts*, PP 1835 (542), p. 5; BG 7 Sept 1809.

88 Below, p. 124; RLD 1833-9; PP 1810-11 (212), pp. 33, 38, 45.

89 Bagwell, *Transport revolution*, p. 49; PP 1835 (542), p. 5.

90 See p. 177 below.

91 BD; BG 13 Apr, 21 Sept 1815.

92 BM, 28 May 1859; www.bristolinformation.co.uk (White Lion); census 1851; BG 14 Jan 1808; BD; census 1841; http://bristolslostpubs.eu (Plume of Feathers); BG 1 Oct 1818; below, pp. 202-3. Niblett sometimes had a business partner (*London Gazette*, 22 May 1832).

93 TNA, E 112/2238, No. 49; BG 25 Mar, 27 May 1824, 13 Jan 1825; TNA, B 3/620, p. 113. In 1825 the Magnet was via Andover.

94 BM 16 May 1825; BG 21 July, 22 Sept 1825. See also William C.A. Blew, *Brighton and its coaches: a history of the London and Brighton road* (1894), pp. 133-46.

95 BG 21 July 1825.

96 BG 2 Nov 1826, 4 Jan, 5 Apr, 7 June 1827, 17 Dec 1829; *Devizes and Wiltshire*

Gazette, 21 July 1825; EFP 7 May 1812; TNA, E 112/2159, Nos. 57 and 58, especially Elizabeth Burch's answer.

97 BD; BG 5 Apr 1827, 16 Oct 1828; Harris, pp. 169, 174, 179.

98 *The Times*, 21 June 1831.

99 Bath RO, 08022/23.

100 John Cary, *Cary's new itinerary* (1810-28); RLD 1832-9; Webb 2, p. 23. See Appendix 1.

101 PP 1834 (483), pp. 23, 26, 29-30, 32; *Report from the Select Committee on Mr Goldsworthy Gurney's case*, PP 1835 (373), pp. 3-6.

102 PP 1835 (313), p. 26; POST 1/304, p. 309; POST 10/256; BG 1 Nov 1821, 4 Aug 1825; POST 10/36.

103 NLW, transcript of diary of Lewis Weston Dillwyn; PP 1837 (70), p. 107; Harris, p. 204; PP 1835 (313), pp. 23-4, 39, 44.

104 *Carriage duties*, PP 1830 (686), pp. 2-5; Institution of Civil Engineers, T8V 60 (HC), statement of passengers.

105 Freeman, 'Stage-coach system', pp. 277-9; BD; BG 3 May, 21 June 1827, 11 July 1833.

106 POST 10/36; Webb 2, p. 40; ABG, 25 Apr 1836; *Brighton Patriot*, 19 July 1836; *Jackson's Oxford Journal*, 7 May 1836; *Cambridge Chronicle*, 1 Apr 1836; *Windsor and Eton Express*, 2 Jan 1836.

107 BG 20 Nov 1834; BD 1834; Harris, pp. 169-71.

108 BG 11 Nov 1824, 30 Nov 1826, 14 Apr 1836; RLD 1837; above, p. 109; PP 1810-11 (212), p. 46; *Select Committee on Acts regarding turnpike roads and highways in England and Wales*, PP 1819 (509), p. 15 (somewhat inconsistent); PP 1831 (324), pp. 73, 90, 93, 95.

109 Above, p. 99; BG 11 July 1833; PP 1810-11 (212), p. 33; PP 1819 (509), p. 15; RLD 1834-6. See also PP 1810-11 (212), p. 45.

110 POST 96/21, f. 53, 8 Dec 1788; PP 1810-11 (212), pp. 12, 17, 34, 41; PP 1808 (315), pp. 210-11; PP 1835 (313), pp. 55, 69, 73; *Report from the Select Committee on post communication with Ireland*, PP 1831-32 (716), p. 78; *Second report from the Select Committee on postage*, PP 1837-38 (658), p. 339. See also *Caledonian Mercury*, 2 Jan 1836 (17 cwt, formerly 20 cwt). Compare Harris, p. 99.

111 PP 1835 (313), pp. 49, 52.

112 *Ibid.*, p. 73; PP 1810-11 (212), p. 42; PP 1835 (313), p. 60, 72; PP 1831 (324), p. 93.

113 Youatt, *Horse*, pp. 35-6 ; below, p. 302; *The Times*, 24 May 1836; BD; PP 1835 (542), p. 5.

114 PP 1831 (324), p. 117; W.J. Reader, *Macadam: the McAdam family and the turnpike roads 1798-1861* (1980), pp. 58, 223.

115 *Ibid.*, p. 127; Wiltshire and Swindon RO, G18/990/1, 24 Dec 1821; Brenda J. Buchanan, 'The Great Bath Road, 1700-1830', *Bath History*, vol. 4 (1992), p. 88; PP 1819 (509), pp. 14, 16; Appendix 4. The Beckhampton trust voted not to employ McAdam (Wiltshire and Swindon RO, 1371/1, 18 Nov 1818).

116 PP 1819 (509), pp. 15-17; PP 1835 (313), p. 43. See also *Report from Select Committee on Mr. McAdam's petition*, PP 1823 (476), p. 27.

117 Alan Crosby (ed.), *Leading the way: a history of Lancashire's roads* (1998), pp. 140-8; Gerhold, *Road transport*, p. 140; PP 1831 (324), p. 50; Wiltshire and Swindon RO, 542/3, 8 Dec 1818, 26 Dec 1820; Reader, *Macadam*, pp. 53, 152; Buchanan, 'Great Bath Road', p. 88.

4

Passengers, coachmasters and horses

Passengers

THIS CHAPTER LOOKS in more detail at what was involved in running a coach between Bristol and London between the 1760s and 1830s, and what it was like to be a passenger. A general impression of who travelled by stage coach can be obtained from diaries and occasional comments in advertisements and elsewhere. Passengers varied from one coach to another. Johnson noted in 1827 that 'Persons of the first distinction travel by the mail-coaches ... persons who depend upon the regularity, security and comfort of the mail-coach, and being less likely to meet with disagreeable passengers'. Chaplin observed in 1835 that when the mail coaches began to Bath, Bristol and other places, they carried 'officers in the army, and merchants and gentlemen', but such people now travelled by day coaches at more convenient times. The New Company's coaches, in contrast, were said to carry 'all the lower-class passengers' because of the low fares. Advertisements sometimes referred to business travellers. Snell & Co's coaches in 1777-80 were said to reach London in time to do business at the exchanges, and in 1824 the advantages of the Chronometer were not just cheapness but the fact that it reached

57 'Flying breakfast, or the contents of a night coach', 1792. It is 5 am, and the
coachman is summoning the passengers back to the coach.

London 'in excellent time for the meat markets'. In 1827 the General
Stage-Coach Company stated that it had consulted 'professional
and mercantile gentlemen' about the timing of its night coach, and
the Monarch claimed to ensure that 'Professional gentlemen may
calculate to five minutes their arrival in Town'.[1]

The diarist most consistently informative about his fellow
travellers was the poet, Thomas Moore, who always travelled inside
in the faster day coaches. Examples from 1818 to 1837 included 'a
jolly old farmer', 'a clergyman, whom I at first took for a clothier',
a lady he suspected to be a teacher of music, 'an elderly military
gentleman', the wife of a coach-owner in Bond Street, a naval lord,
'two shrewd solicitors', an 'odd fellow' going to Ireland to demand an
explanation from a man who had struck him in a coffee house, an
Irish MP, an actor, a radical parson, a naval lieutenant, an Irish Peer, 'a
little Harrow boy', 'Linley, the great violincellist' and a concert singer.
On one occasion he found Lord Arthur Hill travelling as an outside
passenger (in February).[2]

LIGHT SUMMER TRAVELLING, ONLY SIX INSIDE.
CHILDREN HALF PRICE.
Just room for one Madam. ... Well I vow I have run all the way like a Lamp-lighter, till I am all over in such a Heat you can't think.
Published 1.st September 1797, by LAURIE & WHITTLE, 53 Fleet Street, London.

58 *A large lady about to join five other large passengers in a six-inside coach, 1797.*
The coachman is saying 'Just room for one Madam'.

In 1824, after travelling in the York House coach with two
gentlemen (one a naval lord) and a lady, Moore noted 'What a change
has taken place in coach company within these few years!'[3] Evidently
more well-to-do passengers used the faster stage coaches as they
speeded up, perhaps encouraged both by greater speed and by the
sorting of the poorer passengers into the cheaper coaches. At the same
time the social range of coach passengers must also have increased in
the other direction with the establishment of slow coaches and the
decline in coach fares relative to wages. In the 1760s, it would have
taken a craftsman around 14 days to earn the average outside fare for a
return trip between Bristol and London. That figure fell continuously
to nine days in the 1810s and eight days in the 1830s (only five days
for the slowest coaches).[4]

The experience of stage coaching changed as journey times were reduced, but many of the things that concerned passengers remained the same. The source for this is diaries and journals, but it needs to be remembered that travellers tend to record mishaps and discomfort rather than trouble-free journeys. An exception was the Rev John James of Bridgend, travelling to London with his daughter in February 1834, who noted that 'We had a comfortable journey in going & coming'. The only problem was that his daughter lost a silk umbrella worth 20s. in the coach.[5] The diarists varied in their reasons for travel. For example, the Rev James Woodforde visited relations (but also enjoyed himself in London and Bath on the way), the Rev John Skinner travelled in pursuit of antiquities, Henry Ellis travelled for business reasons and Thomas Moore came to London for London society and to meet his publishers. Only four diarists recorded five or more coach journeys between London and Bristol or Bath – Woodforde five between 1786 and 1795, Skinner nine between 1813 and 1833, Moore 73 between 1818 and 1841 (usually from Calne or

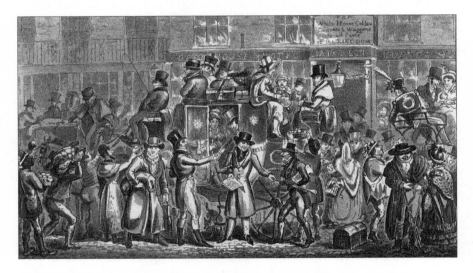

59 *The New White Horse Cellar, Piccadilly, where many Bristol and other coaches called to pick up or set down passengers (drawing by Cruikshank).*

Devizes) and Lewis Dillwyn 51 (but providing little detail) between 1818 and 1840.

It continued to be of the utmost importance who one's fellow travellers were and whether they were interesting or irritating company. When Moore travelled down in the White Lion coach to Bath in 1819, 'one of the passengers a pretty girl, going alone to Bath – found her to be a Miss Maxwell, cousin to Sir Murray – she had been travelling in Italy & France for two years – a very pleasing girl – told her who I was before we parted, & she asked me to call on her – had just read Lalla Rookh [his poem] through – & *looked* her praises of it – have seldom got over twelve hours of travelling more agreeably'. In 1834, having encountered in the Emerald two intelligent women who had travelled abroad, he observed that 'Some fifty years since, drawing-rooms and boudoirs could seldom produce such cultivated female society as is now to be found in stage-coaches'.[6]

The same year, also in the Emerald, Moore noted 'a madman, his keeper & son my companions – the poor man's hands tied together – but very harmless. (The stench, however, all the way, most dreadful.)' In 1813 Skinner's journey 'was rendered rather unpleasant by the presence of a Scots woman with an infant at her breast'. In 1827 he had two agreeable companions but also a third, 'vulgar in his manners, and gross in his person', who said, among many other things, that 'he would in half an hour settle all the differences between the Catholics and the Protestants if it were only left to him'. The companions of the actor, William Macready, in the mail coach in 1837 were 'very great asses, talking much nonsense about politics, and vehement Tories'. One remedy was not to talk at all. Samuel Taylor Coleridge, after travelling from Bristol to London in 1807, wrote that 'I do not think, that half a score sentences were interchanged from the time we entered to the minute of our arrival – tho' it was the sleep of silence, not the silence of sleep'. In 1795 Woodforde travelled from Bath to London in company with an MP

Rev John Skinner in the York House coach from Bath to London, 15 May 1827

[Left Bath 6 am] We had a pleasant drive, the day being fine, to Marlborough, where we stopped to breakfast. One of our fellow travellers was an officer, just returned from Ireland, and gave me some interesting details respecting the present state of the country; another was an intelligent young man, who had been abroad and seemed to have made classical observations on what he had seen at Rome &c: but a third companion was of a different cast: vulgar in his manners, and gross in his person: he declared speaking of the Catholics; That in his opinion the Pope of Canterbury was as bad as the Pope of Rome; that both alike a humbug; that every man ought to profess his own religion, without the assistance of the priest, and he would in half an hour settle all the differences between the Catholics and the Protestants if it were only left to him … [Skinner responded] Both my companions joined in corroborating what I had said; and the man sat sulky and surly, till we got rid of him, much to our satisfaction, at Newbury.

Source: British Library, Add 33,697, pp. 134-6.

known to him, but 'as he did not acknowledge me, I did not him'. The mixing of different classes created great opportunities for comic embarrassment, as in the case of the cockney tailor recounted by Henry Ellis (page 123).[7]

The size of one's fellow travellers also mattered, especially to inside passengers. Woodforde encountered in a four-inside coach in 1793 'a very fat woman with a dog and many band boxes, which much

Thomas Moore from Buck Hill (near Calne) to London, 27 August 1838

Went to Buckhill in a fly & took the coach to town – day hot, and the coach crowded, there being two children besides the four adults – a *row* had occurred before I joined, in consequence of one of the passengers of the room having usurped the place of the other, and the ejected gentleman (who was a powerful fellow) having collared & shaken the other, without waiting, as the latter alleged, to hear his explanation or give him time to resign the place – The collared gentleman, who was a little fellow, continued to be wroth during the whole journey, and at every stage renewed his demand of the other's address who, however refused to give it. Of the two, I felt rather in favour of the small gentleman, as the other, after showing himself a bully at first was evidently anxious to shirk the ulterior consequences. On our arrival in town, the collarer (who was accompanied by a rather suspicious looking elderly lady) having called a hackney-coach to convey away himself & his luggage, the little fellow having again reiterated his demand of the other's address, called aloud to his servant and ordered him to follow that hackney coach in a cab & not to quit it till he had ascertained where the pretended gentleman was set down ... off they set together, leaving me very much disconcerted at not being able to follow & learn the result of the adventure.

Source: Wilfred S. Dowden (ed.), The journal of Thomas Moore, vol. 5 (1988), p. 1992.

Samuel Taylor Coleridge from London to Bath, 26 December 1801

I left London on Saturday morning 4 o/ clock – & for 3 hours was in such a storm, as I was never before out in: for I was a top of the coach – rain & hail & violent wind with vivid flashes of lightning ... However, I was armed cap-a-pie, in a compleat panoply, namely, in a huge, most huge, Roquelaire, which had cost the Government 7 guineas – & was provided for the emigrants in the Quiberon Expedition, one of whom falling sick stayed behind & parted with his cloak to Mr Howel who lent it to me –. I dipped my head down, shoved it up, & it proved a compleat tent to me. I was as dry as if I had been sitting by the fire –. I arrived at Bath at 11 o clock at night.

Source: Earl Leslie Griggs, Collected letters of Samuel Taylor Coleridge, *vol. 2, 1801-1806 (1956), p. 778.*

incommoded us'. Coleridge, travelling from Bristol in 1807, found the coach 'quite full, all lusty men but one, & he together with one of the lusty travellers having great coats on, or rather huge coats that ought at least to have payed half-price, I was terribly cramped, my shoulders in a pillory and my legs in the stocks – in consequence of which my feet and legs are more swoln than I ever remember them to have been on a similar occasion.' Skinner recorded that the York House coach in 1821 'happened to have some very large men, who fully occupied the interior before I got in, it being ordained to hold six instead of four, which proved most inconvenient to myself who sat in the middle'. He found another Bath coach in 1827 to be 'much crowded, there being two females, when I first got into the vehicle,

A traveller from Bath to London in the Regulator in 1816

I started at six on a winter's morning outside the Bath 'Regulator', which was due in London at eight o'clock at night. I was the only outside passenger. It came on to snow about an hour after we started – a snow storm that never ceased for three days. The roads were a yard deep in snow before we reached Reading, which was exactly at the time we were due in London. Then with six horses we laboured on, and finally arrived at Fetter Lane at a quarter to three in the morning. Had it not been for the stiff doses of brandy swallowed at every stage, this record would never have been written. As it was, I was so numbed, hands and feet, that I had to be lifted down, or rather hauled out of an avalanche or hummock of snow like a bale of goods. The landlady of the 'White Horse' took me in hand, and I was thawed gradually by the kitchen fire, placed between warm pillows and dosed with a posset of her own compounding. Fortunately no permanent injury resulted.

Source: Quoted in Arthur Groom, Old London coaching inns and their successors *(n.d.), p. 34.*

and two more were afterwards introduced, so that the squeeze was insufferable; however, what can't be cured, must be endured.'[8]

Securing a suitable seat was a worry even for outside passengers. Thomas Letts in 1833 'ascended the back part of Cooper's Old Company's Coach' towards Bristol, evidently as an outside passenger. Five other passengers were there, all invalids or claiming to be, though he thought in some cases this was 'an excuse for their want

Thomas Moore from London to Calne, 24 December 1829

Started for home – a deuce of a journey – on Marlborough Downs was within an inch of being upset, having gone off the road, which was untraceable from the drifting of the snow – got out with all speed, the leaders of the six horses that drew us being already down in a hollow & the heavily loaded coach within an inch of following – when the coach was righted took in two poor girls (milliners apparently from their smart dress) who had been all along outside – the rest of our way to Calne very slow & perilous, the coachman being obliged to get down continually to see if we were still keeping the road – in the mean time one of the milliners & myself (she being seated directly upon me) kept up a conversation about Paris (with which she was very conversant) ... arrived safely at Calne.

Source: Wilfred S. Dowden (ed.), The journal of Thomas Moore, *vol. 3 (1986), pp. 1271-2.*

of disposition to accommodate'. Letts insisted on a particular seat because he needed support for his bad back; 'The lady opposite me was too nervous to sit outside & the young woman on my right could not ride backwards whilst two others (gents) next the lady felt it necessary in consequence of a severe cold to protect themselves from the chilling north west wind which was blowing a martial gale'. He added that 'a good jostling over the Stones, an occasional interchange of sentiment or observation and a unanimous agreement that it was a very <u>raw</u> morning, made us tolerably good friends before 20 miles was covered'. In 1833 Macready, travelling in an Exeter to Bristol coach, chided himself for being 'guilty of a display of ill humour because a gentleman, a Quaker, claimed, on the right of pre-occupation, the back seats!' Moore recorded a row over places which outlasted the journey.[9]

Another major concern was the weather, especially for outside passengers, though Samuel Curwen's account of his diligence journey in 1777 indicates that being inside offered only limited protection (page 63). Images of stage coaches are so familiar that it is easy to forget how extraordinary it was that they carried passengers without any protection from the elements, in all seasons and weathers, often at night and across the downs. On one long-remembered occasion in 1836, a night of intense cold and unceasing rain, three outside passengers were found to be insensible when the Bath coach arrived at Chippenham. Two were in fact dead and one died shortly afterwards. A really thick coat could provide some protection, as Coleridge found. As for rain, no arrangement of umbrellas by the outside passengers could prevent them being soaked. Great heat, usually accompanied by dust, was also unpleasant, as Colonel Richard Starke found in 1815. Travelling from Swansea towards Bristol in 1834, Macready noted that 'the day was Indian in its sultriness, I had no book, no power of going outside, no capability of thought – patient perspiration was my business through the day, and I went through it like St. Lawrence on his gridiron.'[10] On the other hand, in reasonable weather passengers often enjoyed the scenery. It was perhaps not long after the Irish passengers of 1752 lamented the absence of glass windows that such windows became general. Outside passengers of course always had unimpeded views.

Not surprisingly, passengers sometimes referred to being 'fatigued' by their journeys. In 1789 Woodforde reached London 'rather tired and fatigued', adding that 'Poor Briton [his servant] was very wet in the night and was very much jaded riding in the outside'. In 1795, on the other hand, the weather was fine, and 'We were not much fatigued with our journey or otherwise indisposed, tho' travelling all night'. In 1834, after setting off at 5.30 am from west of the Severn and reaching London at 6.30 the following morning, Lewis Dillwyn went to bed for three or four hours.[11]

Other concerns included securing a place at all (sometimes all the coaches were full),[12] luggage becoming lost, beggars (though there is only one reference), the timing of stops for refreshments and the cost of refreshments. Dr Campbell in 1775 thought the 30 miles westwards from Newbury more full of beggars than anywhere in England: 'for miles together the coach was pursued by them, from 2 to 9 at a time – almost all of them children – They are more importunate than in Ireland or even Wales.'[13] Refreshment stops became shorter, but passengers could of course bring their own food and drink. Typically a day coach would stop for breakfast (if setting off before about 7 am) and for dinner, whereas a night coach might stop for a late supper or early breakfast. Woodforde provides some examples. In 1786, when the journey was from 7 pm to 10am, the only meal was breakfast at 4 am. In 1789, during an up journey lasting from 4 pm to 11 am, the only meal was supper at Newbury at about midnight. Unfortunately, Woodforde 'was very ill in the night soon after we got into the coach after supper at Newbury, as I eat hearty of ham and chicken'. In 1793, the down journey in a day coach was from 5 am to 10 pm, broken by breakfast at Maidenhead with coffee, tea and strawberries, and dinner at Newbury.[14]

The diaries provide little evidence for two of the passengers' fears – accidents and highwaymen – but they record only a tiny number of journeys. Examples of accidents are plentiful in other sources. In July 1827, for example, the Bath mail coach was overturned between Reading and Newbury 'in consequence of the horses taking fright and bolting from the road into a gravel-pit'. A naval officer travelling inside was killed and the coachman, the guard and an outside passenger were injured. James Malcolm, travelling in the mail coach to Bristol in 1805, was pleased to find the coach a new one, until told by a fellow passenger that the reason was that the old one had been destroyed in an accident days earlier when the reins of the leading horses broke. Over time, greater speed made accidents more likely, while improved roads and coaches with a lower centre of gravity worked in the opposite direction. Lord William Lennox, writing in 1876, said he could fill pages with stage coach accidents in which people had been killed or severely injured. Such accidents 'were principally caused through the carelessness of the drivers, a refractory team, a coach that had not been thoroughly inspected before starting, and occasionally by a coachman who had imbibed a considerable quantity of strong ale or fiery spirits'. On the other hand, when precautions were taken, accidents were 'comparatively speaking, few'; he himself had travelled by almost all the fast coaches between London and Bath and other places and had never met with any accident.[15] Similarly, neither Moore nor Dillwyn, the diarists who recorded the most stage coach journeys on the Bristol road, were involved in accidents.

As for highwaymen, robberies of stage coaches seem to have become less frequent after 1771. There are reports in 1777, when £400 was stolen near Bath, 1780, when two Bath coaches were robbed on Hounslow Heath, and 1783. Again just one or two highwaymen were involved each time, though it was claimed (rather improbably) that a gang of 15 was involved in an attempted robbery in 1782 thwarted by a coach guard. One highwayman about whom something is known was Thomas Boulter, born at Poulshot near Devizes in about 1748 and at first a miller and then a grocer. His career in crime lasted from 1775 to 1778, when he was executed. In 1777 he robbed two Bath diligences and a Bath machine, failing on one occasion to carry out his threat to shoot a man who resisted him. The last attempt to hold up a stage coach on the Bristol road seems to have been in 1792, when two highwaymen approached the Bath mail coach near Salt Hill, but rode off when the guard levelled his blunderbuss at them.[16]

Robberies of more vulnerable travellers, such as those in post-chaises, continued. A number of factors seem to have reduced the threat from highwaymen, some affecting all road traffic and some stage coaches alone. They included the Bow Street foot patrols operating intermittently from the 1760s, the increased use of guards on stage coaches from 1784, the larger number of passengers in and on each coach and the greater speed and quantity of road traffic.

Coachmasters

IN THE FIRST century of stage coaching coach firms tended to have only a few proprietors, reflecting the fact that services were less than daily, but the numbers varied. The main Bristol and Bath firm generally had just one owner in 1709-25, but four or five in 1681-90 and five in 1728. The latter became approximately the norm: examples are the five to seven partners of Day & Co and Glasier & Co in the 1750s and 1760s, Snell & Co's eight in 1781, the Mercury's six in 1788, the mail coach's four in 1797, seven in 1828 and six in 1839, the Magnet's six in 1824, The Age's four in 1833 and the Monarch's six in 1834. Numbers were sometimes higher in the 1770s and 1780s: Gevaux & Co had nine proprietors in 1776 and Glasier & Co 13 in 1775 and 15 in 1784, probably reflecting the increased number of services and in Gevaux' case shorter stages.[17] However, it was never a simple matter of one proprietor per stage, as it was easy for a proprietor to horse a stage in each direction, and evidently feasible to horse stages remotely. For example, the Monarch's six partners in 1834 had shares ranging from ten miles up to the 24¼ miles of Nelson in London and the 34 miles of Niblett in Bristol. There were also a few exceptional firms run by just one or two coachmasters, as discussed below.

There were two changes in the character of coach firms on the Bristol road, partly reflecting national trends. The first, early

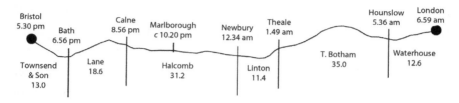

60 *Plan of the mail coach in 1827, showing the proprietors, the distances they horsed the coach (in miles and furlongs) and the times of the up coaches. (Source: Post Office Archives, POST 10/203, p. 5.)*

in the history of stage coaching, was a change in both the locations and occupations of coachmasters. Unlike elsewhere, carriers did not become involved in Bristol coaches, but hackney coachmen (all Londoners) were involved and soon ceased to be, while innkeepers, who may not have participated at all at first, became dominant. The change in locations was partly related: the proportion of coachmasters who were Londoners declined, while the proportion at intermediate places (counting Bath as intermediate) rose; there were none at Bristol. This reflected the fact that the business which stage coaching complemented best was innkeeping (because of the trade brought to the inns) and that the best location was an intermediate one, from which teams and men could best be supervised. These changes took place especially early on the Bristol road, by 1672, whereas elsewhere they are only visible in the period 1715-40.[18] By the 1750s coachmasters who were not innkeepers seem to have been unusual.

The situation changed again in the 1770s and 1780s. Firms started to have proprietors in Bristol and London,[19] and being a middle-ground man began to become less desirable. In Bristol's case this reflected not just the increased number of services but also the growth of regional coach services. Bristol was no longer just the end of a route, but was the hub of numerous onward connections. Increasingly coachmasters must have thought of their own businesses in terms of nodes from which routes diverged, rather than routes. In London's case the reasons were different, as it had always had a network of services and it was more a destination than a place of transfer between coaches. The main cause was probably just the increasing number of London services and therefore the ability to create a large business which would have greater bargaining power and resilience in the face of competition. In fact, whether at London, Bristol or Bath, the larger firms with a range of services must increasingly have been at an advantage, especially when competition was fierce. The middle-ground men, in contrast, generally had fewer opportunities for expansion and, as coaches speeded up, they tended to lose the advantage of passengers eating and drinking at their inns, though there were some notable exceptions to this picture.

The Bristol-London coach firms run by a single coachmaster or just two seem to have no parallels elsewhere. In 1819 William Horne, one of the main London coachmasters, stated that he worked one coach (which was the Night Regulator) all the way from London to Newbury, with Pickwick of Bath working it from Newbury to Bristol.[20]

The two firms run or largely run by a single coachmaster were both based at Thatcham, reflecting its location about half way between Bristol and London. Edward Fromont horsed most of the route himself but sometimes had partners for the stages nearest London and Bristol, though even then he supplied the vehicles himself, at a cost of 2d per mile to the firm as a whole. In 1819 he stated that he worked coaches 500 miles a day on the Bath road, which suggests he was then working 103 of the 122 miles between London and Bristol himself,[21] and in 1821 he had over 200 horses. His coaches were horsed near Bristol by Richard Coupland, evidently in return for Fromont having a substantial share in Coupland's Regulator. At the London end, in 1814 Fromont sold the right to work his Defiance and Express coaches between London and Hare Hatch, reckoned as 36 out of 127 miles, to William Smith of Hounslow and John Smith for the substantial sum of £720. However, Fromont took over the working of those stages himself three years later when the Smiths were in financial difficulties.[22]

Fromont made extensive use of family members. Until her death in 1803 his wife Mary received money for him at Thatcham (by 1806 he was claiming she had withheld money from him), and his daughter Maria took on that role subsequently. Fromont's stepson Henry Dibben ran Gerrard's Hall in London, acting as his bookkeeper and manager there. In 1806 Fromont went to law with Dibben over the London accounts, claiming that Dibben had withheld money on the argument that Fromont 'was a speculating man and might embark all his money in trade'. Nevertheless, the Fromonts and Dibbens continued to be associated in stage coaches together until 1841, when Fromont's daughter and Dibben's son were both horsing the New Company's night coach. Fromont stated in 1806 that he was 'unable to write or read except that he hath of late learned to write his name', to which Dibben replied that Fromont 'can read and write though but imperfectly'.[23] Other coachmasters unable to write included William Halcomb of Devizes in 1799, Richard Coupland of Bristol in 1829 and William Lawes of Chippenham in 1849, and, although this was unusual for coachmasters,[24] it is a reminder that the business was still about managing horses and men rather than sitting in an office writing accounts.

The other Thatcham firm was Thomas Cooper's from 1828. In 1833 Cooper was sharing the route with Richard Lovegrove of Reading, who horsed the coaches from Theale to Brentford, but that may have been a recent arrangement. Cooper then had 186 horses and Lovegrove 70, a total of 256. Stanley Harris, looking back on the coaching era in 1885, said that Cooper was the only man he had heard of working such a long route by himself, and emphasised how arduous and hazardous it must have been: 'I fancy that this inability to frequently inspect his stock and business all up and down the road subjected Cooper to a great deal of loss, notwithstanding that he was a very active man and seemed always to be about'. Harris considered that Cooper also suffered by not restricting the luggage his passengers could carry and charging for any excess. Commercial men took advantage of this, travelling to London by mail and returning on

61 Cooper's Cottage, Thatcham, later known as Beverley House, as it appeared before its demolition in 1958.

Cooper's night coach with their purchases, and one coach was found at Beckhampton to weigh four and a half tons. This and relatively high speeds contributed to heavy wear and tear on the stock. According to Harris, 'there was generally at Thatcham a large number of temporarily disabled horses ... it was by no means an unusual thing for Mrs. Cooper to turn up her sleeves and make bran-mashes upon an emergency for some of the horses'. Costs were therefore high, but so were fares (Table 2), and Cooper's coaches were popular and well-filled.[25]

Cooper expanded his business (perhaps unwisely) by opening a hotel at Bristol in 1831. In 1833 he went bankrupt. After that the proprietors were Chaplin in London, horsing the coaches between London and Thatcham, and Niblett and Lane of Bristol and Bath respectively, horsing from Thatcham to Bristol. Cooper retained some sort of managing role at Thatcham and continued to describe himself as a coach proprietor.[26] Fromont's 200 or more horses and Cooper's 186 (or around 256 when he ran the entire route himself) were probably among the largest stocks of horses held by any coachmasters outside London. While Cooper eventually went bankrupt, Fromont's success shows that single-handedly running all or most of a Bristol-London coach service was not a reckless ambition.

Coach businesses differed in character at each place. At Bristol, from the 1780s, proprietors often had a network of regional services, horsing a stage or several stages on a number of different routes, as discussed in the next chapter. At first they sometimes horsed the London coaches only for the 13-mile stage to Bath, as in Weeks's case in 1784, when an advertisement for Glasier & Co lists seven London partners, some of them in fact based at Newbury, seven Bath partners and Weeks separately as the Bristol partner. This suggests that there was an upper district between London and Newbury, a lower district between Newbury and Bath and a separate district run entirely by Weeks between Bath and Bristol.[27] The only Bristol firm for which the number of horses is recorded is the relatively small one of William Clift, with 46 horses in 1837.

The Bath proprietors also had regional networks, and even in the 1830s their businesses may have been as large as the Bristol ones. Thomas King, a partner of Glasier and then Day, was said to have made £1,000 a year from his coach business up to his death in 1774, and to have left a personal estate of £5,000. The goodwill of his coaching business (excluding the stock) was sold for £800.[28] The most familiar name among the Bath coachmasters is Pickwick, who is believed to have given his

62 *Eleazar Pickwick (1748/9-1837), coachmaster at Bath from 1779 to 1837. His career spanned almost the entire coaching age. He was Mayor of Bath in 1826. James Woodforde noted of Pickwick's White Hart Inn in 1795 that 'a very excellent house it is, everything so good & neat &c'.*

63 The York House Hotel, one of Bath's most prestigious coaching inns, in 1829 (drawing by R. Woodroffe).

name to Dickens' novel. Eleazar Pickwick (Fig. 62) was a coachmaster at Bath from 1779, becoming innkeeper at the White Hart. He prospered, acquired Bathford Manor House and left £20,000 on his death in 1837. His coaching interests passed to his cousin or nephew, Moses Pickwick.[29] A third example is William Lane's business at the White Lion in 1837. It included shares in mail coaches to Exeter, Bristol, Cheltenham, Birmingham, Portsmouth, Southampton and London and other coaches to Southampton, Weymouth, Cheltenham, Oxford and London. His London coaches were the mail coach, the Monarch and the Regulator, in all of which he worked with Isaac Niblett, together with the York House coach from Bath to London. Part of Lane's business was sold for £1,106 in 1837, a quarter of what remained for £1,200 in 1840 and the remainder for £1,248 in 1842.[30]

The London coachmasters quickly established a strong position from the 1780s onwards. As early as 1791, of 21 London innkeepers with seven or more coaches using their inn, seven were themselves involved in all or most of those coaches, including Boulton and Whalley, both part of Glasier & Co, and Mountain and Ibberson, both part of what had been Snell & Co. In the last two decades of stage coaching, London coachmasters most often had 300 to 400 horses (Waterhouse, Horne and Eames in 1819, Chaplin in 1827 and Robert Nelson in 1835), though some had fewer (Robert Gray's 150-200 in 1825, Peter Mountain's 200 in 1827 and 140 at the George and Blue Boar, Holborn, in 1831). Two businesses (and probably also a third, Edward Sherman's) became exceptionally large: William Horne had 700 horses by 1825, and William Chaplin, the greatest coachmaster of all, had 1,200 in 1835, used on 'about 68 different concerns or lines of different coaches'.[31] All the main London coachmasters had interests on the Bristol road in the 1830s: Chaplin in the two mails, the Emerald and from 1833 Cooper's coaches, Sherman in the Regulator, Horne in the Night Regulator, Robert Nelson in the Monarch and the York House

64 Portrait of William Chaplin (1787-1859), the greatest of the London coachmasters, who operated several of the Bristol coaches.

65 Photograph of Benjamin Horne (1804-70), son of William Horne and one of the three most important London coachmasters in the 1830s. His Bristol coach was the Night Regulator.

coach to Bath, Sarah Mountain in The Age and Robert Gray in the White Hart coach to Bath.[32] Many of these coach partnerships are likely to have been dominated by them, but a major provincial proprietor such as Niblett also had a strong bargaining position. The only ways to avoid the embrace of the London coachmasters were to buy or lease a London inn and install a relative there, as Fromont did, or to use one of the lesser London inns, as Cooper did. In the 1830s Cooper's coaches (until 1833) and the New Company's day coaches were the only ones without a London proprietor.

The most elusive figures are the middle-ground men. They were rarely listed in advertisements after the 1780s, though from the 1820s some of them were recorded when they advertised their stock for sale (Appendix 4). Their businesses may have grown as the number of coaches increased, but they no longer dominated their firms. As already indicated, when coaches speeded up they derived less benefit from coach passengers stopping at their inns and became more reliant on their earnings from horsing the coach. Indeed it seems to have become hard to find suitable middle-ground men, at least for the mails, which were the most firmly prevented

66 *The Bear Inn at Devizes, as it appears today.*

from making extra stops for refreshments. When Botham of Salt Hill threatened to give up the Bristol and Bath mails in 1826, on being criticised for loss of time, Johnson observed that 'neither I nor his partners know where to look for a successor'. Johnson's successor described the two mails in 1836 as 'sadly weak in the middle for contractors'.[33]

The middle-ground men's businesses varied in character. At Devizes and Marlborough they might have separate coaches from those places to London. The most important here were the Halcombs. William Halcomb senior of Devizes (1734-1801) was a chaise driver in 1761 and an innkeeper by 1766, eventually succeeding Thomas Lawrence at the Bear in 1780. In 1769 he was involved in a line of post-chaises

67 Portrait of Thomas Lawrence, father of the famous portrait painter. Lawrence was innkeeper at the White Lion in Bristol in 1772, setting up short-lived coaches to Exeter and Leicester. He then moved to the Bear in Devizes, becoming a partner in Glasier & Co. His son later referred to his father's 'essentially worthy nature', but lamented having inherited 'much of my father's carelessness'. After Thomas Lawrence's bankruptcy in 1780, William Halcomb took over the Bear.

with William Day and others, and in 1774 and 1779 in coaches to London. He was said to have 'honourably acquired a handsome fortune' at the Bear, and was described by his son-in-law as 'a warm-hearted, generous, forgiving fellow'. One son, William, ran the Bear from 1799 to 1812, and another, John (Fig. 68), ran the Castle, Marlborough, from 1790 to 1831, assisted by a third brother, James, and later succeeded by his sons William and Thomas. The Halcomb interest apparently extended from Devizes to Hungerford, and separate coaches from Devizes to London and from Cheltenham to Salisbury or Southampton run by the Halcombs and others are recorded in 1810-12 and 1836, together with one from Swindon to London in the latter year. In 1837 William Halcomb's coach interests included shares in the Regulator from Bristol to London, the York House coach from Bath to London, the Bath mail and the Star (probably Bath to Reading).[34]

68 *John Halcomb (1763-1831), innkeeper and coachmaster at the Castle Inn, Marlborough, from 1790 to 1831.*

Towards the other end of the route, middle-ground men might have interests on several diverging routes from London. For example, when William Waddell of Maidenhead left the coach business in 1832, he had ten horses working the Regulator and Emerald coaches which ran from London to Bristol, 12 horses working the Berkeley Hunt and Magnet coaches (London to Cheltenham) and other horses working the Alert coach (London to Oxford).[35]

In the centre of the route, proprietors were less likely to be working other routes, but might still have large businesses. One of the largest, mentioned already, was that of Maria Fromont at Thatcham, with 90 horses in 1841. The business established by George Botham, innkeeper at the George and Pelican, Speenhamland, from 1799, was also large. When he died in 1827, he had 20 horses forming four teams for the mail coach, eight horses forming two teams for the Regulator, nine horses forming two teams for the Sovereign, 15 horses forming three teams for the York House coach to Bath, 24 post-horses, ten odd horses or horses at grass and a pony. That was a total of 52 horses for Bristol and Bath coaches (all assigned to specific coaches) and 87 horses altogether. He also had farms at Donnington and Ransford, where there were seven farm horses. His widow, Eleanor, who continued the business, later estimated she had made about £500 a year clear profit from 1827 to 1837. She had 100 horses, including post-horses, at the end of 1840, and when the railway came she was involved in the Regulator, Night Regulator and Emerald to Bristol, the York House coach to Bath and the Vivid between London and Newbury. Her stables at Reading, Woolhampton, Halfway (west of Newbury) and Froxfield (west of Hungerford) must indicate the extent of the road she covered. She was later fondly remembered as

69 *The George & Pelican, Speenhamland (Newbury), run by George Botham and then his widow Eleanor from 1799 until 1841 (seen here in 1947). The residential part of the inn was the building in the centre with the hipped roof, but the inn included buildings to the right, not shown in this view, and a large yard behind. It closed on Mrs Botham's bankruptcy in 1841.*

'dear old Mrs. Botham ... with her rich black silk gown and her high white, sort of modified widow's cap'.[36]

Another example is Robert King of Hare Hatch, between Reading and Maidenhead, who was working the Regulator, Emerald

70 *The Windmill at Salt Hill, near Slough. Thomas Botham, previously a waiter at a Windsor inn for ten years, took it over in 1792. In 1828 he had 40 horses for the Bristol and Bath mails and 18 for another Bristol coach. In 1840 his son, William Hallam Botham of Salt Hill, had 28 horses for the York House coach to Bath and eight for the Monarch and the Eclipse to Bristol.*

and Shamrock coaches in 1827. His bankruptcy in 1827 may have been prompted by the outbreak of glanders in that year, as his losses included £1,200 for the deaths of 60 horses. One of his expenses, of £50, reflected the difficulty the middle-ground men experienced through receiving virtually no money from passengers and depending on prompt payment from other partners after the sharing accounts were drawn up: 'Discount on acceptances [of bills] being at all times short of capital.' Lane of Bath purchased King's coach business for £545 (possibly for the goodwill alone). King distinguished himself by keeping no books of account whatever, which caused some difficulty to his assigns.[37]

There were also middle-ground men with fewer horses, such as Henry Thurnwood of Windsor, with nine horses for the Bath mail and nine for the Regent to Bristol, and Mr Walkden, with 17 horses for the New Company's coaches between Slough and Knowl Hill, both in 1829, but it is not possible to be certain that these were their only coach interests. George Collins had just six horses for working the Bristol mail coach 5½ miles from Maidenhead to Slough in 1833, and was possibly a sub-contractor.[38]

Coachmasters did not always horse all their ground themselves. Edward Sherman noted in 1839 that they sometimes contracted for the horsing to be done at a fixed price per mile. He was himself paying someone to horse a coach (probably a Bristol coach) from Maidenhead to Twyford for £4 a mile. An example of this sort of person was Abner Clarkson of Hounslow, coachmaster, formerly a proprietor of the Magnet coach at Newbury. His business, based at Hounslow and Slough, consisted of drawing a Bath coach for a fixed sum per mile per month. In 1829 he had 18 horses and five sets of harness, later sold for £310. He went bankrupt in that year, attributing a loss of £800 to deaths of horses from glanders and farcy between 1827 and 1829.[39]

Competition and collusion

STAGE COACHING IS sometimes described as if competition was not only fierce but also continuous and ruinous. The story of the coachmaster who lowered his prices to nothing and even offered passengers a free bottle of wine for using his coach is often cited. There are plenty of contemporary comments supporting this view. For example, Hasker argued in 1811 that if mail coach contracts were opened to competitive tender the winner would be opposed by the loser 'where he was most vulnerable', reflecting 'the natural competition of their business'. A keeper of coach accounts stated in 1837 that 'very frequently an opposition has been carried on by the old coach-masters from a sort of attachment to the road, a desire to keep it to themselves, and a spirit of party against all intruders, and they have sometimes lost large sums of money'. Coachmasters such as Fromont sometimes described their service as an 'opposition coach'.[40]

The coachmaster carrying for free does indeed appear in contemporary newspapers, but usually only as an amusing story. The one real example found anywhere is a Sheffield to Doncaster coach in 1835, which advertised its fares as 'Inside what you please! Outside, ditto!'[41] Given the closeness of direct or variable costs and total costs, large reductions in fares inevitably resulted in large losses. That sort of competition could only be temporary, until a rival gave up or an accommodation was reached, as passengers well understood. For every coachmaster glorying in opposition, there was one like John Crosby of Bath, putting on a new Bath to Bristol coach in 1794, who emphasised that 'it could not arise from the sordid principle of opposition ... but on the basis of œconomical convenience to the public'.[42] There is no evidence, either, of coachmasters bargaining with individual passengers over fares. The story of Bristol's coach firms contains plenty of competition, but also plenty of collusion, and does not conform to the picture of continuous and furious competition.

From the 1680s to the 1790s there were usually two firms operating between Bristol and Bath and London (other than in 1725 to 1753 when there was just one), so it was worthwhile and relatively easy to collude over fares, as in the 1760s, or to band together to fight off a new entrant. A new entrant sometimes prompted a merger of the older firms, as in 1755 and 1775. There were large short-term reductions in fares to drive off new competitors in 1765, when the aim was achieved, and 1781, when it was not. Snell & Co claimed in the latter year that after Glasier & Co had reduced their fares from 'the old price' of 28s. to 21s., an attorney acting for Glasier & Co had asked them if they would agree to raise them to the old level. Glasier & Co responded with a sworn affidavit from the attorney who stated that, on the contrary, he had discussed coach fares with J. Porter, one of the proprietors in Snell & Co, and Porter had proposed that, if Glasier & Co would advertise that they were raising the fare, Snell & Co would do the same and the advertisements would appear together. Glasier

& Co had indignantly rejected this proposal.[43] Evidently this attempt to collude over fares failed, but probably only because Glasier & Co believed low fares were giving them an advantage against a weaker opponent.

One restraint on fares was the risk of encouraging new entrants. Entry to the trade was fairly easy, as a couple of teams to run a stage or two is unlikely to have strained the pockets of a substantial innkeeper. New coach firms were set up in 1754, 1755, 1756, 1765 (two), 1774, 1779, 1781 and 1784. The importance of established 'connections' as an obstacle to new competitors was far less than in carrying because there were fewer regular customers accustomed to using the same firm and less trust was required. The lack of change in productivity when the number of firms increased in the 1790s suggests that the new entrants or the threat of them had been effective in restraining fares.[44] Nevertheless, it seems to have been hard for new coach firms to establish themselves in the face of competition from incumbents. One of those nine new firms (that of 1754) soon merged with the established firm, and only two others survived for more than a few years (Day's of 1756 and Snell's of 1781).

From the 1790s, once the main firm (formerly Glasier's) had broken up, there were more separate firms, and there was a correspondingly smaller ability to collude and much less incentive to reduce fares below cost for competitive advantage. Instead, the adjusting of fares was more of a fine tuning, no doubt in response to changing provender prices, success or otherwise in filling the coach and the pricing decisions of competitors. For example inside fares in the Regulator in eight years from 1818 to 1833 were 45s., 48s., 38s., 42s., 45s., 40s., 38s. and 35s., with outside fares varying in a similar way.[45] The cheapest coaches remained the cheapest and the dearest remained the dearest. Nevertheless, the continual changes in fares, the occasional alteration of inside fares but not outside ones or vice versa, the emphasis in many advertisements on cheapness and the fact that coachmasters advertised fares at all are all indications that there was genuine competition over price as well as speed. New Bristol-London coach ventures continued to be established, in 1801, 1802, 1806, 1815, 1824, 1825 and 1828, as well as some Bath-London ones, and four of these seven survived at least a decade – Fromont's Express, the Triumph, the Company's and the New Company's of 1801, 1815, 1825 and 1828 respectively. The rise of Niblett eventually reduced the number of separate establishments at Bristol to three, but that was probably enough for a competitive situation to continue.

While prudent coachmasters avoided ruinous price competition, this did not mean that competition was a gentle affair, particularly against anything new. Instead it was carried on by other means. When Thomas Cooper contracted to horse the Company's coaches in 1825, the Bath coachmasters attacked him through his posting business, requiring other innkeepers to remove their line of posting from his inn, and for good measure doing the same to his mother-in-law at the Angel in Chippenham.[46] When John Bland, a Scotsman, acquired a Bristol warehouse in 1835 and took over the Rummer in 1837, horsing the New Company's coaches and many regional ones, he was evidently regarded as a threat to be dealt with. Years later, he and Isaac Niblett liked to reminisce about how Niblett had tried to force him out of business and he had frustrated those attempts, calling forth 'many a hearty laugh':

> The proprietors of a London coach line, in which Mr. Niblet was interested, effected a clever engagement, by which the parties at the intermediate stages who horsed Mr. Bland's coach were on a given day to withhold from him the requisite supply of horses, so that on his vehicle arriving at somewhere short of midway to the great metropolis it should be brought suddenly to a standstill. Tidings of this clever stroke of generalship coming to the ears of the gentleman so plotted against, he got some of his large stage wagons, placed

horses and harness in them, and sent them on to other stables in the towns in which the default was to be encountered. The effect was that when the parties in the secret of the planning company were looking out in the expectation of witnessing and exulting over their rival's discomfiture, they were thunderstruck at witnessing his coach drive on to the newly-selected quarters, ribands streaming from the heads of its team, and the guard playing with all the vigour of which his bugle and lungs were capable the triumphant strains of "See the conquering hero comes". On another occasion, when Mr. Bland was about starting a coach to Plymouth, some of his opponents engaged a band of roughs to stop the vehicle about a mile from its destination and cut the traces of the horses. Discovering the plot, Mr. Bland filled a coach with powerful pugilists from "outside the gate", despatched it direct to the intended field of action, and routed the "Plymouth brethren", to their infinite astonishment and disgust.

What is really significant is what happened next, which must have happened many times before: 'It was now found that Mr. Bland was much too cute to be readily got over, and soon after an arrangement was come to by the rivals.'[47]

One of the lessons of that story is the importance of good intelligence, both about what rivals were up to and about their financial health. The latter helped determine whether they could be forced off the road, whether one or more partners could be persuaded to defect or whether some sort of accommodation would be wiser. Undoubtedly much time was spent keeping an eye on competitors, scrutinising, for example, the state of their horses and the number of passengers in their coaches.

The most important question is whether competition was sufficient to ensure that the gains from increased productivity were passed on to passengers in the form of lower fares or shorter journey times. Certainly some of the gains were passed on, as Fig. 25 shows, but any that were not would not show up there. There are three reasons for believing that the gains largely were passed on. The first is the extent of the benefits to passengers as measured in Fig. 25. The second is the way that changes in fares and speeds between Bristol and London approximately followed those on other London routes, since it is unlikely that coachmasters throughout the country could all have appropriated most of the gains for themselves. Indeed John Farey argued in 1831 that stage coaching 'affords a less profit on the capital and trouble of management probably than any other sort of business which is carried on with spirit in this country'.[48] The third is that for much of the time there was clearly genuine competition, even if sometimes intermittent in the earlier decades. In the 1820s and 1830s, in particular, there were always three or more separate firms, several new entrants established themselves and there was constant adjustment of journey times and fares.

Costs and revenue

A S INDICATED EARLIER, the stage coach's balance sheet contained some items falling to the individual coachmaster and some to the partnership as a whole. Among the costs, the dominant item, horse provender, was paid for by the individual proprietor, and much depended on his skill in purchasing the best quality at the best price. He also paid the other costs relating to the horses – shoeing, harness, purchase of new horses, horsekeepers and rent of stables. Purchase of new horses was another important test of the coachmaster's skill, not so much because of the money expended as because whether the horse was a good worker and a moderate feeder powerfully influenced subsequent costs. In some partnerships, the individual proprietors or several of them together also paid for the coaches, and the coach was changed along the route. For example, when Woodforde travelled from London to Bath in 1795 the coach was changed at Newbury, suggesting that the firm concerned was organised into an upper district and a lower one with their own coaches and coachmen.[49] This seems to have become less common in the nineteenth century, perhaps because there was less time to change the coach during refreshment stops and perhaps because coaches were then hired by the mile, usually from London coachmakers, instead of being owned. The tendency was to assign costs to the individual proprietors if at all possible, so as to minimise their reliance on others managing costs effectively.

The costs falling to the partnership were relatively minor, and most were predictable from week to week. Some of them could scarcely be managed at all, such as tolls, though these were never a major cost. Tolls probably increased over time,[50] and they varied from one road to another. Benjamin Horne in 1837 put the average per mile there and back on his 16 routes at 5.4d, ranging from 3.3d for Norwich up to 7.6d for Birmingham, which suggests that the level of tolls related approximately to the difficulty of maintaining the road. The sum he indicated for Bristol was 4.5d, slightly below the average. Chaplin stated a very low charge of 1.3d per mile there and back between London and Newbury, and the lowness of tolls on at least part of that stretch is supported by other evidence. It indicates that further west, where the road was more challenging, the tolls per mile were substantially higher.[51]

Mileage duty, introduced by the Government in 1779, was equally predictable. It rose from ½d per mile in 1779-82 to a peak of 4½d per mile for four-horse coaches in 1822-32. In about 1830 it accounted for around 13% of costs. From 1832 onwards, when the duty varied according to capacity, coachmasters tended to declare capacity of four inside plus 11 outside in summer and four inside plus eight outside in winter, and there was no rebate if they actually carried significantly fewer passengers.[52]

By the nineteenth century the cost of coaches was predictable too, following a change in practice. Until the 1790s coachmasters normally purchased their coaches, but it became the practice to hire them at a fixed price per mile from the coachmakers, or in a few cases for the London coachmaster, such as Sherman, to own them and charge his partners in a similar way for their use. The coachbuilder paid for any repairs and renewals unless damage was clearly the fault of the driver (for example through accidents such as overturning). A London coachbuilder, James Whitbourn, stated that when he had been an apprentice, up to 1794, every coachmaster had had his own coaches. That places the change in the period from the mid-1790s onwards, which suggests it may have been inspired or at least encouraged by the Post Office's contract with Besant in the 1780s for a uniform design of patent coaches paid for by the mail coach contractors per mile travelled. William Horne explained in 1827 that 'Very few of the coaches are our own; we used to have so much trouble with coachmakers' bills that I have very few myself ... we rather choose to hire.' Evidently contracting out the supply of coaches was seen as advantageous by coachmasters. It certainly gave the coachbuilder an incentive to provide a thoroughly roadworthy coach, though he might also wish to provide a heavier and sturdier one than the coachmaster wanted. Typical charges in the 1820s and 1830s were 2½d or 3d per mile. A stage coach then cost about £140 and lasted about five years, by which time a far greater sum had been spent on repairs. The best coachbuilders were in London, but Williams of Bristol was also highly regarded. As the coachmasters did not usually maintain their own coaches they did not employ their own wheelers, but it seems to have been common for them to employ their own smiths, whose main work was probably shoeing.[53]

Other costs were coachmen and guards, who (other than for 'no fees' coaches) could be paid low wages because of the tips they received from passengers, and a few minor costs such as bookkeeping and rent. The fact that many costs were fixed per mile and that capital costs and overheads were minimal meant that it was relatively easy to work out whether a coach was covering its costs and to determine the income needed to cover a particular level of provender prices. In the long term nearly all costs could be varied by buying or selling horses and changing the level of service, but buying and selling horses was troublesome and costly and therefore not worthwhile in the short term, and making a service less than daily was an unattractive proposition almost never resorted to on the Bristol road,[54] so it was hard to reduce costs when loading was poor.

The cost structure of coach firms changed over time. As tolls and duties rose, the importance of provender costs declined somewhat. Taking the two best examples of costs on other roads, from 1761 and 1829, provender costs declined from 66% to 41% and total horse costs from 81% to 56%, while tolls and duties increased from 5% to 25%. This also increased the proportion of joint costs, from 19% to 43%.[55] The evidence from the Monarch between Bristol and London, consisting of a sharing account covering two weeks in June 1834, suggests that the change was somewhat less pronounced. Making assumptions about the number of horses and the individual proprietors' costs, the breakdown of expenditure was provender 48%, other horse costs (horsekeepers, shoeing and new horses) 15%, harness 4%, coaches 5%, coachmen and guards 8%, duty 11%, tolls 8% and rent 2%.[56] The calculation suggests that the Monarch made a small loss in the two weeks covered, with costs of about £423 and income of £414.

All revenue accrued to the partnership as a whole, except the small charge for booking parcels in London. Obviously the main item was passenger fares, which depended both on the level of fares and on success in filling the coach. Cooper stated in 1834 that the average number of passengers in a four-horse coach on the Bristol road throughout the year was nine (though more in his own coaches), and in a mail coach five (three in and two out). This indicates that about two-thirds of capacity was filled, a view shared by other coachmasters in the 1830s.[57]

71 *The booking office at the Golden Cross, Charing Cross, London, 1839 (drawing by Cruikshank).*

There was also income from parcels and luggage. In 1835 it was estimated that the income from 'parcels and packages' between Bristol and London was 40s. per journey, roughly equivalent to the fare of one passenger inside a fast coach and perhaps 15% of revenue.[58] Charges declined, in contrast to fares: in 1768-81 they were 1d or 1½d per lb (depending on the speed of the coach) and in 1825-35 they were normally 1d per lb, though more for bulky and light goods and a minimum of 1s. or 1s.6d for small parcels. Waterhouse and Horne stated in 1825 that the charge had fallen from 1½d to 1d per lb in the previous five years as a result of competition, especially from vans.[59] Waterhouse and other coachmasters from London, Bristol, Bath and Marlborough established a Bristol-London van service in 1827, perhaps for that reason, though perhaps also to oppose the General Stage-Coach Company, which was advertising for goods.[60] Only the slower coaches ever explicitly advertised the carriage of goods. When Fromont established his opposition coaches, he temporarily brought the parcel price down to 6d; the Chronometer charged 6s. per cwt in 1824, equivalent to about 0.6d per lb; and the New Company in 1833 was willing to carry small parcels for 4d. Fromont referred particularly to 'samples, patterns, and other similar packages', highlighting the coaches' importance to businesses, and also to parcels sent by lawyers.[61] Apart from passengers' luggage, items recorded as having been carried by Bristol-London coaches included West Country cloth, fur caps, hat bodies, pearl earrings from a London jeweller, bankers' parcels and pheasants. Letters should have been carried only by the mail coaches, but coachmasters found it hard to resist illegally carrying them in other coaches, and in 1800 Weeks was prosecuted by the Post Office for doing so. Items conveyed as post by the mail coaches included the London newspapers, and the development of the press was closely linked to the development of road transport.[62]

Horses and teams

AS ALREADY EMPHASISED, the coachmaster's key decisions related to his horses, and some of these have been examined already.[63] How many should be kept? What sort of horse should they be? How fast should they go? How long should their stages be, and how often should they run them? How much should they be fed? All these matters needed to be reconsidered as the roads were improved and speeds increased.

Coachmasters sometimes used one horse per double mile[64] as a rule of thumb in the 1820s and 1830s, but in practice the calculation was more complicated. The number was obviously affected by the speed, the weight drawn and the quality of the road. Waterhouse stated in 1827 that the mails needed more than one horse per double mile, and both he a few years earlier and Chaplin in that year reckoned that, while a horse per double mile was needed within 50 miles of London, only four-fifths as many were needed for the same speed beyond that distance.[65]

Advertisements for horse sales indicating the stock held for specific stages make it possible to test these statements for the Bristol road in 1828-43 (Appendix 4). Usually they emphasise that the horses were 'a genuine stock' used for that coach, though it is conceivable that sometimes an odd horse or two was left out. The fastest coaches generally had somewhat more than one horse per double mile (except close to London), such as the two mail-coach examples at 1.09 and 1.17 and Cooper's at 1.05. Slower ones such as The Age, the New Company's night coach and the Prince of Wales had fewer, the examples from those being from 0.83 to 0.88. The differing numbers of horses underlay the variation in fares at different speeds in Table 2. In several cases the numbers kept followed exactly the principle set out by Horne that ten horses were needed to keep eight horses constantly at work.[66]

One obvious anomaly is the fewer horses required per double mile between Hounslow and London even for fast coaches such as the mails – 0.77 to 0.79 in the three examples.[67] Although in 1819 the London coachmasters emphasised that the roads within 50 miles of London were bad and required more horses than elsewhere, Horne observed that the one between London and Hounslow, formerly 'extremely bad', had become 'good', through better construction and through better materials,[68] and that was clearly reflected in the numbers of horses kept. As for the contrast between roads under and over 50 miles from London, there is no sign on the Bristol road that coaches more than 50 miles from the capital could be worked with many fewer horses, and the contrast may have been drawn mainly from roads leading north.[69] Similarly, although Horne stated in 1819 that if he were to work his Bristol coach westward from Newbury, 'I should keep short-legged horses, because of the hills', there is no sign of variation in the size of horses along the road.[70]

Horses per double mile in the 1830s can be compared with those required in the seventeenth and early eighteenth centuries. About 0.6 horses were then required per double mile in summer and 0.8 in winter,[71] compared with about 0.8 to 1.1 regardless of season by the 1830s. Meanwhile capacity had at least doubled and speed had more than doubled. As discussed above, much of the increase in horses per double mile may have coincided with a substantial increase in capacity around 1805.[72] The fact that the increase in horses per double mile between the seventeenth century and the 1830s was fairly small despite the much greater speed and capacity was a major ingredient in the growth of productivity discussed earlier. There was a related change in the number of miles covered by teams per week. Examples from 1681-1739 were usually between 80 and 93 miles in summer and 90 to 120 in winter, though the latter was for six-horse teams. In the examples from 1831-43 where the number of teams is clear, miles per week ranged from 58 to 88, but almost all except slow coaches or between Hounslow and London were from 60 to 73 miles.[73] Teams therefore covered somewhat fewer miles per week in the 1830s, but, again, at much higher speeds and with larger loads.

As coaches became faster, stages became shorter, though the link was not automatic or unvarying and coachmasters were not always agreed on the best length of stage for a given speed. Four broad overlapping periods can be identified. Nationwide, until the 1750s or 1760s, stages throughout the country were typically 20-25 miles in summer and 29-36 miles (an entire day's journey) in winter. Some summer stages on the Bristol road conformed to this between London and Reading, but most were somewhat shorter (Fig. 12). In the second period, from the 1750s, the longer stages on the Bristol road near London were reorganised so that all were from 13 to 18 miles, and these stages were used in both summer and winter (Figs.

72 Mail coach horses being changed at night, c.1840.

15 and 26). In the third period, from the 1770s, faster services such as
Gevaux' diligences and the mail coach (except in its first few years) had
stages ranging from nine to 14 miles and averaging 11 miles (Figs. 35
and 43), though the two-horse mail coach in its first years and possibly
also the Balloon coaches had even shorter stages of six to eight miles.
Glasier & Co used the same, longer, stages for its diligences as for its
machines in 1775, probably because the existing stages determined
the structure of the partnership and perhaps because the diligences
were not expected to last. Stages of ten or 11 miles remained common
for fast coaches even in the 1830s. For example the two known stages
of Cooper's coaches between Brentford and London and Thatcham
and Theale were 10.3 and 9.1 miles.[74]

In the fourth period, from the 1820s, some firms reduced their
stages to about six miles, though teams then ran two stages of that
length in place of one. Coachmasters disagreed about whether that
was better than a 10 or 11 mile stage once a day, and it may have made
little difference to the number of horses needed per double mile. An
inspector of mail coaches stated in 1827 that the average mail stage
was ten miles and that he recommended to the contractors that they
work shorter stages, but they preferred them as long as possible
'for their own benefit; at least they calculate upon a benefit, which
I do not, because if the stages are long, of course it must wear the
horses out sooner'. Horne stated in 1827 that his longest stage was 12
miles, 'but we generally make two sixes where there is a twelve-mile
stage'; this required more horses, 'but we think that they last longer,
because if we have a twelve-mile stage nothing but a good horse will
do, therefore we cannot use them so long'. Three references to the
Monarch in 1838-40 suggest stages of 5.1 to 7.8 miles, and George
Collins horsing the mail coaches between Maidenhead and Slough
in 1833 cannot have had a stage longer than 5.5 miles. His horses
must have worked both up and down every day, covering 77 miles per
week, though Collins had six horses in order to keep four at work.[75]

Stages became shorter even for the slower coaches, though the distances did not decline so much. In 1814 the first three stages from London of Fromont's Express and Defiance coaches averaged only 11.8 miles each, and several slow coaches in 1835-43 had similar stages of 11.9 to 14.0 miles.[76]

The simplest possible arrangement of teams was that of Richard Lovegrove, horsing the Monarch between Maidenhead and Colnbrook in 1831. His eight horses were evidently two teams, each travelling 9.3 miles up one day and down the next, covering 65 miles a week. Horses treading the same stage every day got to know the route well. When, in 1799, the coachman of the Bristol mail became so benumbed with cold that he fell off the coach near Reading and the guard was unable to stop the horses, the horses proceeded four miles to Hare Hatch where they were to be changed and then stopped, having safely passed two waggons and with the passengers unaware that anything was amiss.[77]

There is no doubt that in the nineteenth century the horses in fast coaches were rapidly worked to death, as coachmasters themselves acknowledged.[78] When John Skinner used what seems to have been one of the Company's coaches in December 1826, he noted that it travelled with the velocity of the Mail 'till one poor horse dropped down, and was with difficulty got again on his legs'. Later, when descending the hill to Bathford,

> another horse fell, and in the course of a minute, after three loud groans, breathed his last. "It would have been a bad job", said the coachman, soliloquizing on the event, "if thou hadst a soul to be saved; but as it is, it cannot be helped". Thinks I to myself, it might have been helped, if you had not driven the poor animal like a mere machine, beyond his strength, – and ruptured a blood vessel on his heart, which I doubt not was the immediate cause of his death. The three remaining horses however conveyed us in safety to the Christopher Inn.[79]

There is no reason to believe this sort of event was typical of fast coaches, but in 1835 it was common for mail coach guards to report in winter 'horses weak and not fit for the stage'. When the Bristol mail coach was accelerated for the last time in 1836, the superintendent of mail coaches observed that 'if the animals could plead they would surely be advocates for rail roads'.[80] The horses paid with their lives for the fast coach travel of the 1820s and 1830s.

How long did stage coach horses last? They were probably about five years old when first harnessed to a coach. Several coachmasters emphasised in 1819 that the stock used within 50 miles of London did not last more than three or four years, whereas further from the city coach horses would last six years. As Horne explained, 'first, the work is lighter, and next, the food is better; besides which, the lodging of them is better – the stables are airy and more healthy; they have not so often diseases in the country as we have in London.' This did not mean that all the horses died; rather that they were sold on for less demanding work. In 1827 Chaplin, who changed a third of his stock every year, stated that 'I have thought it better not to stop till they get old, but when I find them failing in their limbs or constitutions to patch them up and sell them, and get in a fresh horse'.[81]

Coachmen, guards and horsekeepers

As Lord William Lennox explained, the coachman had far more to do than simply guiding the horses along the road:

> To become a downright good coachman, a man should be able to put the team together, so as to alter a trace or a bit during the journey; he must take care that every horse does his work, and must keep the jades up to the collar. He must then be careful to ease his horses up a hill, spirting down one, and taking advantage of any level piece of

road, make up for the slower pace of a heavier one. He must also learn how to handle his whip, so as to flip off a horse-fly from his leaders, and to double thong a refractory wheeler when gibbing or refusing to work; he must remain perfectly placed upon the box, even amidst danger never losing his head or his temper, always remembering that upon his presence of mind depends the fate of his passengers.[82]

The Duke of Beaufort contrasted the two coachmen who drove the York House coach alternate days between London and Marlborough in the 1830s:

> James Adlam was not nearly so good a coachman as Jack Sprawson ... . Adlam made his wheel-horses do all the work the first half of the stage, and when they were beat made the leaders pull both the coach and the beaten wheel-horses, so that he got the whole lot well tired before the end of the stage, and in spite of going faster he was always late – always a minute, sometimes five, sometimes more. Jack Sprawson made his horses work level, never seemed to be going so fast, and yet was always punctual to a minute. ... He was universally liked and respected by every one, which I cannot say of the other man.[83]

According to Lennox, the character of stage coach drivers changed as the old heavy coaches gave way to faster ones. The driver 'was formerly a man of enormous bulk, with a rubicund face, greatly addicted to strong ale, often indulging in language the reverse of parliamentary', whereas 'the fast coachmen were well-conditioned, in many instances well-educated men, who could sing a song, and tell a good story to while away the time'. Leonard Rudd, looking back to 1830 fifty years later, said that they had 'that good address and civil manner which gave confidence to timid ladies ... as a rule they were sober men: and some of them coffee-drinkers only on the road. I do not remember being driven by any man on a public coach the worse for liquor.' Harris recalled that 'Cooper's coachmen were mostly large powerful men, but he ultimately found out that smaller yet quicker and more active young men were better.'[84]

73 Portrait of a mail coachman, drawn by Thomas Anderson Rudd of Reading in about 1820.

The usual organisation of coachmen in all periods seems to have been that they worked up one day and down the next, rather than accompanying a coach throughout its journey. Baldwin's coachmen in 1725 covered the whole distance between London and Bath, two of them travelling 327 miles every week, but that was specifically contrasted with the practice of other firms. A more normal distance was then 45 to 50 miles per day in summer, or about 270 to 300 miles per week, but less in winter.[85] As coaches speeded up, coachmen could cover more miles per day, but their miles per week did not increase in proportion to the higher speed, probably because more care and attention was needed to drive a fast coach safely. In 1786-95 Woodforde normally tipped two coachmen, who in at least two cases changed at Newbury, indicating about 61 miles a day, taking about nine hours, and 430 miles a week. In 1834, the Monarch had four coachmen, two driving up and down between Bristol and Newbury (63 miles) and two between Newbury and London (59 miles), which were then typical distances for coachmen.[86] As in 1786-95 a week's work was about 430 miles, but it now took only about seven hours a day. The Monarch's arrangement was probably typical of the faster

Bristol coaches, but the York House coach to Bath, with a slightly shorter route, managed with three coachmen, two alternating between London and Marlborough (77 miles) and one between Bath and Marlborough (32 miles each way), covering about 540 and 450 miles a week respectively. The Bristol mail coach differed by having five coachmen, perhaps because its high speed, lack of stops and night running made the 63 miles westwards from Newbury too hard for one man. Two coachmen drove up and down between London and Newbury, just as in the Monarch's case, but west of Newbury there were three coachmen, two between Newbury and Calne (31 miles) and one driving up and down between Calne and Bristol (32 miles). One advantage was that the mail coach's contractor between Newbury and Calne could appoint and supervise his own coachmen. When Waller was contractor there, two of his sons drove the mails and then his son-in-law for 25 years.[87]

An example of what this sort of arrangement meant in practice is provided by Cooper's day coach. Jack Stacey for several years drove up and down on alternate days between London and Thatcham, lodging at Cooper's Cottage:

> The situation was easy and pleasant; he left Piccadilly every other morning, including Sundays, as the coach ran every day, at seven o'clock, and reached the Cottage at ten minutes to one, when the coach stopped for the passengers to dine, and his day's work was finished. The next day he got on the box again at the Cottage, at two o'clock, and drove up to town, reaching Piccadilly at the Old White Horse Cellar at ten minutes to eight.[88]

Coaches which had guards organised them differently. The Monarch, a night coach, had three guards, each of whom stayed with the coach for an entire journey there and back and had every third night at rest. This meant 14 hours up, from 5.15 pm to at least 7.15 am and then a similar 14 hours down the next night, followed by a night's rest. The Post Office regarded ten to 12 hours for two nights followed by a night's rest reasonable, which is perhaps why until at least 1820 it split the Bristol route, with the guards changing at Marlborough.[89]

One horsekeeper was considered necessary for every seven to ten horses. Their hours reflected the need to prepare the horses for their stage and to look after them following the stage. When William Price, horsekeeper at Robert Gray's Bath stable at the Bolt in Tun inn in London, gave evidence in a case of theft in 1828, he stated that he had left the stable at 11.15 pm and had returned the next day at 4.40 am.[90] The lives of everyone in the coach trade were dominated by its insistent routine and uncompromising hours.

Notes

1   *Mail coach contracts*, PP 1835 (313), pp. 24-5, 77-8; Harris, p. 169; FFBJ 29 Nov 1777, 1 Apr 1780; BG 11 Nov 1824, 5 Apr, 7 June 1827.

2   Wilfred S. Dowden (ed.), *The journal of Thomas Moore*, 5 vols (1983-8), pp. 87, 167, 189, 632, 636-7, 714, 725, 982, 1012-13, 1401, 1779, 1789, 1849, 1958.

3   *Ibid.*, vol. 2, p. 714.

4   Wage rates from E.H. Phelps Brown and Sheila Hopkins, 'Seven centuries of building wages', *Economica*, n.s., vol. 22 (1955), p. 205.

5   Cardiff Central Library, MS 3.799, 24 Feb 1834.

6   Dowden, *Journal*, vol. 1, pp. 186-7, vol. 4, pp. 1612-13.

7   *Ibid.*, vol. 4, p. 1597; British Library, Add 33,647, 17 May 1813; *ibid.*, Add 33,697, pp. 134-5; William Toynbee (ed.), *The diaries of William Charles Macready 1833-1851* (1912), vol. 1, p. 210; Earl Leslie Griggs (ed.), *Collected letters of Samuel Taylor Coleridge* (1959), vol. 3, *1807-1814*, p. 40; John Beresford (ed.), *The diary of a country parson* (1924-31), vol. 4, p. 239; above, p. 123.

8   Beresford, *Diary*, vol. 4, p. 39; Griggs, *Collected letters*, p. 40; British Library, Add 33,658, 27 Jan 1821; *ibid.*, Add 33,697, pp. 193-4.

9   NLW, MS 22,340B, pp. 1-2; J.C. Trewin (ed.), *The journal of William Charles Macready* (1967), p. 7; above, p. 145.

10 Above, p. 63; Lord William Lennox, *Coaching, with anecdotes of the road* (1876), pp. 149-50, with Daphne Phillips, *The Great Bath Road* (1983), p. 109; above, p. 146; Nathaniel Sheldon Wheaton, *Journal of a residence during several months in*

London (1830), p. 318; above, p. 109; Toynbee, *Diaries*, vol. 1, p. 181.

11 Beresford, *Diary*, vol. 3, p. 140; *ibid.*, vol. 4, p. 240; NLW, transcript of diary of Lewis Weston Dillwyn, 21-2 April 1834.

12 e.g. *ibid.*, 11 Feb, 21 Apr 1834, 10 Apr 1837.

13 James L. Clifford (ed.), *Dr Campbell's diary of a visit to England in 1775* (1947), p. 87.

14 Beresford, *Diary*, vol. 2, p. 255, vol. 3, p. 139, vol. 4, pp. 39, 209-10.

15 Lennox, *Coaching*, pp. 107, 110, 154-5; Anthony Beesom, *Bristol in 1807* (2009), p. 183.

16 *London Evening-Post*, 4 Oct 1777; *Gazetteer & New Daily Advertiser*, 13 May 1780; *Morning Herald and Daily Advertiser*, 19 Aug 1782; *Public Advertiser*, 6 Jan 1783; [James Waylen], *The highwaymen of Wiltshire* (n.d.), pp. 13-14, 33, 42, 54; *General Evening Post*, 14 June 1792.

17 Above, pp. 19, 21-2; Figs. 15, 26, 27, 35, 36, 43, 60; FFBJ 27 Oct 1781, 6 Nov 1784, 12 Apr 1788; Webb 2, p. 33; Harris, pp. 200, 204.

18 Gerhold, pp. 105, 109-11; above, p. 18.

19 Above, pp. 65, 67-8.

20 *Select Committee on Acts regarding turnpike roads and highways in England and Wales*, PP 1819 (509), p. 15.

21 On the basis of two daily London-Bristol coaches and a London-Bath one three times a week, as in 1821 (*The Times*, 14 Dec 1821; BD).

22 TNA, C 13/2778/82; PP 1819 (509), p. 17; *The Times*, 20 Nov 1821; *English Reports*, vol. 130, pp. 271-2.

23 TNA, C 13/89/36; RLD 1832-9; *The Times*, 21 July 1841.

24 Wiltshire Heritage Museum, MS 1360-1; Bristol RO, FCW/1826/3, frames 5-6; TNA, PROB 11/2099, William Lawes; TNA, PROB 11 for other coachmasters.

25 *The Times*, 4 Feb, 4 & 11 Mar 1833; Harris, pp. 172-8; Institution of Civil Engineers, T8V 60(HC), p. 38.

26 BD 1832, p. 298; *The Times*, 4 Feb 1833; Harris, p. 180; Institution of Civil Engineers, T8V 60(HC), p. 38.

27 FFBJ 6 Nov 1784; TNA, PROB 11/1296, John Harris; FFBJ 15 July 1780; BM 8 Apr 1837.

28 TNA, E 112/1927, Nos. 198, 205.

29 Webb 1, pp. 48-9; Godfrey F. Laurence, *Bathford past and present* (1985), pp. 33, 35; website of Somersetshire Coal Canal Society (www.coalcanal.org); TNA, PROB 11/1899, Eleazar Pickwick. Eleazar's will describes Moses as his cousin.

30 TNA, C 14/1259/L86; TNA, C14/407/L42.

31 *Universal British directory*, vol. 1 (1791); PP 1819 (509), pp. 13-15; *Report from Select Committee on conveyance and porterage of parcels*, PP 1825 (498), pp. 13, 16; PP 1835 (313), pp. 41, 45, 66, 75, 79; *The Times*, 4 Apr 1831.

32 RLD 1832-6; BG 28 Mar 1833 and 1831-6 *passim*; above, p. 156.

33 POST 10/256; POST 10/36.

34 Wiltshire Heritage Museum, MSS 1287-8, 1289, 1360-1, 1362; FFBJ 5 Aug 1769,

3 Dec 1774, 25 Dec 1779; Henry Hunt, *Memoirs of Henry Hunt, Esq* (1820), vol. 1, pp. 297, 301; *Salisbury and Winchester Journal*, 11 Feb 1799, 30 Apr 1810, 30 May 1836; *Hampshire Advertiser*, 5 Mar 1836; TNA, C 14/1259/L86.

35 *The Times*, 23 Jan, 27 Feb, 23 June 1832.

36 *The Times*, 19 & 27 July 1841; *Bath Chronicle*, 17 Oct 1799; TNA, B 3/788; Duke of Beaufort, 'The Brighton, Bath, and Dover roads' in Beaufort, *Driving* (1890), p. 244.

37 TNA, B 3/2860.

38 *The Times*, 4 July, 3 Oct 1829, 10 Apr 1833; Parliamentary Archives, Lords evidence 1848, vol. 7, p. 114.

39 *Report from the Select Committee on turnpike trusts*, PP 1839 (295), p. 12; TNA, B 3/1130; above, p. 110. See also PP 1835 (313), pp. 29-30; Harris, p. 246.

40 *Report from the Select Committee on mail coach exemption*, PP 1810-11 (212), pp. 9, 40; *Report from the Select Committee on internal communication taxation*, PP 1837 (456), p. 39; Fig. 47.

41 *The Times*, 2 Jan 1813 (col. 3c); *Leeds Mercury*, 16 Oct 1819; *Sheffield Independent*, 5 Dec 1835. See also ABG 27 Mar 1797 (col. 2b) for a Wolverhampton-Birmingham coach said to be carrying for nothing.

42 FFBJ 29 Mar 1794.

43 Above, pp. 18-19, 21-2, 36-7, 60-5; FFBJ 3 & 17 Nov 1781.

44 Otherwise there would have been an apparent increase in productivity in the 1790s as excessive fares were eliminated.

45 i.e 1818, 1820, 1825, 1826, 1827, 1829, 1832 and 1833. Fares for the New Company's day coach in 1828, 1828/31, 1832, 1833, 1834/6 and 1838 were 45s., 38s., 28s., 30s., 30s. and 36s. inside and 21s., 18s., 14s., 14s., 16s. and 18s. outside.

46 *Devizes and Wiltshire Gazette*, 14 July, 4 Aug 1825.

47 BD; census 1851, 1861 (for Sully, Glamorgan); BM 12 Nov 1870.

48 *Report from Select Committee on steam carriages*, PP 1831 (324), p. 55.

49 Beresford, *Diary*, vol. 4, p. 210.

50 See e.g. PP 1819 (509), p. 13.

51 *The seventh report of the Commissioners appointed to inquire into the management of the Post-Office Department*, PP 1837 (70), pp. 70, 108, 116. In 1794 Fromont's waggons paid 2.67d per mile there and back between London and Colnbrook and 2.84d between Thatcham and Bristol, but only 1.00d between Colnbrook and Thatcham (TNA, C 12/205/21).

52 *Report of the Commissioners of Inland Revenue*, PP 1870 (C.82-I), pp. 28-9; Samuel Salt, *Statistics and calculations essentially necessary to persons connected with railways or canals* (1845), p. 83; Harris, p. 407; PP 1837 (456), p. 17; coach duty lists in RLD 1832-9.

53 PP 1835 (313), pp. 34, 36-8, 42, 46-9, 51, 64, 76-7. But see *ibid.*, p. 36, for the mileage system being established earlier. For coachmasters employing smiths: Bath RO, BC 134/198 (for Pickwick); TNA, PROB 11/1882, Thomas Botham

(for Botham); Peter Allen, *Around Thatcham in old photographs* (1992), p. 75 (for Fromont); BM 15 Apr 1837 (for Clift).

54 After 1793 the only Bristol-London coaches running less than six times a week were the Royal Sailor in 1805-6, the Economist in 1824 and the Chronometer in 1826-7 (all three times a week).

55 TNA, E 134/8GeoIII/East10; Salt, *Statistics and calculations*, p. 83.

56 Harris, p. 200. Assumptions are that the coach had 0.9 horses per double mile, provender cost 2s.6d per horse per day (see PP 1835 (313), p.39) and other horse costs were 15%, harness 4% and rent 2%.

57 Institution of Civil Engineers, T8V 60(HC), p. 38; PP 1837 (456), pp. 2, 17; *Minutes of evidence ... railway from London to Birmingham*, PP 1831-32 Lords (181), p. 29.

58 *Great Western Railway Bill: minutes of evidence*, Lords PP 1835 (81), p. 419. See PP 1831-32 Lords (181), p. 30, for a similar relationship on the Birmingham road (£2 received for parcels; inside fare £2.6s.). The 15% is on the assumption of three inside passengers at 40s. each and six outside ones at 18s. each.

59 Fig. 27; FFBJ 4 Feb 1775, 15 July 1780, 27 Oct 1781; PP 1825 (498), pp. 9-11, 13; BG 27 Apr 1826, 3 May, 7 June 1827; 28 Mar, 11 July 1833, 5 Feb 1835. Robert Gray claimed to be charging 1½d per lb in 1825 (PP 1825 (498), p.16).

60 BG 7 June 1827.

61 BG 8 July 1802, 11 Nov 1824, 5 Dec 1833. See Dorian Gerhold, *Road transport before the railways* (1993), pp. 183-4.

62 Lords PP 1835 (81), p. 29; *Proceedings of the Old Bailey* website, t17880227, t18020918, t18150111, t18340220; *English Reports*, vol. 172, p. 1145; FFBJ 26 April 1800; J.H. Chandler (ed.), *Wiltshire Dissenters' meeting house certificates and registrations 1689-1852*, Wiltshire Record Society, vol. 40 (1985), p. xx; George Boyce *et al* (eds.), *Newspaper history from the seventeenth century to the present day* (1978), pp. 89-90, 101.

63 Above, pp. 8-12, 24, 25, 27-8, 72-3, 82-4.

64 See above, p. 72.

65 PP 1835 (313), pp. 44, 47; PP 1819 (509), p. 13. In 1820 Waterhouse reckoned only 0.67 horses per double mile were needed for a hard and good road without steep hills (*Second report from Select Committee on the road from London, by Coventry, to Holyhead*, PP 1820 (224), pp. 24-5).

66 PP 1835 (313), p. 39.

67 Also only 0.84 overall for the New Company's day coach over a longer stretch including Hounslow-London.

68 PP 1819 (509), p. 14. See also *ibid.*, p. 16.

69 Appendix 4; PP 1835 (313), p. 44.

70 PP 1819 (509), p. 15; above, pp. 82-3.

71 Gerhold, pp. 202-5, but correcting the figures to relate to seven days a week rather than six and excluding services under 40 miles. The ranges were 0.47 to 0.83 in summer and 0.61 to 0.94 in winter.

72 Above, pp. 106-8.

73 Gerhold, pp. 202-5; Appendix 4.

74 Gerhold, pp. 142-3; above, pp. 26-7, 44, 75-6, 89-90; Appendix 4. According to Harris (p. 297), Cooper's coaches had six changes of team for the 56 miles between Thatcham and London, indicating 8.0 mile stages, but he perhaps meant six teams (9.3 miles per stage), which would be more consistent with the other evidence.

75 Charles G. Harper, *Stage-coach and mail in days of yore* (1903), vol. 2, p. 176; *Eighteenth report of the Commissioners of Inquiry into the collection and management of the revenue*, PP 1829 (161), p. 442; PP 1835 (313), p. 40; Appendix 4; Harris, p. 136. See also PP 1835 (313), pp. 36-7, 47.

76 TNA, C 13/2778/82; Appendix 4.

77 Appendix 4; R.C. Tombs, *The Bristol royal mail* [1899], p. 31.

78 PP 1819 (509), p. 15; PP 1820 (224), pp. 24-5; PP 1835 (313), pp. 41, 47.

79 British Library, Add 33,695, pp. 187-8.

80 PP 1835 (313), p. 57; POST 10/36.

81 PP 1819 (509), pp. 13-16; PP 1835 (313), p. 44.

82 Lord William Lennox, *Coaching, with anecdotes of the road* (1876), pp. 175-6.

83 Beaufort, 'Brighton, Bath and Dover roads', pp. 242-3.

84 Lennox, *Coaching*, pp. 171-2; Berkshire RO, D/EX 1373/1, ff. 23-4; Harris, p. 179. See also *Report from Select Committee on the observance of the Sabbath Day*, PP 1831-32 (697), p. 133.

85 Above, p. 29; Gerhold, p. 118.

86 Seven examples on other roads in 1809-28 range from 48 to 73 miles.

87 Harris, pp. 200-3; Beaufort, 'Brighton, Bath and Dover roads', pp. 242-3.

88 Harris, p. 297.

89 Harris, p. 201; *First report from the Select Committee on postage*, PP 1837-38 (278), p. 123; *Proceedings of the Old Bailey* website, t17950416, t18200628.

90 PP 1831-32 (697), pp. 129, 133, 215; *Proceedings of the Old Bailey* website, t18281204.

5

Regional and local coaches

The Union coach to Hereford

THE UNION FROM Bristol to Hereford provides a well-recorded
example of a regional coach, thanks to a legal dispute.[1] It began
in August 1802, running three times a week. Its route, not previously
served except briefly in the 1780s, crossed the Severn by the Old
Passage and proceeded via Chepstow and Monmouth. The journey
lasted from 7 am until the evening of the same day, suggesting an
overall speed no greater than about five miles per hour. The two
proprietors were William Williams of Bristol, coachmaster, and James
Bennett of Hereford, innholder. Williams had 31 miles (Bristol to
Monmouth) and Bennett 18 miles (Monmouth to Hereford), and
receipts were divided in proportion in the usual way. Williams had
14 horses for his share, equivalent to just over one horse per double
mile, despite the low speed. Both his horses and his four coaches
must have been divided into two groups on either side of the Severn.
Assuming the same number of horses per mile, Bennett had eight,
making a total of 22 for the whole route.

The cost of keeping the horses is not recorded, being an individual
cost, and the same applied in this case to the coaches, but the shared
costs are recorded. They were largely the same from month to month.

In the four weeks from 17 January 1804 they were £10.10s.0d for tolls, £9.12s.0d for stage coach duty, £7.4s.0d for passengers crossing the Old Passage, £4.4s.0d for coachmen's wages and 10s.6d for oil for greasing coach wheels. The one shared cost which varied was the ferry crossing, the partnership account being charged 1s.6d per passenger. This money apparently came to Williams, as he claimed his 'large passage boat' worth £150 was used by the coach business. After the partnership ended Williams sought to charge other costs to the partnership account, including the cost of 15 journeys to Chepstow, Monmouth and Hereford on coach business (evidently once a month at a guinea a time), 3 guineas a month for booking passengers and parcels, rent of coach office, writing of accounts and £10 for a lost parcel.

Receipts for passengers and parcels for each return journey to Hereford and back from mid-January to late March 1804 varied from £2.14s.0d to £14.16s.5d. The numbers of passengers crossing by the ferry indicate an average loading of 4.4 during this winter period (3.9 towards Hereford and 4.9 towards Bristol), but average loading rose from 4.0 to 4.5 and then 4.9 in the three periods covered, suggesting that it was higher in summer. The vehicle was a post coach, which probably had four inside places and at least as many outside ones. Income and loading together indicate that the fare was relatively high. Why there were more passengers travelling towards Bristol than towards Hereford in each of the three periods is unknown. Williams and Bennett quarrelled in March 1804 and for a time both ran their own coaches in competition the whole distance. Williams evidently retired defeated. The Union coach continued to run under Bennett and his successors until 1827.[2]

The Union coach indicates that regional services were similar to London ones in most respects, but with some differences, mostly reflecting the more limited custom. The organisation was similar, with a division of the road into miles and allocation of surplus receipts according to miles covered. They were usually on a smaller scale, though the stock of an individual proprietor might be comparable to that used for a stage in a London coach. The regional coach might be less frequent. At certain periods it was likely to be dearer and slower, though there was much variety. It was more likely to be a monopoly, as in the Union's case, though there were sometimes competitors on alternative routes – for example Bristol to Hereford via Gloucester.[3] The final destination was not always clear, since a proprietor with more than one coach route or co-operating with other coachmasters could advertise several coaches as a single service, as Bennett and later owners did in describing the Union's destination as Shrewsbury and even Holyhead.[4]

Bristol's regional network

AFTER 1730, BRISTOL acquired no new regional services for nearly 30 years. Then two important ones were added within a few years: to Birmingham in 1759 and Exeter in 1764. Their importance partly reflected that of the two cities, which had populations of about 24,000 and 16,000 respectively in 1750,[5] but also the connecting coaches available to more distant places – from Birmingham to Manchester, Liverpool and elsewhere and from Exeter to Plymouth. Both new services started tentatively – no more than a weekly coach to each place at first – but the two routes always accounted for at least a third of the regional services.

New destinations added subsequently included Weymouth in 1779, Gosport via Southampton in 1780, Milford Haven via Swansea in 1787, Hereford in 1802, Abergavenny and Barnstaple in 1809, Leicester in 1810, Cheltenham in 1813, Brighton and Minehead in 1822, Brecon in 1830 and Liverpool in 1831, in several cases preceded by an earlier coach which failed to become established. A network

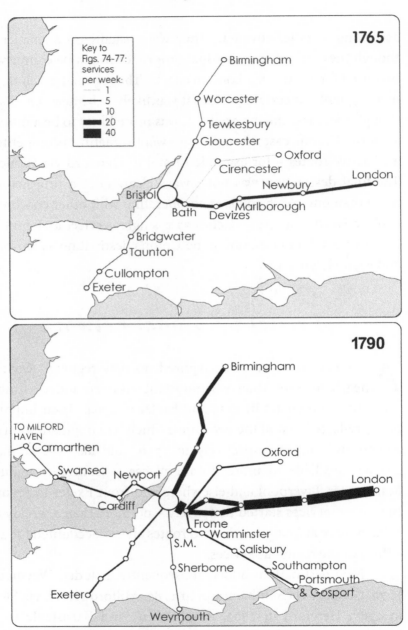

74-77 *Plans of coach routes from Bristol indicating their frequency in
1765, 1790, 1816 and 1836. Services to Stroud (nine in 1816, six in 1836)
and Chalford (six in 1836) have been omitted for lack of space. London
services in 1790 and 1816 have been evenly divided between the two*

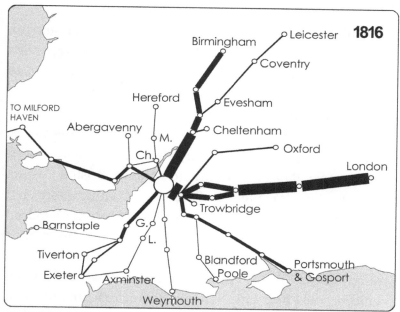

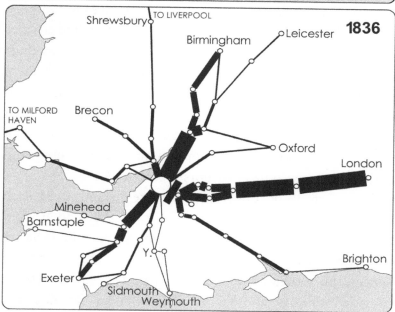

*routes for want of information. Some services eastwards may have been
Bath ones connecting with Bristol-Bath coaches. Key: Ch – Chepstow; G
– Glastonbury; L – Langport; M – Monmouth; SM – Shepton Mallet; Y –
Yeovil. (Sources: Local directories; newspaper advertisements.)*

of regional mail coaches was established in 1785-7, to Portsmouth, Oxford, Bath, Birmingham and Milford Haven, and expanded piecemeal thereafter, though not always successfully. Local services of 20 miles or less began to appear in 1779, and coaches to nearby coastal resorts multiplied in the nineteenth century.

Bristol's network intersected with the networks of other towns, especially Bath, and this complicates any attempt to count services. In 1782, for example, Bath had coaches to London, Bristol, Oxford, Birmingham, Exeter, Weymouth, Salisbury, Southampton and Gosport, Worcester and Shrewsbury, Frome and Gloucester.[6] Indeed Bristol and Bath were so close that the services advertised were often the same, either because a coach actually passed through both (as most of the London ones did) or because the frequent coaches between the two could be used as a link. Thus a Bristol coachmaster with Bristol to Bath coaches could claim to provide services to Gosport, Oxford and other places by transferring passengers at Bath to coaches for those places. Services approaching either city from the south or north might have a branch to the other or at least an arrangement for transferring passengers to a connecting coach.[7] Even experienced coach travellers could be caught out: when Thomas Moore took what he thought was a Cheltenham to Bath coach in 1835, he 'found that it took me round by Bristol, where I stopped a quarter of an hour, and was from thence conveyed in a two-horse coach to Bath'.[8]

Similarly, there were connections at more distant places, such as Birmingham. Partnerships with nothing on the road beyond Birmingham could advertise their coaches as serving Manchester and Liverpool by virtue of such connections, and almost invariably advertisements for coaches from Bristol purporting to serve those places provided timings and fares only as far as Birmingham. Also, some advertised services were branches rather than separate departures from Bristol, such as the coaches to Minehead which met the Exeter to Bristol coaches at Bridgwater. These interconnections

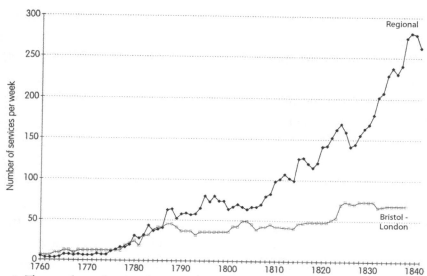

78 *The numbers of regional services per week from Bristol covering more than 20 miles, 1760-1841. For comparison, the numbers of Bristol-London services are also shown. (Sources: Local directories; newspaper advertisements.)*

increased as regional services multiplied, and perhaps also reflected improved timekeeping. They are one of several reasons why coach services listed in directories should never be counted uncritically, as explained in more detail in Appendix 1. From the point of view of the historian counting services the onward links artificially inflate the numbers. From the point of view of passengers it may sometimes have made little difference that they were connections rather than direct services, provided the connections worked perfectly, but there is abundant evidence that passengers disliked being transferred between vehicles,[9] and it is unlikely that the advertised links always meant a quick transfer and a guaranteed place.

In this chapter an attempt has been made to identify coach services genuinely setting out from Bristol, and, as far as numbers are concerned, to eliminate the double-counting inherent in directory listings. The resulting figures are mapped for four dates in Figs. 74 to 77 and are shown as a whole in Fig. 78. Bristol's regional services multiplied much faster than the London ones. There were more regional services than London ones from 1787, and the gap widened massively and almost continuously from 1808. The timing of growth differed from that for London services, for reasons examined later. In particular, the period of stagnation ended for regional services in about 1808 and thereafter there was almost continuous growth.

The impact of turnpikes

IT IS SOMETIMES argued that there was a direct connection between turnpiking and the development of coach services.[10] However, in Bristol's case the dates demonstrate that there was no simple relationship between the creation of a trust and the running of the first sustained coach service (Table 3). The earliest stage coaches managed without turnpikes at all. From 1759 all new services operated on fully turnpiked roads, and the Birmingham and Exeter services started only a few years after their roads were fully turnpiked, but in all other cases there was a long time lag. This is hardly surprising in view of the different timescales of the two processes: a dense network of turnpike roads was created during the 'turnpike mania' of the 1750s and 1760s, whereas the development of regional coach services was a longer-term process over many decades. Turnpiking of a road was not enough to conjure a coach service into existence, and many turnpike roads never saw a stage coach until decades after being turnpiked, or at all.

That does not of course mean that turnpikes were not important, as the example of Bristol-London coaches has demonstrated. By improving the roads they improved the economics of stage coaches, making it possible for them to run cheaper and faster. That, together with rising population and prosperity, helped to make stage coaches viable where they had not been before. In other words, the contribution

Table 3. Turnpikes and coach services from Bristol

Route	Route fully turnpiked	First coach service[1]	Years from full turnpiking to coach service
London	1744	1657	–
Oxford	1758	1701[2]	–
Gloucester	1727	1721	–
Birmingham	1756[3]	1759	3
Exeter	1759	1764	5
Weymouth	1761	1779 (1768)	18
Southampton	1761	1780	19
Milford Haven	1771	1787	16
Hereford	1758	1802 (1780)	44
Abergavenny	1758	1809 (1794)	51
Barnstaple	1786	1809	23
Leicester	1757	1810 (1772)	53
Poole	1766	1815	49
Minehead	1765	1822	57

Sources: Turnpike Acts; William Albert, *The turnpike road system in England 1663-1840* (1972), pp. 202-223; O. Bryan Morland, *An introduction to the infrastructure of the Industrial Revolution in Somerset* (1982); Arthur Cossons, 'Warwickshire turnpikes', *Birmingham Archaeological Society, Transactions and Proceedings*, vol. 64 (1946), pp. 53-100; *Victoria history of the counties of England – Wiltshire*, vol. 4 (1959), pp. 254-71.

Notes:
1 Dates in brackets indicate services which soon disappeared.
2 Coach summer only at first.
3 85% of route turnpiked by 1727.

of turnpikes to the development of regional coach services was linked to the longer-term improvement of the roads rather than to the dates when trusts were established, and improved roads were not the only reason for that development.

Bristol coachmasters and regional coaches

GEORGE SEASON OF Bristol was a founding proprietor of the Bristol to Exeter coaches in 1764, and Thomas Lawrence set up short-lived coaches to Exeter and Leicester in 1772, but the first Bristol proprietor with a substantial regional network was John Weeks at the Bush. He had services to Birmingham from 1775, Exeter from 1777, Gosport from 1782, and Weymouth and Oxford from 1784, in addition to his London coaches.[11]

By 1783 the Bush and the White Hart were sharing the Birmingham and Exeter services, and the pattern was set for more than 30 years, with Weeks, Poston and Coupland dominant at Bristol. In 1785 there were five Bristol inns with London coaches and seven with Bath coaches, but only two with Birmingham and Exeter ones. New services to Birmingham and Exeter were probably even more strongly resisted than new ones to London, and a newcomer demonstrated his intention to establish a significant coaching business regardless of the opposition by challenging on those routes. The pattern was only slightly disturbed in the 1780s by the establishment of mail coaches, most of which were horsed by John Wheeler at the Rummer, since after his death in 1793 the mail coaches were largely secured by the Bush and the White Hart.[12]

The first major challenge was from the White Lion under Thomas Luce. The White Lion had had coaches only to London, Bath and the New Passage, but Luce added Exeter in 1795 and Birmingham in 1796, as usual with partners along the routes. This prompted fierce competition. He was driven off the Exeter road for the time being (he or others using his inn later tried three more

GENERAL COACH-OFFICE,
PLUME OF FEATHERS, WINE-STREET,
BRISTOL.

THE following LIGHT POST COACHES start from the above Office:—

Birmingham, the TRAVELLER Light Post Coach, leaves every Morning (except Sundays) at Seven o'clock, through Gloucester, Cheltenham, Tewkesbury, and Worcester, to the Albion Hotel, Birmingham, at Seven o'clock, where Passengers and Parcels are immediately forwarded to Manchester, Liverpool, Shrewsbury, Chester, Holyhead, and all parts of the North.

A New COACH to Derby, Nottingham, and Sheffield, every Morning (except Sundays) at Quarter before Seven.

A New COACH to Leicester and Coventry, every Morning at Seven.

Exeter, the TRAVELLER, every Morning at Quarter before Seven, through Bridgwater, Taunton, Wellington, and Tiverton, to Congdon's Hotel, Exeter, where Passengers and Parcels are forwarded to Totness, Plymouth, Truro, Falmouth, and all parts of Cornwall.

Barnstaple and Southmolton, the only DAY COACH from Bristol, leaves every Morning at Quarter before Seven, and arrives at Barnstaple at Nine o'clock the same Evening. Fares, Inside 25s. Outside 12s.

Bridgwater, Dunster, Minehead, and Taunton, the SPECULATOR, Mondays, Wednesdays, and Fridays, at Quarter before Nine in the Morning.

Oxford, the CHAMPION, every Morning (except Sundays) at Quarter before Eight, through Sodbury, Didmarton, Tetbury, Cirencester, Bidbury, Burford, and Witney, to the Mitre Inn, Oxford, where it arrives at Half-past Six in the Evening; where it meets Coaches to Buckingham, Northampton, Cambridge, and all parts of the North.

Weston-super-Mare, the RISING SUN, New Light Four-inside Coach, leaves every Sunday, Monday, Wednesday, and Friday Mornings, at Quarter before Nine; and returns from Weston-super-Mare for Bristol and Bath the same Afternoon, at Half-past Four, and arrives in Bristol at Quarter past Seven, and the Greyhound Inn, Bath, at Nine in the Evening.

London, the TRIUMPH Light Four-Inside Coach, every Afternoon at Four o'clock, through Chippenham, Marlborough, Newbery, and Reading, to the New White Horse Cellar, Piccadilly; the Angel, St. Clement's; White Horse, Fetter-Lane; and Bull and Mouth, Bull and Mouth-Street, early the next Morning; leaves the Bull and Mouth at Six o'clock, and the White Horse Cellar at Seven o'clock the same Evening for Bristol.

Bradford, Trowbridge, and Westbury, Light COACH, every Afternoon at Half-past Three o'clock.

COACHES to Bath at Quarter past Eight, Nine and Ten in the Morning; at Three, Half-past Three, Four, and Quarter past Seven in the Evening

Parcels and Luggage forwarded by the above Coaches at very Reduced Prices.

Performed by WM. CLIFT & Co.

Who inform their Friends and the Public, that the above Coaches shall be conducted equal to any Coaches in the Kingdom; and will not be answerable for any Parcel, Package or Passengers' Luggage, above the value of Five Pounds, unless entered and paid for accordingly.

79 Advertisement by William Clift of his coaches from the Plume of Feathers in 1824. It makes less attempt to magnify the number of services than some of his other advertisements, but the Exeter and Barnstaple services are clearly the same departures, and so probably are the Birmingham, Derby and Leicester and Coventry ones. (Bristol Gazette, 13 May 1824.)

times), but his Birmingham service continued until a compromise some years later.[13]

The next challengers were William Williams, using various inns, from 1802 until his death in 1816, and Charles Bessell at the Swan from about 1807 to 1816. Williams seems to have been cautious about the Exeter and Birmingham roads, apart from taking over what had been Luce's Birmingham coach and starting a coach to Exeter using an indirect route via Axminster. His other ventures, mostly short-lived, were to Hereford, Portsmouth, London and south Wales.[14] Bessell also started cautiously with a Leicester coach in 1810, but the ferocity which this aroused among the Birmingham proprietors seems to have resulted in him hitting back with a Birmingham one in 1811. Only Williams' coaches to Hereford and to Exeter via Axminster and Bessell's Leicester coach endured.[15]

The competitive situation was transformed by William Clift. He became innkeeper at the Plume of Feathers, Wine Street, not then a coaching inn, in 1816. In 1820 its only coaches were to London, Bath and Stroud. The following year Clift launched his challenge, acquiring a stake in the recently-established Traveller to Birmingham and starting his own Traveller coach to Exeter, as well as short-lived coaches to Poole and Trowbridge. In addition to the Feathers, Clift had a large property around a courtyard in Temple Backs including stabling for about 50 horses. What made Clift distinctive was that he seems never to have compromised with the established proprietors, and proudly proclaimed that he was engaged in 'opposition'. In 1821 he thanked the public for their support since embarking on 'opposition coach business, by which travelling has been facilitated and its expenditure reduced; the different roads laid open to a fair competition, and monopoly by any party rendered impossible – an evil severely felt by the public before the starting of the undermentioned coaches'.[16] As we shall see, this was no idle boast. In 1828 he stated that public support had enabled him for years 'to keep down a monopoly among the proprietors of public conveyances' from Bristol, with a consequent effect on fares. In response to Townsend and Niblett denouncing his allegation of collusion as 'a wilful deception' and a 'foul and unjust charge', Clift stated that

> he has single handed (although every Coach Office in the City has been opposed to him), kept in check an overgrowing monopoly among the coach masters in Bristol, and is astonished at the effrontery of Townsend and Son, who state theirs to be an independent Office, knowing they are connected with every other General Coach Establishment. W.C. is proud to state that his Office is alone perfectly unconnected with any other.[17]

The London, Bath, Birmingham, Exeter and Stroud routes remained the basis of Clift's business, but 11 other generally short-lived destinations were added, most years seeing at least one new service. The only new ones lasting more than four years were to Weston-super-Mare, to Coventry and to Exeter, Sidmouth and Lyme via Axminster, but no route was safe from a Clift challenge. In the 1830s he sometimes acquired a stake in an existing service, but these seem to have been the weaker ones.[18] In 1837 Clift had just 46 horses, together with four coaches, but this would be consistent with horsing five or so daily services for one stage out of Bristol. He went bankrupt in that year, for reasons unknown. Perhaps he had simply overreached himself in establishing new services or in cutting fares, or he had failed to withstand new competition from John Bland, discussed below. Clift subsequently entered into partnership with his former rival Isaac Niblett as 'hackney masters and black work proprietors' ('black work' being funeral work). The last information available is the dissolution of that partnership in December 1841, and even the date of his death is unknown.[19]

80 *The Greyhound, Broadmead, Bristol, used by John Bland, seen here in the 1880s.*
The inn still stands, but not the building to its right.

New competitors appeared even before Clift's demise. The most important was a Scot, John Bland, who was both a coachmaster and a carrier, at first in association with Robert Leonard. His coaching bases were the Rummer and the Greyhound (Fig. 80). His services are first recorded to Clevedon in 1834 and then a wide range of destinations from 1835 to 1840, including Exeter in 1836 and Birmingham in 1837. The obituary already quoted indicates that Bland was a very different man from Clift, and that the established coachmasters soon reached an understanding with him, probably in 1839. After that only a handful of mainly short-distance coaches were not controlled by Townsend, Niblett or Bland, and by 1841 Niblett was a partner in Townsend's business at the Bush.[20] However, there would have been little point in struggling to establish a new business against strong competition when the railways were about to wipe out the coach trade, and but for the prospect of railways Bland might have been more independent.

In almost all their services the Bristol coachmasters were in partnership with other coachmasters along the road, and their bargaining power must have varied from one route to another. It also varied from one coachmaster to another, according to the size of their connection and the perceived extent of their resources. For example, when John Land of Exeter wanted to expel Thomas Thompson from the Bristol-Exeter partnership in 1804 for reasons unconnected with coaching, the Bristol partners, Weeks and Poston, had no interest in the quarrel but decided that Land would be the more dangerous enemy of the two and therefore acquiesced.[21] A complication was that Bristol coachmasters were sometimes in partnership with each other on one route but in opposition on another. For example, in 1810 Weeks was involved with Bessell in the Leicester coach to which Poston and Coupland took strong exception, but Weeks, Poston and Coupland continued to run Birmingham coaches together. Coupland was allied with Fromont in newly-established coaches to Exeter while continuing to run the old-established Exeter coaches with Weeks and Poston. Meanwhile Bessell, Weeks, Poston, Coupland and Fromont were involved in various competing London coaches.

Coach routes

Birmingham

THE BIRMINGHAM ROUTE was Bristol's most important after the London one. The first coach ran in April 1759, under John Turner, a Gloucester coachmaster, and Thomas Shakell of Birmingham, a warehouse-keeper for London waggons. Its route was that which Birmingham coaches almost invariably followed subsequently, via

Gloucester, Tewkesbury, Worcester and Bromsgrove. It was twice weekly in summer, taking two days for the 87 miles, and weekly in winter, taking three days. In summer the two coaches met at Gloucester and then returned to Bristol or Birmingham, which suggests that Turner horsed the coach between Bristol and Gloucester and Shakell did the same between Gloucester and Birmingham, probably with two teams each and one change of team each day. The winter timing was then typical for journeys without changes of team. Judging by the changes of proprietor and frequency from year to year the coach had a chequered existence at first, and by 1762 neither of the original proprietors was still involved. By 1764 there were partners in three cities, for the first time including Bristol: Thomas Garmston at Worcester, John Turner (again) at Gloucester and Thomas Wilts at Bristol (later succeeded by Francis Sawyer). By 1765 the coach was taking a day and a half.[22]

What happened next was described nearly 40 years later by John Weeks:

> When J.W. first took to the Bush Tavern, in the year 1772,[23] there was no coach, either to London, Exeter, Oxford, or Birmingham, in less than two days; that J.W. used all his interest with the proprietors of these two-day coaches to accommodate the public, by running the distance in one day, which met with a positive refusal, and a threat at the same time to throw him into the King's Bench, if J.W. dared to put a coach upon the road in opposition. Notwithstanding J.W. opposed all their threats, and worked coaches at very reduced prices, and by his exertions, after sinking a large sum of money, he made them comply with his wishes to run coaches to the above places in one day; but not before he was under the necessity of working a coach to Birmingham for two years every day, all the way himself, at the reduced fare of 10s.6d. inside, and 8s. outside [1.4d and 1.1d per mile], allowing each passenger a dinner and a pint of wine at Gloucester, out of that small fare.[24]

When this was written Weeks was one of Bristol's most important coachmasters, and he naturally emphasised his selfless desire to serve the public. All that is certain in his account is that he established opposition coaches which performed the journey in one day and later reached an agreement with the established coachmasters ('he made them comply'). The Birmingham service of 1775 was Weeks's first, and he used diligences to cut the journey time to 16 hours. His prices were in fact higher than Sawyer & Co's had been – the standard 3.0d per mile of the diligence, the advertised price never falling below 2.9d per mile – and he seems from the start to have had a partner in Birmingham. Sawyer & Co responded by running post-chaises, taking 17 hours, at 2.9d per mile, and cut the fares in their ordinary coaches from 2.5d to 1.8d per mile. Competition thereby served the purpose of providing one-day journeys and raising speeds, to 5.1-5.4 miles per hour in 1775 and 6.0-6.2 from 1781. It also reduced the fares, though only temporarily. If strong opposition to a new competitor failed to force him off the road, the next tactic was

The Original Flying **DILIGENCE,**
From BRISTOL to BIRMINGHAM,
(In O N E D A Y)

SETS out from the Bush-Tavern, opposite the Exchange, in Corn-street, every Tuesday, Thursday and Saturday, at Four o'Clock in the Morning precisely, Breakfasts at Glocester, and meets the BIRMINGHAM DILIGENCE (which sets out from the Castle-Inn, at four o'Clock the same Mornings) at the Green Dragon on the Lawn; returns to Glocester to Dinner, and arrives at Bristol the same Evening at Eight o'Clock.

Each Passenger to pay Three Pence a Mile, and to be allowed Ten Pounds Weight of Luggage, but all above to be paid for. Parcels and Passengers received, and carefully delivered. The most respectful Attention will be paid to the Commands of the Encouragers of this Undertaking, to merit their Favours and Recommendation.——The Proprietors will not be accountable for Cash, Bills, Writings, Jewels, Plate, &c. unless entered as such, and paid for Accordingly.

N.B. The above Diligence meets the Sheffield and Coventry Diligence every Evening at the above Inn,
Performed by
JOSEPH PIPER, Castle-Inn, Birmingham.
WM. KINGS, Crabb-Mill, Bromsgrove.
J. THOMPSON, Crown-Inn, Worcester.
WM. RAYER, Booth-Hall, Glocester.
FRANCIS HATHEY, Bell, Newport.
JOHN WEEKS, Bush, Bristol.
N.B. The Exeter Diligence in and out Three Times a Week as usual.

81 Advertisement for the Birmingham diligence in 1778. The change of vehicle half way along the route suggests that the firm was organised as two separate partnerships. (Felix Farley's Bristol Journal, 14 February 1778.)

usually collaboration. In this case that was achieved by 1782 at the latest, when the two firms jointly advertised an increase in fares. By 1785 the enduring pattern was established of services on alternate days from the Bush and White Hart inns (by 1787 under Weeks, Poston and Coupland).[25]

When the mail coach to Birmingham was established in 1787, it did no more than match existing journey times of 14 to 15 hours (5.8 to 6.2 miles per hour). The time-bills were made out for 13 hours, but Hasker noted that until at least 1797 it always arrived an hour later. John Wheeler of the Rummer at first horsed the stages as far as Newport (18 miles), but after Wheeler's death in 1793 they were horsed by Weeks and Poston. In 1796 Hasker indicated that if the mail coach was to be routed through Thornbury as had been proposed, the proprietors would have to be persuaded rather than instructed to do it, because 'all the inn keepers and coachmaster[s] from Bristol to Birmingham are in [a] company thirty four in number, and if they should say they will not a new connection cannot be found'.[26]

The company was challenged in 1796 by Luce & Co with their Jupiter light coach to Birmingham, Manchester and Liverpool (Fig. 82). Unusually, proprietors were listed all the way to Manchester and Liverpool and through fares (but not precise arrival times) were specified. The company responded by reducing its fare to half the Jupiter's (only 1.45d per mile inside). Luce & Co cautioned the public against this practice by 'a set of monopolisers that have long taken upon them to assume an exclusive right to the Bristol and Birmingham road'. Luce & Co claimed to have the only direct coach to Manchester and Liverpool, despite the 'notorious falsehood' by the monopolisers in claiming that they too had a Manchester coach. By this Luce & Co perhaps meant only that a single partnership covered the entire route,

82 (opposite) Claim and counter-claim for Luce's Jupiter coach to Birmingham and the older service, 1796. (Felix Farley's Bristol Journal, 5 November 1796.)

BRISTOL, October 26, 1796.

BUSH, WHITE-HART, & RUMMER TAVERNS.

THE Public are most respectfully informed, that a New and Elegant POST-COACH, to carry four Insides, will commence running on MONDAY Morning next, at Four o'clock, and continue to run every MONDAY, WEDNESDAY, and FRIDAY, at the same Hour, at the reduced fare of Ten Shillings and Sixpence Inside, and Seven Shillings Outside.—Likewise a POST-COACH from the White-Hart, the same Mornings, at the same Fares, to the Swan and Castle-Inns, BIRMINGHAM, from whence Passengers and Parcels are immediately forwarded to *Shrewsbury, Sheffield, Leeds, Halifax, Liverpool, Manchester,* and all parts of the North of England.—Also, a DAY COACH to BIRMINGHAM every Morning at Four o'clock, and Royal MAIL every Evening at Seven.

⁎ Small Parcels 1s. each, larger ones 1d. per lb. in all the above Coaches.

EXETER COACH every Morning at Five, and DILIGENCE every Morning at Seven, immediately after the arrival of the Birmingham Mail.

WEEKS and Co. *Bristol,*
HART and Co. *Birmingham.*

☞ The Proprietors will not be accountable for any Money, Bills, Plate, or Jewels *of any value,* nor for any Parcels or Passengers' Luggage *of more than £5 value,* unless the same be ascertained, *regularly book'd and paid for accordingly.*

⁎ The Public are respectfully informed that the other Party advertising the only Coach to *Manchester,* is a gross Imposition on the Public, as we have a Coach from *Birmingham* to *Manchester,* in particular, every Evening at Ten o'clock, as well as to all parts of the North.

COACHES.

The Public are cautioned against

A DECEPTION,

WHICH an arbitrary set of Monopolizers have attempted to impose on them, by an Advertisement in the *Bristol* and other Papers, contradicting truth, and substituting a

NOTORIOUS FALSEHOOD!!!

Respecting certain conveyances to *Birmingham, Manchester, Liverpool, &c.* but, however, in order that Travellers may not be misguided, nor deceived, they are most respectfully and positively assured, let what may be said to the contrary, that the ONLY DIRECT COACH by way of *Birmingham* to *Manchester* and *Liverpool,* is the New

JUPITER LIGHT COACH,

Which sets out every MONDAY, WEDNESDAY, and FRIDAY MORNING, at Four o'clock, from Mr. LUCE's,

WHITE-LION INN, BRISTOL,
TO THE
SARACEN's-HEAD INN, *Birmingham,*

Where it arrives at Seven o'clock the same Evening, and proceeds on WITHOUT THE LEAST DELAY to *Manchester* and *Liverpool,* and arrives at each place early the next day.

Inside Fare from *Bristol* to *Liverpool* £2 2 0 each.
Outside Ditto . . . . . Ditto 1 1 0 ditto.
Inside Fare from *Bristol* to *Manchester* 2 2 0 ditto.
Outside Ditto . . . . . Ditto 1 1 0 ditto.

Performed by

LUCE, EVETT and Co.

N. B. The Public are requested to notice, that party Shafts, from a Set of Monopolizers that have long taken upon them to assume an exclusive right to the Bristol and Birmingham Road, is directed against this Undertaking, by reducing the Fares those Days on which the Jupiter runs, and taking their usual Advantage on the Public, Four Days out of Seven. To avoid Imposition this Caution is inserted, and the Bristol Jupiter Light Coach, submitted to the Public for Support, and will be continued on the above reasonable terms, being the Medium betwixt an extravagant Price, and reduced ones that cannot be continued.

Bristol, Nov. 4, 1796.

WHITE-LION INN.

Bristol, Birmingham, Manchester, and Liverpool

JUPITER LIGHT COACH,

WILL set out for the First Time on WEDNESDAY next *October* 26, and continue to go every MONDAY, WEDNESDAY, and FRIDAY MORNINGS, at Four o'clock, to the

Saracen's-Head Inn, Birmingham,

Where it arrives at Seven o'clock the same Evening, and there meets the MANCHESTER HAWK LIGHT COACH, and LIVERPOOL EXPEDITION POST COACH, which proceeds on at Nine o'clock the same evenings, and arrives at the above places early the next day.

The Public are respectfully informed, that the JUPITER is the only direct Coach by way of *Birmingham* to *Manchester* and *Liverpool,* where places from the WHITE LION INN, may be secured certain throughout by this conveyance. Carries only Four Insides.

From Bristol to Birmingham, inside, £1 1 0 each.
Outside Ditto . . . . 0 10 6 ditto.
Small Parcels, 1s. each ; larger 1d. per pound.

The Proprietors of this Undertaking solicit patronage and support, which it will be their invariable study to merit by a continued assiduity in adopting the most eligible mode of Travelling, for the convenience and interest of the Community at large, on fair and reasonable terms ; and are the Public's obedient humble servants,

T. LUCE, White-Lion Inn, *Bristol.*
SPENCER, Booth-Hall Inn, *Glocester,*
RIDLER, Hop-pole Inn, *Tewkesbury,*
SMITH, Bell-Inn, *Worcester,*
EVETT, Saracen's Head Inn, *Birmingham,*
MILLAR, Roebuck-Inn, *Newcastle,*
WHITEHEAD, Spread-Eagle Inn, *Manchester,*
STANTON, Crown-Inn, *Liverpool.*

☞ Will not be accountable for Cash, Bills, Plate, Writings, Valuables, &c. nor Passengers' Luggage, unless regularly booked, and their value ascertained and paid for accordingly.

Bristol, October 21, 1796.

as their own advertisement states that passengers were forwarded from Birmingham by the Hawk and Expedition post-coaches to Manchester and Liverpool respectively. It took a long time in this case for an accommodation to be reached. In 1801 identical high fares (4.3d per mile inside) were advertised almost simultaneously for the Jupiter and the established coaches, and fares were jointly advertised for them in 1803. The Jupiter seems eventually to have been replaced by an arrangement whereby the White Lion booked Manchester passengers to be carried on Birmingham coaches from a different inn.[27]

There were other challenges in 1803, 1805, 1811-13 and 1815-16, but none was successful. That of 1803 perhaps prompted the closer co-operation between the proprietors of the Jupiter and the older coaches, as well as exceptionally low fares (1.45d per mile inside). Bessell & Co's Eagle coach of 1811-13 competed on speed, at 6.4 to 7.3 miles per hour. The company's Birmingham coaches, reorganised in about 1811 into the Wellington in the mornings and the Hero in the afternoons, were slower – 5.8 to 6.2 miles per hour in 1814-19.[28] Which coach formed the basis for Southey's fictional account of 1807 about a long coach is unclear.

The first successful competitor was the Traveller in 1820. Its speed was higher than the company's, at 6.6 miles per hour in 1820 and 7.3 in 1821-2. The response was evidently fierce. In 1821 Clift noted that it was continuing even though the 'monopolists' had reduced their fares to ruinously low levels, bought off three of the people who worked it and then more than doubled their fares. That was apparently when Clift became involved.[29] Clift and Co proved an exception, as they never reached an agreement with the established proprietors.

There followed a period of relative stability, despite Birmingham's continuing rapid growth. The only changes were the brief appearance of Rogers & Co's Rocket in 1824 and the longer-lasting Tally Ho (later the Criterion) in 1832, both via Evesham and Alcester instead of

83 A long coach, drawn by Pyne, 1803.

A fictional account of a Spanish gentleman in a Bristol to Birmingham coach, 1807

We waited in Worcester for the coach from Bristol to Birmingham, which passes through in the afternoon, and in which we were tolerably sure of finding room, as it is one of those huge machines which carries sixteen within side. Its shape is that of a coffin placed upside-down; the door is at the end, and the passengers sit sideways. It is not very agreeable to enter one of these coaches when it is nearly full: the first comers take possession of the places nearest the door at one end, or the window at the other, and the middle seats are left for those who come in last, and who for that reason, contrary to the parable of the labourers in the vineyard, may literally be said to bear the heat of the day. There were twelve passengers already seated when we got in; they expressed no satisfaction at this acquisition of company; one woman exclaimed that she was almost stewed to death already, and another cried out to the coachman that she hoped he would not take in any body else. The atmosphere of the apartment, indeed, was neither fresher nor more fragrant than that of a prison; but it was raining hard, and we had no alternative. The distance was only two stages ... the easy work of five hours; but I never before passed five hours in travelling so unpleasantly. To see any thing was impossible; the little windows behind us were on a level with our heads, the coachman's seat obstructed the one in front, and that in the door-way was of use only to those who sat by it. Any attempt which we made at conversation by way of question, was answered with forbidding brevity; the company was too numerous to be communicative; half of them went to sleep, and I endeavoured to follow their example, as the best mode of passing away time so profitless and so uncomfortable. But it was in vain; heat, noise, and motion, kept me waking. We were heartily rejoiced when the coach arrived at Birmingham and we were let loose.

Source: Don Manuel Alvarez Espriella [Robert Southey], Letters from England (1807), vol. 2, pp. 110-13.

Worcester and the Tally Ho probably just a branch from a Leicester coach. The number of services rose following the opening of the railway from Birmingham to Manchester in 1836, reaching 47 a week in 1838. After Clift's bankruptcy in 1837, the Mail, Wellington, Hero, Traveller and newly-established Railroad were all in the hands of Niblett and Townsend. John Bland, who took over the Criterion, was by 1839 jointly running a service with Niblett and by the end of 1840 jointly advertising his services with Niblett and Townsend, leaving Bristol and Birmingham coaching firmly in the hands of a single grouping once again.[30]

The story of the Bristol to Birmingham road shows how difficult it was to challenge an established monopoly, but also that, if the newcomer was able to withstand the initial period of strong hostility he had a good chance of reaching an accommodation, especially if another newcomer appeared. Continuing competition required either a succession of new entrants or someone stubbornly independent and tenacious, such as Clift. There were impressive reductions in journey times, from a probable 23 hours[31] in 1759-74 to between nine and 11½ hours in 1827-40 (from 3.9 miles per hour to 7.6-9.7). There was much less differentiation by speed than on the London route, since there had been no Fromont running slow coaches. Information on fares is sparse, but fares were probably restrained by competition only intermittently in the earlier period and more consistently from 1820.

Exeter

THE FIRST BRISTOL to Exeter coach ran in June 1764, taking two days for 77 miles, with an overnight stop in Taunton. It was at first once a week, and possibly summer only. One-day journeys were advertised in 1765, but that was not repeated. Unlike in the Birmingham case, the initiative evidently came from the Bristol end of the route, as the proprietors were George Season at Bristol and others at Cross, Bridgwater, Taunton and possibly Cullompton (Fig. 84). In late March or April of 1767 and 1768 the coach was being drawn by six horses, which was unusual in any period for coach teams in summer, and seems to indicate that the road was a difficult one, though six-horse teams did not necessarily continue for the whole summer. Certainly it had high fares: 21s., or 3.3d per mile in 1764-72. Like many later Bristol-Exeter coachmasters Season & Co claimed to be serving Plymouth too, though there were no proprietors south of Cullompton. One of their passengers was the industrialist Matthew Boulton, on his way to visit Cornish mines in November 1779. The Bristol-Exeter

Exeter MACHINE,
In ONE DAY,
And the next Day to *Plymouth*;
To DINNER,

BEGAN to fet out on Monday the 18th Inft. March, from the George-Inn at Temple-Gate, and the Bell-Inn in St. Thomas-ftreet, Briftol, and continue going every Monday and Wednefday Morning at Four o'Clock ; and from the Oxford-Inn, without Eaft-gate, Exeter, every Tuefday and Thurfday Morning, at the fame Hour.——Infide Paffengers to pay

To Bridgwater	-	-	-	0	10	0
Taunton	-	-	-	0	12	6
Exeter	-	-	-	1	1	0
Plymouth	-	-	-	1	13	0

To be allowed 14lb. Weight of Luggage, all above to be paid for after the Rate of One Penny per lb. Outfide Paffengers in Proportion, but allowed no Luggage. Half the Money to be paid on taking Places, the Remainder on entering the Machine.

For the greater Conveniency of Outfide Paffengers, the Proprietors have fo conveniently contrived it, that if the Weather fhould prove wet, it will not affect them, by Means of a Covering, by which they will continue as dry as if in the Infide of the Coach.

As by this Conveyance Gentlemen, Tradefmen, &c. will have the moft early Correfpondence with their Friends ; and as it is the firft Attempt of the Kind ever fet on Foot from this City, the Proprietors, to render it ftill more agreeable to the Citizens, propofe to convey all fmall Parcels, under a Pound Weight, for Sixpence each, which will be delivered the fame Night.

No Money, Plate, Jewels, Writings, or other Things of Confequence, will be paid for, if loft, unlefs entered and paid for as fuch.   Performed by

George Seafon, Briftol.
Capel Tripp, White-Part, Crofs.
Thomas Daffon, Globe, Bridgewater.
Chriftopher Lutley, George, Taunton.
———————— Cullumpton.

84 Advertisement for the Bristol to Exeter coach, 1765. (Felix Farley's Bristol Journal, 30 March 1765.)

coaches became noted for their carriage of fish, 'to the annoyance of passengers'.[32]

Events on the Birmingham road were repeated here. In 1777 John Weeks, together with Daniel Ross, the manager of his post-horses, and Richard Lloyd, an Exeter innkeeper, established diligences to Exeter. They took just a day in both summer and winter, with the same fare as Season & Co had charged. Not later than 1780 an agreement was reached between the new company and the old, and by 1783 the pattern of services was identical to that on the Birmingham road: alternate days from the Bush and the White Hart (the inn used by Season). The merged firm was not successfully challenged until 1808, and its coaches continued from the two inns until about 1839, rebranded as The Times. The structure of the firm in 1797 (Fig. 85) reflected its history: Weeks and Land from one firm (or succeeding members of that firm), Poston and probably Pulsford from the other, and Thompson given a half-share at Exeter later to entice him away from a competitor.[33]

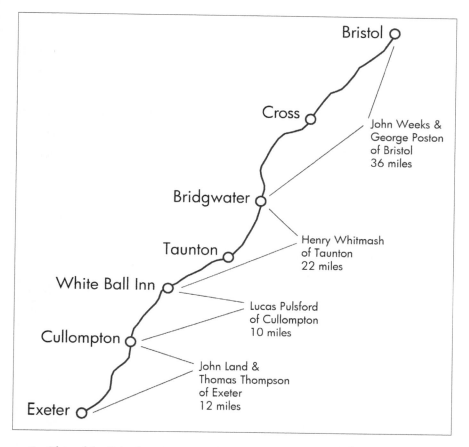

Bristol

Cross

John Weeks &
George Poston
of Bristol
36 miles

Bridgwater

Henry Whitmash
of Taunton
22 miles

Taunton

White Ball Inn

Lucas Pulsford
of Cullompton
10 miles

Cullompton

John Land &
Thomas Thompson
of Exeter
12 miles

Exeter

85 Plan of the Bristol to Exeter coach in 1797, showing the division of the road
between the partners. (The division at White Ball Inn is deduced from the mileages.)
In 1819 the structure seems to have been unchanged, the proprietors being John
Townsend and Richard Coupland of Bristol, Henry Whitmash of Taunton, Blampin
of Cullompton (who had married Pulsford's widow) and John Clench of Exeter.
Grace Blampin still had a share in 1830. (Source: TNA, E 112/1420, No. 397.)

There were challenges in 1783, 1795-7, 1798-1800 and
apparently 1802.[34] All four had a drastic effect on Weeks & Co's fares,
which fell to about half before returning to the original level once the
danger was past. For example, in 1795, when Luce & Co set up the
Royal Caroline diligence, Weeks & Co's fare fell from 27s. to 12s. Luce
announced that

The question is, whether Weeks and Co. by a temporary reduction of prices, shall, or shall not, destroy all competition for conveyance of passengers, &c. between Bristol and Exeter; and having thus established the monopoly they aim at, not only dictate the mode of travelling, by coach or diligence; but (at last advancing the price to any height they please) hold the very purse strings of the public, in their avaricious grasp?

The answer was 'yes'. Not content with reducing the fare, in 1797 Weeks & Co offered Luce's Exeter partner, Thomas Thompson, a share in their business in return for abandoning the diligence, whereupon the diligence disappeared. Weeks & Co's fare then rose immediately to 31s.6d (4.9d per mile).[35] The Exeter service, like the Birmingham one, must have contributed powerfully to the wealth of Weeks, Poston and Coupland.

The next two challenges were less direct and more successful. The Royal Devonshire and Freemason coaches were by mid-1810 a network of coaches serving Bristol, Bath, Taunton, Exeter,

To the PUBLIC in General.

THE QUESTION IS,

WHETHER WEEKS and Co. by a TEMPORARY Reduction of Prices, shall, or shall not, destroy all competition for conveyance of Passengers, &c. between *BRISTOL and EXETER;* And having thus established the MONOPOLY they aim at, not only dictate the *Mode of Travelling.* by Coach or Diligence; but *(at last advancing the Price to any Height they please)* hold the very Purse Strings of the Public, in their avaricious Grasp?—To prevent such A PERNICIOUS MONOPOLY, (notwithstanding the reduction is made at a time when every requisite for the undertaking is unprecedently dear)

T. LUCE, for Self and Co.

Respectfully informs the Public, that he has adopted the REDUCED PRICES; and that HIS NEW DILIGENCE

The *ROYAL CAROLINE,*

Continues to set out from the *WHITE-LION.* Broad-Street, to *THOMPSON's HOTEL, EXETER,* EVERY Morning at Five o'clock, *(Sunday's excepted)* carrying Three Inside Passengers, at 18s. each, and One Outside at 14s. Luggage, &c. in proportion.
The above Carriage meets at *Exeter* all the Northern conveyances, and parcels &c. will be delivered as directed, immediately on their arrival at their respective destinations.
T. Luce further begs leave to assure the Public, that his utmost vigilance shall be used to defeat the Monopoly his Opponents so ardently desire, being determined to convey on whatever terms they may think fit to offer; and trusts, that such his exertions, with the strictest regard to every other accommodation, at moderate charges, will secure to him the continued favours of a generous and discerning Public.
Bristol, August 24, 1795.

86 *Thomas Luce's denunciation of monopoly on the Bristol-Exeter road in 1795. (Felix Farley's Bristol Journal, 12 September 1795.)*

Plymouth, Devonport, Barnstaple and Minehead. The Bristol-Exeter part began as two separate ventures: the Royal Devonshire of 1808 to Exeter from Luce's White Lion and the Royal Freemason of 1809 to Barnstaple started by Fromont, Coupland and others from the Bell, Thomas Street. Agreement seems to have been reached between the two in 1810, after which the usual pattern was six per week from Bristol, of which three were to Exeter and three divided at Taunton to serve both Exeter (at first via Honiton) and Barnstaple. Whatever the original intention, the Exeter coaches became distinctive in the same way as Fromont's London coaches: they were relatively slow, and also relatively cheap; hence the advertisements for 'the Royal Devonshire cheap coaches'. In 1808-10 their speed was only 4.8 to 5.4 miles per hour, and even in 1830 this had risen just to 5.8 miles per hour, compared then with The Times's 7.7.[36] This meant journeys of just over 13 hours compared with The Times's ten hours. Their slowness was perhaps why they seem to have been tolerated by the established proprietors. As a result, unlike the Birmingham road, the Exeter road saw the same sort of differentiation of coaches by speed and fare as the London one.

The next successful new coach was the Dispatch from the White Lion, started in December 1811 and belonging to Stucky, Williams & Co. Its route was via Wells, Langport, Ilminster, Chard, Axminster and Honiton. This somewhat roundabout route was probably intended to serve the towns on the way and the growing south-coast resorts within easy reach of Axminster and Honiton, especially Sidmouth and Lyme Regis. In fact it may have been essentially a service to Axminster, from which any Exeter passengers could be forwarded in the London to Exeter coaches. One of its advantages was that with very little change it could be converted into a direct Sidmouth or Lyme coach in the summer, and it was indeed advertised as a direct Sidmouth coach in June or July in several years from 1817 to 1832 and as a direct Lyme coach in 1834-5. The route made the coach less of a threat to the established coaches, and this must have contributed to its survival. It seems to have had a middling speed (7.7 miles per hour in 1835). It continued until about 1841.[37]

The next challenge was a head-on one: William Clift's Traveller from the Feathers in 1821. Its speed of 7.0 miles per hour was the same as The Times's, and it followed almost the same direct route, though after the first few months via Tiverton instead of the much smaller Cullompton. Clift continued it under various names until his bankruptcy in 1837, independently of any other Bristol proprietor. On the other hand, at least one of Clift's partners, Joseph Pratt at Exeter, was also involved in a coach with Niblett, so Clift did not have a free hand. That was perhaps why a new coach called the Comet in 1829 was said to have been put on 'to destroy the monopoly which is aimed at'.[38]

From about 1828 there was a proliferation of services, with frequent changes of name and inn. The new services were the No

87 A rare example of a painting of a local coach: the Tam O'Shanter, which ran between Bristol and Exeter in 1836-7. The Scottish name reflects the fact that John Bland was its Bristol proprietor. The artist shows Tam O'Shanter and Souter Johnnie, both characters in Robert Burns' poem, as outside passengers.

Henry Ellis from Exeter to Bristol, 15-16 July 1836

On Friday evening the 15th of July we left home by the old Devonshire Coach for Bristol. ... Two of my companions ... informed us that they "travelled in the piggh (pig) line". ... As they all appear to have been sacrificing pretty freely to their jolly God, their warm heartedness knew no bounds. ... Having to wait some time before the coach was made ready to start, our Irishmen were so noisy that they attracted no small share of attention from the passers by, which was considerably increased by the appearance of a passenger some 14 or 15 stone in weight ... No sooner did he essay to mount the coach with his cumbrous load of flesh, than he was assailed with shouts of laughter by our boisterous companions, who speculating on his weight as they would on that of one of their own porkers began to offer bets thereon ... The coach was crowded, after Mr Woodbury and myself were seated opposite to each other at the back, and the Irishmen sat next to us vis a vis. Thus wedged against these dirty fellows, and seeing that I liked not my neighbour more than he liked his, Mr W. contemplated shifting our quarters and in his blandest manner suggested to one of our swinish associates whether he would not like to sit by the side of one of his friends. "No", said the worthy stilisian; "No, thank you Sir, all men are alike friends to me". ... We had no alternative, but to remain as we were inhaling the perfumes of their breath, and the whiffs of their short pipes the remainder of the way to Bristol. ... The pig merchants were getting in a very excited state, full of the praises of "the big bulley Dan", loud in favour of "Repale", and menacing in denouncing "the bloody Saxon". At every pothouse they imbibed, but nothing was said by us to provoke discussion

... One of them during the night warbled some wild Irish airs with so much natural taste and execution that the effect was truly pleasing.

16 July. We arrived at ... the White Hart Inn at ½ past 6 in the morning, where our companions left us to proceed to the Emrald Isle. We were extremely cold on getting off the coach, and right glad to find a fire, albeit it was in the kitchen, and a regular roaster it was ... Here we partook of a hearty breakfast.

Source: Devon RO, 76/20/5, pp. 59-62.

Wonder, Comet, Exquisite, Invincible, Pilot, Tam O'Shanter, Star, Surprise, Exonian, Magnet, Estafette and Westonian.[39] The number of direct services per week rose from 19 in 1827 to a peak of 41 in 1839, plus six services via Axminster at each date. Niblett and Townsend had 58% of the direct services in 1827, 73% in 1833 and 50% in 1836, whereas in 1839, in alliance with Bland (and following Clift's departure), they had all 41. A monopoly situation was established like that on the Birmingham road, but only shortly before the railway arrived. Before that, there was more competition than on the Birmingham road, with occasional examples of very low fares.

Speeds and fares varied greatly. In 1831-5, for example, speeds ranged from 6.0 to 10.0 miles per hour, hours from 7¾ to 13 and inside fares from 10s. to 21s. Speeds rose in the 1830s from an average of 8.0 miles per hour in 1831-5 to 9.3 in 1836-40, exceeding the average then for London services. The highest speed advertised was the 10.3 miles per hour of Niblett's Estafette in 1839, taking only 7½ hours. The Times, which had middling speeds, accelerated gradually from 6.4 miles per hour in 1819 to 8.1 in 1834.[40] The disappearance of the plodding Royal Devonshire coaches in 1831 reflected the new situation.

The history of coaching on the Exeter route was similar to that on the Birmingham route, especially the difficulty of challenging an entrenched monopoly and the eventual success in doing so in the 1820s. The main difference was the greater range of speeds and fares.

The south coast

WEYMOUTH HAD A well-established summer season by the 1770s, and acquired its first hotel in 1772. From 1794 it also had packet services to the Channel Islands, which were by steam vessel from the late 1820s. [41] There were 'post-chariots' from Bristol to Weymouth in 1768 and diligences from Bath to Weymouth in 1776-7, but the first Bristol to Weymouth coaches which endured began in 1779. These too were diligences, probably reflecting the limited custom. They were three times a week and took 12 hours for the 64 miles. After an unsuccessful attempt in the first year to continue in winter, services were summer-only until the late 1820s, and were usually advertised in May or June. The establishment of this coach provides an interesting example of innkeepers banding together to bring trade to their road, and at first there were no proprietors at either terminus (Fig. 88). Once established, it soon acquired a more typical arrangement of proprietors mostly at the main towns. In 1784 the proprietors stated that they had run the service for the last three years 'to a very great disadvantage to accommodate the public', and 'an opposition' was now started against them, whereas 'the road will not support two coaches'. Nor did it, as no more is heard of the opposition.[42]

The coach of 1779 remained the main Weymouth service, becoming known as the Royal Dorset and continuing until the

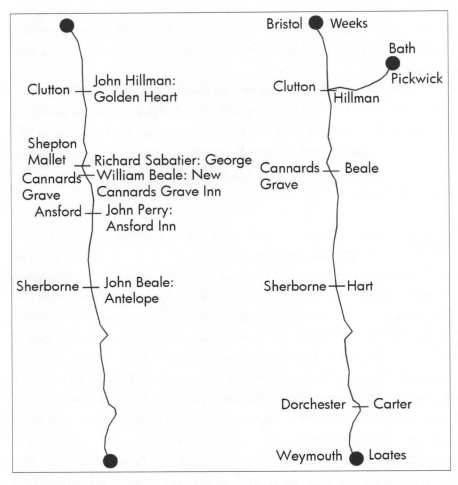

88 Plan of the Weymouth coach, indicating where its proprietors lived in August 1779 (left) and June 1784 (right). Where the Bath branch joined the main route is uncertain. (Sources: Felix Farley's Bristol Journal, 7 Aug 1779, 5 June 1784.)

1840s. The John Bull coach listed at the Bush from 1818 followed a different route via Frome, and seems to have been only a link to a Bath to Weymouth coach of that name. Serious competition apparently began only with Clift's Red Rover coach in 1834. The times of 9½ to ten hours recorded from 1831 to 1839 were not much below the 12 hours of 1779, and Weymouth coaches remained slow, reflecting their predominantly leisure traffic. No services exceeded six miles per hour until 1831, and the highest recorded speed was 6.7 miles per hour in 1832.[43]

The more important route was through Salisbury and Southampton to Gosport and Portsmouth and later Brighton. Bath had diligences to Southampton in 1776, but the first service from Bristol was to Southampton and Gosport in 1780, twice-weekly, taking one day for the 94 miles. By 1781 there was the familiar pattern of services on alternate days from the Bush and the Rummer. A mail coach operated only from 1785 to about 1790. All that survived in the 1790s was a coach six days a week from the Bush to Gosport and Portsmouth, cut back in the mid-1790s and several times subsequently to Southampton only, perhaps indicating that passengers had always been forwarded by another coach from Southampton. Apart from a short-lived new coach in 1801-2, the reappearance of the mail coach in 1808 (though only as a two-horse coach) and extra services by Weeks to Portsmouth in 1815-17, that was all there was until 1831. A petition from the proprietors of the main service about the duty they were paying reveals something that could not have been ascertained from directories: that from at least 1817 to 1826 the apparently daily service to Gosport consisted in fact of three a week from Bristol to Gosport and three a week just from Bath to Southampton. In

89 *Moses Nobbs, who was a guard on the Bristol to Portsmouth mail coach in 1836-7. By the time of his retirement in 1891 he was in charge of the mail at Paddington.*

1831 Niblett started his Red Rover coach to Brighton, apparently in summer only, and in 1838 Bland began the Favourite to Southampton. In 1835 Southampton's cross-Channel passengers were said to be predominantly from Bristol rather than London.[44]

As for Poole, Henry Wallace started coaches to it via Shepton Mallet, Wincanton and Blandford in 1815, but they are not heard of again. Two different services from 1816 to 1824 followed routes through Warminster or Frome. The Royal Pilot from the Bush is the only Poole coach recorded at Bristol for a decade after 1825, but seems to have been no more than a link to a service from Bath.[45] Services to Sidmouth and Lyme branching from the Exeter coach known as the Dispatch have been mentioned already. There were briefly separate Lyme coaches in 1797 and 1832 and a separate Sidmouth coach (the Invincible) in about 1833-6.[46] Coaches to Bridport were advertised in various years from 1821 to 1841, but (except possibly in 1821) all seem to have been branches from other Bristol services at Yeovil, Ilminster or Taunton, as the Bridport mail coach (from Taunton) certainly was.[47]

Oxford, Coventry and Leicester

THE OXFORD ROUTE did not flourish like the other early ones, probably because its early development had been based mainly on occasional travel connected with the university. In 1827 it was said to have few passengers except students at the beginning and end of term. In 1750-5 and 1764-5 only Bath to Oxford services were advertised, and in 1767 Robert Sperinck of Burford was running two services from Bath to Oxford each week and just one from Bristol to Oxford. The latter took one day in summer for the 83 miles via Bath, Tetbury, Cirencester and Burford. Subsequent evidence is scarce until 1784, when Weeks and Carr of Bristol, Masters & Co of Cirencester and Phillips of Fairford began services three times a week, via Sodbury,

Tetbury, Cirencester, Fairford and Faringdon, avoiding Bath.[48]

This coach became the mail coach (via Bath) in 1786, with Weeks, Phillips and Masters among the partners, and had perhaps been established with that aim. However, it soon ceased to be a mail coach when the proprietors refused on grounds of cost to use the patent coaches favoured by the Post Office. The Post Office for its part complained about 'the number of outside passengers carried on it, the frequent temporary loss & irregular conveyance of the bye bags, [and] it so often being overturned'. In 1792 the Post Office relented, and it became the mail coach again, without the patent coaches. By 1797 it had just two partners: Pickwick of Bath with 46 miles and Costar of Oxford with 37 miles. From 1792 to 1817 no coaches other than the mail are recorded (except briefly in 1810), so in this case the mail coach took the place of the existing service.[49]

The time allowed was 13 hours to Bristol and 14 hours to Oxford, half an hour of the difference being accounted for by office work at Cirencester. Hasker stated that the coach 'never has given any trouble; this shews the difference of coachmasters. It never I may say arrives at Bristol later than 6, nor at Oxford later than 10 [the scheduled times being 6 and 9.30] – seldom so late'. The proprietors were satisfactory, but the amount of custom was not, and the Post Office was obliged to continue to allow ten outside passengers instead of the usual four. As Johnson explained in 1827, 'the road is supposed to be incapable of supporting a mail with a less number; there is very little business except at the commencement and termination of the Oxford terms, when a good many students are passing. The thing has been tolerated from time to time rather than incur a greater expense.'[50]

The mail coach faced competition from 1817, when Lane, Ryley & Co of Bath established the Hero, via Bath, Cirencester and Burford. A challenge from Clift and others in 1822-5 (the Champion) was beaten off by taking his Oxford partner into the Hero partnership. After that the Hero for a time followed different routes on alternate days (Cirencester and Burford and Chippenham and Swindon).

In 1827, when the mail coach's contractors were still Pickwick and Costar, the time to Bristol was 10 hours 40 minutes, but the time to Oxford was 14¾ hours, mainly because of a long wait at Bath for connecting services. Johnson noted in 1825 that the coach had given him 'infinite trouble, both as to its hours of leaving Bristol and Oxford, its detention in Bath, and its rate of going on the road, which requires to be sometimes fast and sometimes slow.' He described it as a 'weak and losing concern.' In 1828 the mail coach was abolished and the Post Office made alternative arrangements, including a horse-post between Cirencester and Bath, though the coach itself continued to run, as the Post, apparently merged with the Hero. The last new coach was the Age (later the Favourite) from the Greyhound via Gloucester and Cheltenham in 1834. It claimed to be the only direct coach to Oxford, but perhaps transferred passengers to London coaches at Gloucester or Cheltenham. Its advertised time was 9¾ hours (8.5 miles per hour), the fastest between Bristol and Oxford, but not far below the 11½ hours of 1788.[51]

The Coventry and Leicester route was also a minor one. Both were large towns (with about 18,000 and 23,000 people respectively in 1811), and Bristol wholesalers probably had an important role in distributing Leicester's hosiery goods, but Leicester was less useful for onward connections than Birmingham. Apart from Lawrence's short-lived service in 1772, the first coach, the Telegraph, was started in July 1810 by Bessell of Bristol and partners in Coventry, Leicester and elsewhere. By December Poston and Coupland had responded with a new mail coach to Leicester. Evidently deeper pockets than Bessell's were required to sustain the Telegraph, as Weeks was involved by November and it moved from the Swan to the Bush. Weeks and Bessell emphasised that this was the first ever coach on that road and the only direct one, whereas Poston and Coupland claimed to have had coaches on that road for 30 years. Both claims were partly true: Weeks and

GREAT ACCOMMODATION.
A NEW COACH FROM BRISTOL TO LEICESTER.

THE TALLY HO !!

FOUR INSIDE COACH, leaves the BUSH TAVERN, CORN-STREET, and the SWAN INN, BRIDGE-STREET, every MONDAY, WEDNESDAY, and FRIDAY Morning, at Six o'clock, passing through the following Towns, and arriving at each at the time specified :

Gloucester....... 4 minutes before 10 o'clock.
Allowed there for Breakfast 20 minutes.
Cheltenhan.................. 16 minutes past 11.
Evesham.............. .... 8 minutes past 1.
Alcester................ .... 15 minutes past 2.
Stratford....................... 7 minutes past 3.
Leamington................... 22 minutes past 4.
Allowed for Dinner 25 minutes.
Coventry...................... 11 minutes past 6.
Leicester...................... 26 minutes past 9.

The Proprietors hope, by strict attention to the above time, combining dispatch *with safety*, to merit the support of the Public.

They will not be responsible for any parcel of any description whatever, if it be of more than £5. value, unless it be specified as such at the time of booking it

TOWNSEND & SON.

90 An unusual advertisement giving timings along the route: the Tally Ho! to Leicester in 1829 (Bristol Gazette, 3 September 1829.)

Bessell's was the first direct coach to Coventry and Leicester, but from Bristol to Tewkesbury it used a road on which Poston and Coupland (and Weeks) had for decades had Birmingham coaches. In January 1811 Weeks & Co noted that 'a powerful party are formed against them, consisting of fifteen persons, with a threat of beating them off the road; and should they succeed, it is supposed they will do with the public as they please'. In March Weeks & Co attacked 'a very evil and ill-natured report' that the coach would be given up, emphasising their determination to continue 'so long as there is a horse to be purchased, or a coach wheel to be turned round', and announcing that between a thousand and two thousand gentlemen were determined to support the coach. In May Bessell & Co (but apparently not Weeks) retaliated with a coach of their own to Birmingham.[52]

The outcome was a compromise. In 1813 it was announced that the Leicester coach would in future set off three days a week from the Swan, which was Bessell's, and three days a week from the White Hart and White Lion, where Poston and Coupland were based. The Leicester mail coach and Bessell & Co's Birmingham coach disappeared. Thus the Leicester route acquired exactly the pattern achieved long before by the Birmingham and Exeter routes. The coach became known as the Pilot, and continued until about 1841, changing its route slightly to pass through Cheltenham instead of Tewkesbury. The frequency to Leicester declined to three a week in 1817, and the apparently new Tally Ho! coach in 1829-31 seems to have been no more than the restoration of the other three services a week (Fig. 90). The Leicester route was never able to sustain competing services.[53]

South Wales, Hereford and Liverpool

SERVICES TO SOUTH Wales were complicated by the need to cross the Severn, which required a long and sometimes hazardous ferry crossing. Two ferries were used by coaches from Bristol. Hereford coaches and most Abergavenny ones crossed by the Old Passage from Aust to Beachley (later the site of the first Severn Bridge). The three-mile long New Passage from Redwick to St Pierre (later the site of the second Severn Bridge) was usually used by the coaches towards Swansea.

Telford described the New Passage in 1825 as 'one of the most forbidding places at which an important ferry was ever established; it is, in truth, a succession of violent cataracts formed in a rocky channel, exposed to the rapid rush of a tide, which has scarcely an equal upon any other coast'. The ferry itself was simply an open boat, and Lewis Dillwyn was once exposed to torrents of rain for an hour and a half in it. Delays caused by adverse wind and tide were sometimes many hours. The road was also challenging: in the mid-1820s there were still hills of up to 1 in 6 between Newport and Cardiff and many steep hills elsewhere. Seasonal differences in timing continued late: in 1814 the Cambrian to Swansea started at 4 pm in summer but midnight in winter.[54] Passengers approaching South Wales from London of course had an alternative route via Gloucester.

The first coach from Bristol to South Wales was Weeks & Co's

91 Advertisement for the Milford Haven mail coach in 1788, including the arrangements for crossing by the New Passage. (Felix Farley's Bristol Journal, 5 January 1788.)

Briftol, Cardiff, Swanfea, Carmarthen, and *MILFORD-HAVEN*
M A I L   C O A C H,
BY GOVERNMENT AUTHORITY WITH A GUARD.

THE Proprietors of the above carriage refpect-fully inform the Public, that it began running on Monday the 6th of Auguft, and continues going every day from the

RUMMER-TAVERN, *BRISTOL,*

Directly after the arrival of the Mail Coach from London, and crofs the NEW-PASSAGE in boats conftructed on the fafeft principle for the purpofe, and arrive at Mrs. Huggard's, the Ferry-Houfe in Monmouthfhire, to dinner, at which place good poft-chaifes are to be had to forward paffengers to Chepftow, &c.—The coach paffes through New-port, and fups at Cardiff; goes through Cowbridge, Aberavon, Neath, and breakfafts at Swanfea next morning.

Mondays, Wednefdays and Fridays, it imme-diately proceeds on through Lanelly, Kidwelly, CARMARTHEN, St. Clare, Narbeth, Haverford-weft, to Milford-Haven,—The fame coach returns every evening at eight o'clock from Swanfea; and Tuefday, Thurfday, and Saturday mornings from Milford-Haven; and arrives at the *Rummer, Briftol,* by noon the next day.—From which *Tavern* the mail and feveral other coaches ftart the fame after-noon for London.

By the above conveyance paffengers are certain of directly croffing at the Ferry, of being forward-ed in the moft fafe and fpeedy manner to and from Swanfea, and all intermediate towns, every day; and to Carmarthen, Haverfordweft, and Milford-Haven, three times a week; from which Port, ROY-AL PACQUETS fail every day with the Mail for Waterford, carrying paffengers, packages, &c.

Performed by

CHURCH, New Paffage-Inn,
    BRADLEY, Angel-Inn, Cardiff,
    C. BRADLEY, Bear-Inn, Cowbridge.
    NOTT, Ship and Caftle, Neath,
    CALVERT, Swanfea,
    JONES, Red-Lion, Carmarthen,
    PALMER, Noah's Ark, Brangwithnoar,
    OWENS, Waterford-Pacquet, Milford-Haven

☞ The Proprietors will not be anfwerable for any parcel above the value of 10l. unlefs entered as fuch and paid for accordingly.

The Birmingham Mail Coach, fets off every even-ing from the *Rummer Tavern,* carrying Paffengers and Parcels for that Town, Worcefter, Shrewfbury, Manchefter, Liverpool, Coventry, Derby, Not-tingham, Sheffield, Leeds, &c. &c.

Alfo the London Mail, and feveral other coaches from the above Tavern every day.

N. B. As many perfons have been difappointed at the New Paffage by expecting, if they arrived about the time the Mail Coach did, that they would be entitled to a feat in the Mail Boat; this is to in-form the public, that no perfons whatever can be permitted to crofs in the Mail Boat, but Mail Coach Paffengers, fuch as take places for a longer diftance than the ferry.—If on their arrival at the Paffage-Houfe on the Gloceftterfhire fide the Coach is not full, places may be taken to Newport, &c. by which they will be entitled to crofs with the Mail; and if not full when they arrive at the Paffage-Houfe, on the Monmouthfhire fide, places may be taken to Briftol.

Milford Haven service via the Old Passage and Brecon in May 1787, perhaps put on in an unsuccessful attempt to obtain the mail coach contract. The mail coach began in August that year, daily via the New Passage to Cardiff and Swansea, with three services a week continuing to Milford Haven (Fig. 91). At Carmarthen it met another mail coach from Gloucester and Brecon. The contractors were responsible for organising the crossing at the New Passage, which they did by paying those who rented the passage £150 a year to provide boats and two, four or six men twice a day as required. A further 25s. a week had to be paid to Mrs Huggard, who rented on the Monmouthshire side and feared losing her post-chaise traffic to the mail coach. Hasker stated in 1794 that an hour was allowed in the time bill for the ferry, and sometimes it took two or three hours, but the average was half an hour. The coach served not just South Wales but also southern Ireland. Hasker observed in 1794, when there was a proposal to re-route it through Gloucester, that not passing through Bristol would be a disadvantage: 'Bristol ... is a kind of metropolis to South Wales, the business of the inhabitants lays very much with that City, as does the commerce of Cork, Waterford and the south of Ireland in general. ... I may say half the passengers have concerns with Bristol, Bath, or the west of England'.[55]

Weeks & Co's coach is not recorded after 1787, and a Bristol to Swansea diligence of 1788 was advertised only once. The mail coaches then had a monopoly of direct services between Bristol and South Wales until 1806. Williams & Co's Prince of Wales coach of 1806-13 seems to have been no more than a link via the Old Passage to a new coach with the same name between London, Chepstow and South Wales. The Cambrian of 1810 from the Bush and the Regulator of 1811/12 from the White Lion, both to Swansea (the latter using the Old Passage), were more substantial ventures, and both survived. From 1811/12 the Cambrian, the Regulator and the mail coach shared the business until 1840 without any direct challenge.

Lewis Weston Dillwyn from Bristol to Swansea, 17 December 1819

Started at 6 by the Cambrian coach and breakfasted on the Gloucestershire side of the Passage, where we waited for about an hour and a half for the tide to become more favourable. We crossed in 17 minutes, but the waves were high and some of the passengers were much alarmed by the tossing of the boat. I had taken a daughter of the Revd. D. Williams under my care and delivered her safe at Cowbridge about ½ past 5. The rain had fallen in torrents since yesterday and this added to the sudden thaw had so flooded the country that the roads were in many places almost impassable and the torrents were so violent at Merthyr Mawr that we were obliged to take a circuitous route by Bridgend &c.

Source: NLW, transcript of the diary of Lewis Weston Dillwyn, 1817-52.

Moreover, from 1817 the Cambrian and Regulator were evidently working in co-operation, with coaches on alternating days from two Bristol inns, one of which also accommodated the mail coach. Fares were exceptionally high, probably reflecting both the difficulty of the road and the lack of competition. In 1820 the mail coach's inside fare was reduced from 6.8d per mile, the highest ever recorded for any Bristol coach, to a still expensive 4.8d per mile, and the fares of the Cambrian and Regulator were reduced at the same time to the same level. Colonel Starke, using the Regulator in 1815 as one of six inside passengers plus two children, described it as a 'vile opposition coach', whereas C.J. Thomas, who travelled by the Regulator from Bristol to

The Regulator Post Coach,
FROM
SWANSEA TO BRISTOL AND GLOUCESTER.

THE Proprietors of the above Coach beg to inform their Friends and the Public, that the inconvenience experienced by Passengers wishing to go to London, in consequence of its not arriving in Bristol in time for the London Coaches, having been complained of, the Proprietors, wishing to oblige and facilitate the travelling of Passengers by their Coach, have given directions that, for the future, it shall start from Swansea every Monday, Wednesday, and Friday, at Four o'clock in the Morning, commencing on Monday, the 22d instant, and arrive at

	h. m.		h. m.
Neath, at..............	5 0	Rock and Fountain....	12 25
Pyle	6 30	Chepstow	1 25
Bridgend	7 15	Office Business	0 10
Cowbridge	8 15	Beachley	2 5
Cardiff	9 45	Aust..................	2 30
Breakfast.............	0 20	Bristol................	4 0
Newport..............	11 35		

Passengers to Gloucester will be allowed 30 minutes at Chepstow for Dinner, and arrive at

Newnham at.... 4h. 0m. ; Gloucester at.... 5h. 30m.

By this alteration the Regulator will arrive in Bristol in time for the following London Coaches :—Royal Mail, at a quarter past five, from the Bush ; Monarch, at five, from the White Lion ; Cooper's Company's Coach, at five, from the Plume of Feathers.

☞ Should any Passengers, who may be pleased to travel by this Coach, meet with incivility from any servant belonging to the establishment, or unnecessary delay on the road, they are respectfully requested to signify such misconduct to either of the Proprietors, when immediate steps will be taken to prevent a recurrence of the same.—April 18th 1833

*92 Advertisement for the Regulator between Swansea and Bristol and its branch to Gloucester in 1833, including a detailed timetable. (*Monmouthshire Merlin, *20 April 1833.)*

Newport in about 4½ hours in June 1828, 'had a very pleasant ride through a delightful country'.[56]

While there was little or no competition on the road, there was competition from steamships, unlike on any other route from Bristol. From 1822 there were regular steamship services between Bristol and Newport and by 1823 between Bristol and Swansea. The latter advertised times of nine hours, four or five hours less than the coaches, and fares ranging from 5s. to 15s., far less than the coaches. Lewis Dillwyn recorded times from eight to 11 hours on that service in 1830-8. He recorded times of three to five hours in the Newport-Bristol steamship in 1823-35. In 1823 he preferred the steamship 'as the rain fell in torrents, to crossing the Severn in an open boat at the Passage'. But the steamship journey was not always pleasant: in 1827 the sea was rough and he was wet to the skin and sick. By 1831 it was possible to travel by steamship direct from Bristol to southern Ireland in 22 hours, whereas the mail coach to Milford and the Post Office packet boat took at least 38 hours. Steamship services at sea were seasonal at first, but by the late 1820s they were operating all year. In 1827 Dillwyn was able to use the Newport-Bristol steamship in February and December.[57]

Steamship competition made the mail coach much less profitable, and from 1830 the Post Office had to pay the contractors a higher mileage rate than for the Bristol-London mail coach. Whereas the rate had been 1½d per mile in the 1820s, in about 1834 the contractors demanded 6d per mile, whereupon the Post Office began preparations to replace the mail coach by horse-posts. A compromise of 4d per mile was reached instead. In 1825 Telford had recommended a longer sea crossing for the mail by steamship (rejected mainly on grounds of cost) together with extensive road improvements, which were slow to be implemented. There was a steam packet at the New Passage in 1825, but it had gone a few years later. The Old Passage, on the other hand, was considerably improved in 1826-7, and there was

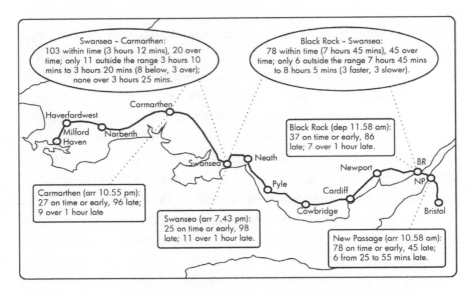

93 *Map showing the actual times of the Milford Haven mail coach down (Bristol to Milford), recorded daily from October 1833 to January 1834, a total of 123 days. Key: NP – New Passage (Redwick); BR– Black Rock. (Source: National Library of Wales, Vivian B133.)*

increasing hostility in South Wales to the New Passage because of the long delays it caused.[58]

That case was supported by a record of the times of the mail coaches down from Bristol to Milford from October 1833 to January 1834 (Fig. 93). Late arrivals at the New Passage after the short journey from Bristol probably indicate late arrivals of the London mail coaches at Bristol or delays in office work there. The real problems began at the New Passage, where only 37% of crossings were completed within the scheduled hour and 3% took more than two and a half hours, the longest being six hours and 42 minutes. With the horse as the method of propulsion this time could not be made up, and contractors were not expected to do so, so delays at the New Passage

94 *(opposite) The Post Office's time bill for the Milford Haven mail coach, 1827. Four different vehicles were used. (Post Office Archives, POST 10/203, p. 61.)*

GENERAL POST-OFFICE.

Lord Frederick MONTAGU, His Majesty's Postmaster-General.

Bristol and *Milford* TIME BILL.

Contractors' Names	Number of Passengers In. | Out.	F.	Time allowed H. M.		
				Dispatched from the Post-Office, *Bristol*, the of	
				182 , at	
				at	*9 . 49 A.M.* by Time-Piece by Clock
				London Mail arrived, at	
				Coach No. sent out	{ With a Time-Piece safe { No to
Townsend & Walker —	10 .. 4	1	10	Arrived at the New Passage, at *10 . 59* Tide Wind On the Water	
				Number of Passengers in the Mail Coach, and no other Persons but such as are Passengers by the Mail Coach are to be permitted to go in the Mail Boat.	
		1	0	Number of Watermen with the Boat. *One Hour allowed for Crossing.*	
				Arrived across the Passage, at *11 . 59* Coach No. gone forward	
T. & H. Smith	14 .. 1	1	34	Arrived at *Newport*, at *1 . 33 P.M.*	
J. & W. Bradley	12 .. 2	1	22	Arrived at *Cardiff*, at *2 . 55*	
			30	*Thirty Minutes allowed.*	
	12 .. 4	1	25	Arrived at *Cowbridge* at *4 . 50*	
E. & C. Bradley	12 .. 3	1	24	Arrived at *Pyle*, at *6 . 14*	
J. & J. Simpson	12 ..		1	20 Arrived at *Neath*, at *7 . 34*	
	8 .. 6		58	Arrived at *Swansea*, at *8 . 32* at	by Time-Piece by Clock
W. & W. Jones			10	*Ten Minutes allowed.*	
				Coach No. gone forward	{ Delivered the Time-Piece safe { No. to
	9 .. 2	1	10	Arrived at *Pontardulais*, at *9 . 52*	
Davies —	17 .. 6	2	12	Arrived at *Carmarthen*, at *12 . 4 A.M.* at	by Time-Piece by Clock
			15	*Fifteen Minutes allowed.*	
				Mail from *Gloucester*, at off at Coach No. gone forward	by Time-Piece
Davies —	16 .. 5	2	15	Arrived at *Tavern Spite*, at *2 . 34*	
				Arrived at *Narberth*, at *about 3 . 30*	
Pugh —	16 .. 1	2		Arrived at *Haverfordwest*, at *4 . 34*	
Pritchard —	7 .. 5		53	Arrived at the Post-Office, *Milford*, the of	
	149 .. 7	19	38	182 , at *5 . 27 A.M.* at	by Time-Piece by Clock
				Coach No. arrived	{ Delivered the Time-Piece safe { No. to

THE *Time of working each Stage is to be reckoned from the Coach's Arrival, and as any Time lost, is to be recovered in the course of the Stage, it is the Coachman's Duty to be as expeditious as possible, and to report the Horse-keepers if they are not always ready when the Coach arrives, and active in getting it off. The Guard is to give his best assistance in changing, whenever his Official Duties do not prevent it.*

June, 1827.——200.

By Command of the Postmaster-General,

CHARLES JOHNSON,
Surveyor and Superintendent.

had a direct impact on arrival times at Swansea and Carmarthen. But for those delays, the regularity of the service would have been extremely impressive, especially as these were winter months. From Black Rock to Swansea, where the scheduled time was seven hours and 45 minutes, only three services were more than 20 minutes over the time. Between Swansea and Carmarthen, where the scheduled time was three hours and 12 minutes, only one service took more than ten minutes extra and even that was only 13 minutes late. The summer times would undoubtedly have been more reliable still. Instead of re-routing Swansea's mail via Gloucester, as requested, the Post Office responded to the complaints by transferring the mail coach to the Old Passage and speeding it up.[59]

Competition from steamships explains the absence of new services between Bristol and Swansea. When a new coach, the Western Railway, was eventually established from the Rummer in December 1840, competition on the road seems to have lasted less than a year, and by August 1841 the Bush, White Lion and Rummer were jointly running the Cymro coach to Swansea instead.[60]

As for the route to Abergavenny and Brecon, in 1794-8 there were coaches from Bristol to Abergavenny through Raglan, connecting with the Gloucester-Carmarthen mail coach. Then there was a gap until the Telegraph coach was set up in 1809 to Abergavenny (and later Brecon), using an indirect route via Newport and Usk. In 1830 the Telegraph was superseded by the Welsh Fusilier to Brecon, following the direct route through Raglan. It had proprietors at Bristol, Beachley, Chepstow, Abergavenny, Crickhowell and Brecon. There was competition for the first time when Clift & Co established the Paul Pry to Brecon in 1831. By 1833 it was known as the Retaliator, and Clift was allied with Jonathan Edwards, who had a network of coaches from the Castle Hotel, Brecon, serving Aberystwyth, Merthyr, Swansea and Builth Wells. On Clift's bankruptcy it passed to Niblett. When Niblett advertised a new coach to Brecon in 1842, he described it as 'a sovereign remedy for slow travelling, so much complained of in that part of the country'[61]

Another route passed through Chepstow, Hereford and Shrewsbury towards Chester, Holyhead and Liverpool. Coaches on this route were most often recorded in directories as Hereford services, sometimes with a remark such as 'from whence coaches proceed daily to Shrewsbury & Holyhead'. However, in 1780-7, when services on the route were first recorded, fares were listed as far as Shrewsbury and proprietors as far north as Bridgnorth, and in one case all the way to Holyhead. After a gap, the Union coach operated between Bristol and Hereford from 1802 to 1827. Niblett re-established direct services to Hereford in 1829, which continued to about 1842. Competing coaches were run by Clift & Co in 1834-5 and Bland & Co in 1838-40.[62]

In 1831 a more ambitious service was started: a direct mail coach from the White Lion to Liverpool via Hereford, Shrewsbury and Chester, albeit as two separate contracts for the roads north and south of Shrewsbury. This was apparently made worthwhile by the improvement of the Old Passage and a new road between Chepstow and Monmouth, and it cut the distance from 187 miles via Birmingham to just 161 miles. By 1838 the continuation of the southern section was in doubt, partly because of the imminent completion of the railway to Birmingham but also because, according to the contractors, 'the middle part of the road was so weak'.[63] The other Liverpool coach advertised in the late 1830s, the Hibernia, was in fact a link with the famous Cheltenham-Liverpool coach of that name.[64]

Other coaches

As ALREADY INDICATED, many destinations listed in directories turn out on closer inspection not to be separate services, but instead places *en route* or reached by connecting services or branches (see Appendix 1). The same or similar departure times are often the clue, as are indirect routes. On the other hand, a named coach was usually a genuine service, and occasionally an apparently implausible service may have been a real one. For example, entries in Bristol directories for coaches to Reading might be expected to refer to London services, and usually did, but from 1818 to 1824 departure times not matching those of any London coach suggest a separate service, and it even had a name – the Star. In practice it may been essentially a Bath to Reading coach, possibly connecting with a Bristol to Bath one, and it continued as a Bath to Reading coach until 1843. A Bath directory of 1829 which lists the Star adds that from Reading, 'passengers are forwarded by light post coaches to Town at any hour the following day', suggesting that it served people who would otherwise have used the two-day coaches in order to break the journey.[65]

Bristol's second-oldest regional route was to Gloucester, and the Gloucester coach associated with the first Birmingham coach had a continuous history from 1765 or earlier to the end of stage coaching. In response to Cheltenham's rapid growth it became a Gloucester and Cheltenham coach in 1813, later known as the Phoenix, and in 1832 an afternoon coach called the Exquisite was added. Occasional challenges were beaten off, apparently none lasting more than three years, until in 1834 the proprietors quarrelled and started competing with each other (Fig. 95). There was of course competition from coaches travelling further, especially Birmingham and Leicester coaches. Speeds were always high to Cheltenham, with 9.6 miles per hour being recorded as early as 1822, and 10.8 in 1836. In 1833 the Phoenix was conveyed by five teams, changing at Alveston, Newport, Whitminster Inn (or thereabouts) and Gloucester, an average of nine miles per stage.[66]

There was a coach to Stroud from minor inns from 1794 to 1819. A second service, known as the Dart or the Royal Dart, began in 1813 from one of the major inns, the White Hart. In 1820 the Bristol and Stroud proprietors evidently quarrelled, briefly setting up

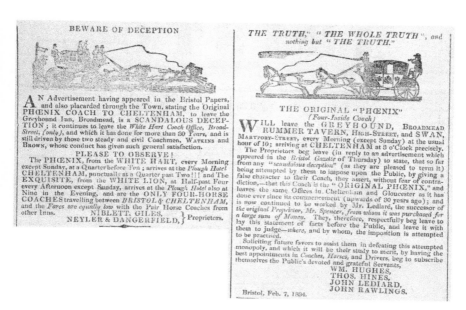

95 *Competing claims to be the original Phoenix to Cheltenham, 1834 (Bristol Gazette, 20 February 1834.)*

rival services, and thereafter the survivor was known as the Original Dart. By 1828 it was run by William Clift of Bristol and Richard Parker of the George Hotel, Stroud. A former driver, William Moody, tried unsuccessfully to establish his own coach in 1827.[67] Coaches to Wotton-under-Edge, North Nibley or Dursley ran in 1785, 1795-9, 1815-28 and 1836-42.

The Wiltshire cloth towns and Frome also acquired services. Competing coaches to Bradford and Trowbridge were set up in 1815-16. Hemingway & Co claimed in the latter year that their Loyal Clothier from the Talbot was the original Trowbridge coach, and condemned the present 'illiberal opposition'. The Loyal Clothier seems to have prevailed, as there continued to be a coach from the Talbot to Trowbridge until about 1839, then known as the Union. It had to face competition in the 1830s from passenger boats on the Kennet and Avon Canal between Bath and Bradford, taking only an hour and a half, a rare example in England of canals competing for

96 The Talbot, Bath Street, one of Bristol's lesser coaching inns, in the 1830s.
Most coaches listed at the Talbot merely called there to pick up passengers, but
it had a few regional and local services of its own, such as the Union coach to
Trowbridge and the Talbot to Wrington.

passenger traffic. Coaches to Frome are recorded intermittently from 1780 to 1791, but then there is nothing until J. Wheeler's Dove from the Talbot, which ran from 1825 to 1841. In 1835 Wheeler claimed to have an omnibus from Bristol to Salisbury, and there was a Devizes coach from the Bush in 1834.[68]

Barnstaple provides an example of a route where evidence from directories and advertisements needs to be treated with extreme caution, since a branch coach could easily be run from an Exeter service at Taunton or even Tiverton, though advertised at Bristol as if it was a direct coach. Nearly always the ostensible provider of a Barnstaple service also had an Exeter service on the same days at the same times. For example Clift's Barnstaple service was explicitly advertised in the Exeter newspapers (but not the Bristol ones) as a branch from Tiverton.[69] The first services advertised as direct to Barnstaple were the Royal Freemason coaches in 1809, and by the following year there were three services a week from Bristol which divided at Taunton to serve both Exeter and Barnstaple. The Freemason coaches to Barnstaple were slow (4.9 miles per hour in 1809-10, 5.8 in 1822 and 5.5 in 1830), and the limited evidence suggests they were not cheap either. They ceased to run in 1831, but by then there were direct mail coaches, established in 1828 and extended to Bideford in 1836.[70]

Minehead could similarly be reached by branch coaches. The Freemason coaches had what was acknowledged as a branch coach from Bridgwater to Minehead, and the Minehead mail coach advertised from 1834 was a branch from Taunton. On the other hand, the Royal Speculator, which started in 1822-3, does seem to have been a direct coach from Bristol, and continued until 1841.[71] As for Taunton and Bridgwater, in most years from 1797 there were services to one or both of these which were separate from the Exeter services, nearly always from the minor inns.

Some destinations clearly struggled to sustain services, or had to rely on coaches passing through. For example Wells had its own coaches to Bristol only in 1785-7, Cirencester in 1808-9 and 1820, Wotton Bassett in 1825, Sherborne in 1831 and Yeovil and Langport in 1832. Others acquired a service only in the 1830s, such as Calne in 1834 (it was on one of the London routes anyway) and Chalford in 1835.[72]

Local services

THE MOST IMPORTANT of the local routes (defined here as 20 miles or less) was the 13 miles between Bristol and Bath. Indeed it was one of the most travelled coach routes in the country. In 1837 there were said to be 34 coaches each way daily (a figure apparently derived from the records of stage coach duty), compared with 25 on the Liverpool to Manchester road before the opening of the railway there. In the Bristol and Bath case, about half of these were going further, mainly to and from London, but the other half were local services between the two cities. The local ones were run by a mixture of major and minor coachmasters. An example of the latter was Joseph Kennell, described as an

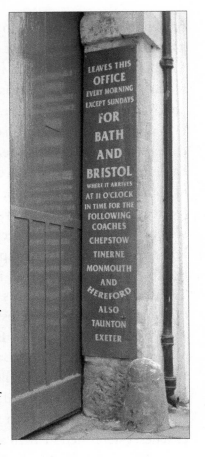

97 Advertisement for the Hope coach between Bristol and Calne, established in 1834, painted on the gateway of the King's Arms, Calne. The words 'The Hope coach' at the top have disappeared in recent times. On the other side of the gateway is an advertisement for the Eclipse coach to London, which dates the two advertisements to 1838-40.

honest and industrious man with a wife and four children to support, for whom an appeal was launched when the coach overturned and

Susan Young from Bristol to Bath and back, 24 October and 1 November 1798

24 Oct. At ten o clock set of in a coach for Bath – had a very agreeable companion Henry Moore a Methodist preacher – found near access to his mind and had some heavenly conversation with him.

1 Nov. At nine o clock return'd to Bristol with 2 men passengers – how different was their conversation from that of Christians – foolish and insignificant although they appeard to be ... what the world calls men of abilities – numbers of times they took the Lords name in vain – how glad I was when the time came to be releas'd from them.

Source: West Glamorgan Archives, D/D JVH 9.

broke his legs in 1788.[73] Bristol to Bath services tended throughout their history to be relatively cheap, reflecting the competitive situation and perhaps also spare capacity on long-distance coaches which shed many of their passengers at Bath.

Matthews's annual Bristol directory seems to provide an incomplete view of the other local services (Fig. 98). Not only are the few advertisements for them not always reflected in directory entries, but the lists based on stage coach duty record a wider range of local coaches in the 1830s. The fact that some were run by minor coachmasters from minor inns and changed from year to year would have made it relatively hard for directory compilers to track them down. On the other hand the local services in 1832-3 included ones to Clevedon, Iron Acton, Olveston, Pucklechurch and Thornbury drawn by a single horse and licensed for four or six inside passengers

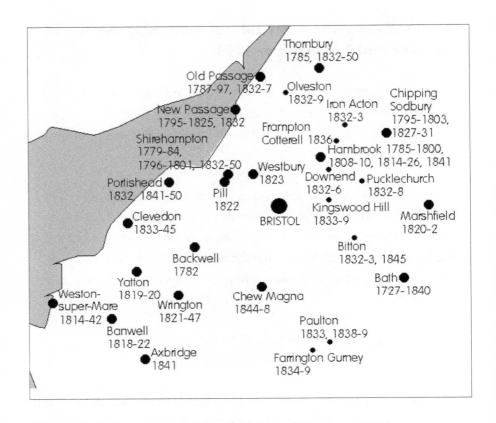

98 *Map of local coach and omnibus services within 20 miles of Bristol, 1779-1850. Many more are included here in 1832-9 than in other years because the tax lists in Robson's London directory for those years are more inclusive than other sources; the smaller circles indicate places with services recorded only there. (Sources: Newspaper advertisements, Bristol directories,* Robson's London directory *(1832-9).)*

only, all recorded in *Matthews's* as vans for goods and passengers or simply as carrying services.[74] This indicates that liability for stage coach duty caught some services which were not really stage coaches, and therefore that *Matthews's* was less incomplete than it seems at first sight.

The first recorded local service (other than the Bath one) was to Shirehampton, via Westbury, Henbury and Kingsweston, advertised intermittently in 1779-84 and 1796-1800 but never listed in a directory. In 1779-84 it was run by Weeks from the Bush, and by 1796 by Luce from the White Lion.[75] Other services, except Weeks's to Flax Bourton and Backwell in 1782,[76] are recorded only when directories begin in 1785. They included one to Hambrook, listed intermittently from 1785 to 1826. Unlike the Shirehampton coach it was not in the hands of a major innkeeper, and the only advertisement records a former servant as proprietor (Fig. 99). In 1841 there were omnibuses to both Hambrook and Shirehampton. There were coaches to the New Passage from 1785 to 1825 (from the Bush) and to Wrington from 1821 to 1847.[77]

Hambrook, Frenchay, and Bristol
STAGE-COACH.

THE above COACH sets out from *Hambrook*, every MONDAY, WEDNESDAY, and FRIDAY, at Eight o'Clock in the Morning, and goes through *Frenchay* and *Stapleton*, to the SWAN-INN, *Maryport-street, Bristol*, where it arrives between Nine and Ten o'clock, and returns again immediately from Bristol, through the above-mentioned Places to Hambrook aforesaid;—from whence it sets out again at Five o'clock in the Evening for Bristol, and returns the same Night, without stopping, from Bristol to Hambrook.

Fare from Hambrook and Frenchay, One Shilling; from Stapleton, Ten-pence;—small Parcels carefully conveyed and delivered.

Performed by

THOMAS SEABORN, *Hambrook*,

Late Servant to *Edward Brice*, Esq; of Frenchay.

☞ The above Coach may be had by the day, on application as above.——Neat Post-Chaises with able Horses, and careful Drivers; also a neat Hearse and Mourning-Coaches may be had at the shortest notice, and on the most reasonable terms, on application to THOMAS SEABORN and Co. *Hambrook.*

99 A rare example of an advertisement for a local coach: the Hambrook coach in 1795. (Felix Farley's Bristol Journal, 26 September 1795.)

The most important local destination came to be Weston-super-Mare. James Wookey of Congressbury, about half-way between Bristol and Weston, advertised a coach later known as the Hope from Bristol to Weston in 1814, at first just once a week during the season. This coincided with the reopening of Weston's first hotel. From 1821 there were winter services as well as summer ones, and by 1828 apparently three or four services daily. In 1825 William Hill of Cleeve, near Congressbury but closer to the half-way point, was joint owner with the Townsends of the Sovereign. Their driver was King, who had a coach office on Ratcliff Hill, Bristol, where the coach picked up passengers. By 1828 Hill also had Wookey's share of the Hope, and in the 1830s he owned the Magnet jointly with its driver, John Harse. The Magnet's horses were changed at the Nelson Inn, Cleeve, dividing the route into two stages of nine and ten miles. In 1837 the owners of the Magnet and the Cuckoo were Hill, William Hurst, Leonard and Bland of Bristol and Reeves, probably the owner of Reeves' Hotel in Weston, which would make him the only Weston person involved in one of its coaches.[78] As for Clevedon, its services began in 1833 and were as numerous as Weston ones the following year.[79]

The number of local services (excluding those between Bristol and Bath) fluctuated widely. The evidence from directories and advertisements indicates from three to 14 a week from 1779 to 1818, other than in nine of those years when there were none.[80] The number was higher from 1819, partly reflecting the growth of services to Weston. It only once fell below 21 and there were peaks of 58 in 1838 and 1841. Little reliance can be placed on the exact numbers, but there clearly was expansion in the local services. On the other hand the frequent changes in them suggest that their economics were precarious. The major coachmasters were involved in some of the early ones (Shirehampton and Backwell) and in services to Weston-super-Mare and Clevedon, but otherwise seem to have considered them not worth the effort, probably because they neither generated much profit nor were significant feeders to the long-distance coaches.

Speeds, fares and productivity

WHY DID THE number of regional services grow so strongly from about 1808, in contrast to that of London services? One reason was that each new destination satisfied demand that had previously been met wholly by other means or not at all, whereas London services were already long-established. The other is that the speeds and fares of regional coaches moved closer to those of London coaches, as did their productivity, making regional coaches viable where they had not been before, and that this process seems to have begun during the period of stagnation in London services.

Average speeds of regional services are shown in Fig. 100, indicating acceleration until the 1780s and in the 1820s and 1830s but little change between the early 1780s and the late 1810s. What is most significant is that regional speeds were 80 to 88% of the London ones from about 1770 to 1810, but 90 to 95% from 1816 to 1835 and higher than London ones in 1836-40.[81] As for fares, these broadly tracked the London ones, but with some variation, as shown in Fig. 101. Overall, fares were similar to London ones in the 1760s and were higher thereafter until the 1820s, when they were similar again.[82] In other words, while speeds caught up with London ones in the 1830s, fares did not rise relative to London ones as a result but instead converged to London levels.

Fig. 102 draws together the information on speeds and fares, together with that on costs, to provide an index of productivity for regional services and compare it with that for London ones. It must be emphasised that the evidence is much less plentiful than for London

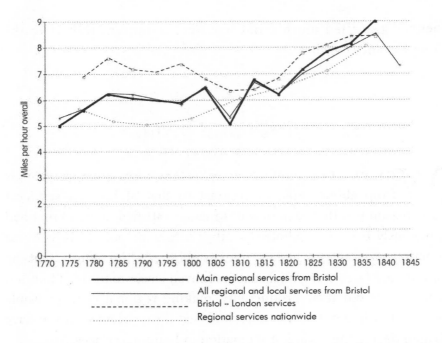

Main regional services from Bristol
All regional and local services from Bristol
Bristol – London services
Regional services nationwide

*100 Speeds of Bristol's regional coaches, 1770-1845. The figures are averages of the
speeds recorded for five-year periods. The thick line for the main regional routes
(353 examples 1762-1840) is probably a more reliable guide than the thin line for
all regional and local services (562 examples 1762-1845); it relates to coaches to
Birmingham, Worcester, Gloucester, Exeter, Plymouth, Southampton, Portsmouth,
Gosport, Hereford, Shrewsbury and Liverpool. A speed is included here only if there
were two or more examples in a five-year period, so both Bristol series have a gap in
1791-5. Bristol-London speeds are included for comparison (the dashed line), as are
the speeds of regional coaches throughout the country, based on work in progress (the
dotted line). (Sources: Local directories; newspaper advertisements.)*

coaches, and the figures are affected by variations from road to road,
in the amount of evidence from each road in each period and in the
degree of competition on each road at any particular time. Two sets
of information are used, and the lines based on them differ from each
other (though not massively) and fluctuate, so any conclusions must
be cautious, but it seems fair to conclude that productivity fell behind
that of London services from the 1770s or earlier, was slowly catching
up from the 1790s and was about the same in the late 1830s.

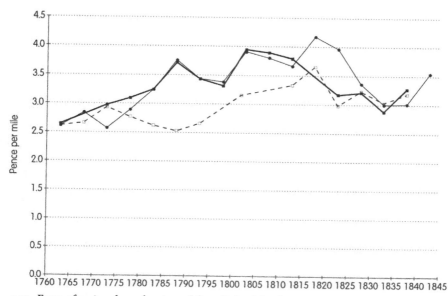

101 *Fares of regional coaches to and from Bristol (in five-year periods), 1760-1845. The thick line relates to main regional routes, the thin one to all regional and local services and the dashed one to Bristol-London services. The fares here are inside ones or, if an outside fare was given, half of the total of one inside and two outside fares. Fares are not shown here for periods when fewer than four are recorded (for main regional routes, 1766-70 and 1816-20). (Sources: Local directories; newspaper advertisements.)*

The situation in the 1770s and 1780s may reflect the lesser degree of competition in regional services, but probably also indicates that the cross roads were improved less than London roads in that period. There is some evidence of increased competition in the 1790s, but the change then seems more likely to have been the result of the cross roads being gradually brought up to the standard of the London roads. Earlier it was indicated that there was less incentive to improve the roads if speeds were not increasing, but that did not necessarily apply if one set of roads, the cross roads, was clearly in poorer condition than another set, the London roads. In Somerset there were 14 Acts adding stretches of road to the turnpike network from 1791 to 1807, which suggests a continuing spirit of improvement as regards the cross roads and a belief based on experience that turnpiking would

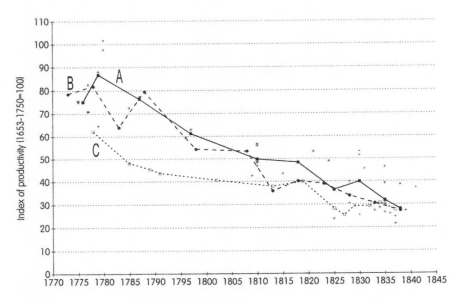

102 *Productivity growth of Bristol's regional services, 1773-1841, calculated as explained in Appendix 2. The evidence is much poorer than for London services, with a substantial margin of error. Line A is based on averages of individual examples of coaches (47 in total) for which both fare and speed are known, in some cases averaging just two examples. Line B is based on averages of all known fares and speeds for five-year periods, and therefore draws on much more information but with the risk that the fares were not typical for the speeds recorded. Periods without at least three speeds and three fares are excluded (i.e. up to 1770, 1791-5 and 1801-5). Line C is the productivity of Bristol's London coaches (from Fig. 25) for comparison. Asterisks indicate the index figures for individual coaches for which both speed and fare are recorded.*

make a difference.[83] Improvement in the cross roads may well have prompted the growth of regional coaching from about 1808. The process of bringing the cross roads up to the standard of the London ones had evidently been completed by the 1830s, and there was also increased competition on Bristol's regional routes in the 1820s and 1830s, eliminating the productivity gap between London and regional coaches. The evidence of speeds and fares nationwide indicates that this development was not peculiar to Bristol coaches and their roads, but took place everywhere, though the timing probably varied from one route to another.[84]

The figures just discussed of course group together a variety of services on different roads, and the differences from route to route are also informative. Routes which were relatively fast in 1819-37 (when their speeds are measured against the five-year averages for regional services) were Cheltenham (16% faster on average), Oxford and Southampton (both 10% faster).[85] A few services claimed to exceed 10 miles per hour in 1826-40, including coaches to Exeter (1829), Oxford (1835) and Cheltenham (1836), all 10.3 to 10.8.[86] Speeds on the Exeter and Birmingham routes varied, and the former was the only one with a range of slow and fast services comparable to the London ones, but they tended to be slightly above average. Slow routes included Weymouth (21% slower), Sidmouth and Lyme (15%), Weston-super-Mare (17%) and the short-distance services in general, except Bristol to Bath.[87] Evidently coaches to the seaside were generally slow, suggesting that for coaches largely or wholly serving leisure purposes reasonable cost mattered more than speed, though this did not apply to upper-class Bath and Cheltenham. From 1823, the only recorded speeds under six miles per hour were to Weymouth in 1823-7, Weston-super-Mare in 1828, Exeter (the Royal Devonshire) in 1830, Lyme in 1832, Portishead in 1842 and Brecon in 1844.[88]

Fares inevitably varied far more than speeds, occasionally falling to 50% of the five-year averages during periods of intense competition.[89] The lowest inside fares recorded were to Gloucester in 1765 (1.4d per mile), Birmingham in 1791, 1796-8 and 1804 (also 1.4d), all reflecting strong competition, and Weston-super-Mare in 1835 (1.3d), reflecting both strong competition and low speed. The highest were both for mail coaches – 5.8d per mile to Birmingham in 1801 and 6.8d to Milford Haven in 1820. No other fares exceeded 4.9d. These figures are of course the extremes, and the identification of highest and lowest fares from scattered dates ignores changes in costs.

It might be reasonable to assume that the regional coaches had lower capacity than the London ones, but the evidence suggests little difference, at least in the 1830s, the only period for which there is comprehensive evidence. In 1836, apart from the mail coaches (restricted to four or five outsiders) and the omnibuses, all of Bristol's regional and local coaches carried four insiders and two-thirds were licensed to carry eight outsiders, like many London coaches, with the others carrying 11 outsiders or, more often, five outsiders. There were some two-horse regional services in the 1830s, to Portsmouth and Cheltenham,[90] but the first certainly and the second probably were among the coaches carrying fewer outside passengers. The omnibuses, none of which except the Frome one travelled more than 11 miles from Bristol, carried from four to nine insiders and no outsiders. Three omnibuses recorded in advertisements in 1837-41 (to Gloucester, Bath and Bristol Hotwells) carried eight, ten and 14 inside passengers and five, six and four outside ones respectively.[91] Earlier references are to a Bridgwater coach able to carry six inside and ten outside passengers in 1814, and coaches to Weston-super-Mare and Exeter (two) in 1821-3 all able to carry four inside passengers and six, eight or ten outside ones.[92] Looking back further, diligences were used later on regional services than London ones, but none of the later ones was successful and there were none after 1797.

Another conclusion is that, as with Bristol to London coaches, there was a strong tendency towards combination and monopoly, and, while it was reasonably easy to start a regional service, it was hard to challenge an entrenched monopoly successfully. The Birmingham and Exeter roads quickly set the pattern of two or more Bristol coachmasters and their partners along the road sharing a route and defending it against interlopers. The impact on fares is most clearly demonstrated by the Exeter road between 1783 and 1802. The Exeter, Birmingham and Oxford routes all provide examples of established firms enticing away the partners in new ones. Some roads had too little custom to sustain competing services. On the other hand, challenges were reasonably frequent, even on the Birmingham and Exeter roads, high fares were likely to attract competitors, some challenges were successful, and from 1820 to 1837 William Clift ensured a reasonably competitive situation generally. It was thanks to Clift and his partners, as well as to the turnpike trusts responsible for the cross roads, that in the 1830s the speeds, fares and productivity of Bristol's regional coaches converged with those of its London coaches.

Notes

1 TNA, E 112/1948, No. 958; BG 26 Aug 1802.
2 *Ibid*; BG 12 April 1804; BD.
3 e.g. BG 9 Dec 1819.
4 BG 12 Apr 1804, 1 Oct 1807, 21 Feb 1811; BD.
5 Jan de Vries, *European urbanization 1500-1800* (1984), p. 270.
6 R. Cruttwell, *The new Bath guide* (1782), pp. 72-6.
7 See Appendix 1.
8 Wilfred S. Dowden (ed.), *The journal of Thomas Moore*, vol. 4 (1987), p. 1679. See also *ibid.*, p. 1723.
9 From advertisements emphasising that only one coach was used (e.g. FFBJ 11 Mar 1780, 27 Oct 1781).
10 e.g. Eric Pawson, *Transport and economy: the turnpike roads of eighteenth century Britain* (1977), pp. 281-4.
11 FFBJ 9 June 1764, 20 June 1772, 24 June 1775, 22 Feb 1777, 2 Nov 1782, 5 June, 2 Oct 1784.
12 Below, pp. 208, 214; BD; POST 10/24, pp. 128-9, 135.
13 Below, pp. 208-10, 215-16.
14 BG 26 Aug 1802, 23 June 1803, 26 June, 11 Sept 1806, 12 Mar 1807, 8 June, 13 July 1809; BD; online index to *The Cambrian*, 9 Nov 1816.
15 BD; BG 8 June 1809, 20 Sept 1810, 2 May, 13 June 1811, 4 June 1812.
16 Above, p. 110; BD; BG 17 May, 12 July, 4 Oct 1821; BM 15 Apr 1837.
17 BG 16, 23 & 30 Oct 1828.
18 The Exeter coach via Axminster, the Pilot to Leicester and The Age to London.
19 BM 8 Apr 1837; BG 13 April 1837; *Morning Chronicle*, 4 Dec 1841.
20 BG 3 Apr 1834; BD; above, pp. 114, 168-9. Niblett and Bland were jointly

horsing a new Birmingham coach in 1839 (BG 22 Aug 1839).

21 TNA, E 112/1420, No. 397.

22 ABG 19 Mar, 16 Apr, 22 Oct 1759, 3 Mar, 21 & 28 Apr 1760, 12 Oct 1761, 8 Mar, 18 Oct 1762, 21 Mar 1763, 2 Apr 1764, 4 Mar 1765; FFBJ 6 Feb 1773.

23 Actually 1773 (FFBJ 1 May 1773).

24 FFBJ 14 May 1814.

25 FFBJ 24 June, 1 July, 30 Sept 1775; ABG 20 Aug 1781, 7 Jan 1782; FFBJ 1 Feb 1783; BD 1785.

26 FFBJ 7 July 1787; POST 10/366, pp. 115-18; POST 10/24, p. 135; BD; POST 10/26, p. 322.

27 FFBJ 29 Oct, 5 & 12 Nov 1796, 2 & 9 May 1801, 18 Aug 1803; BD 1807-24; below, pp. 288 & 292, n. 7.

28 BG 2 June 1803, 15 Mar 1804; ABG 26 Mar 1804; BG 10 Jan, 14 Mar 1805, 2 May, 14 Nov 1811, 16 July 1812, 29 July 1813; ABG 21 Mar 1814; BG 1 June, 13 July 1815, 1 & 8 Feb 1816; BD.

29 BG 8 June 1820, 8 Feb, 17 May 1821, 3 Oct 1822.

30 BG 2 Sept 1824; BD 1833-8; Fig. 90; BG 22 Aug 1839, 3 Dec 1840.

31 On the assumption of 3.8 miles per hour overall.

32 FFBJ 9 June 1764, 30 Mar 1765, 28 Mar, 4 Apr 1767, 14 Sept 1771; EFP 1 Apr 1768, 3 July 1772, 11 Mar 1780; Birmingham City Archives, MS 3782/12/107/11; BG 2 Nov 1815; EFP 18 Oct 1827. Other Bristol-Exeter services are recorded in 1772 and 1780 (FFBJ 20 June 1772, 26 Feb 1780).

33 EFP 28 Feb, 19 Dec 1777; TNA, C 12/2120/20; FFBJ 11 Mar 1780, 16 Feb 1782, 15 Feb 1783; BD; BG 8 Apr 1819; TNA, E 112/1420, No. 397.

34 The evidence for the 1802 challenge is the decline in Weeks & Co's fares from 32s. to 15s. (EFP 4 July 1801, 4 Nov 1802).

35 EFP 4 June 1795; FFBJ 12 & 26 Sept 1795; TNA, E 112/1420, No. 397; EFP 2 Feb, 6 Apr 1797.

36 BG 24 Nov 1808, 3 Aug, 7 Sept 1809, 8 Feb, 6 & 20 Sept, 13 Dec 1810, 16 Sept 1830; EFP 13 July 1809; *Taunton Courier*, 8 Feb, 24 May, 22 Nov, 6 Dec 1810, 7 Feb 1811; BD 1808-32.

37 BG 12 Dec 1811, 3 July 1817, 30 July 1818, 7 June 1827, 28 July 1831, 5 July 1832, 28 Aug 1834, 26 Nov 1835; BD 1814-41. It was launched as an Axminster coach in October 1811, was advertised as an Axminster coach in 1829 and 1830 and was licensed only between Bristol and Axminster in 1833 (*Sherborne Mercury*, 21 Oct 1811; BG 17 Dec 1829, 1 Apr 1830; RLD 1833).

38 BG 4 Oct 1821, 14 Feb, 18 July 1822; EFP 13 Sept, 18 Oct 1827, 11 June 1829.

39 BD. This list ignores subsequent changes of name.

40 BG 8 Apr 1819; BD 1835; EFP 23 May 1839.

41 Maureen Boddy and Jack West, *Weymouth: an illustrated history* (1983), pp. 61, 87.

42 FFBJ 4 June 1768, 15 June 1776, 10 May 1777, 7 Aug, 18 Dec 1779, 5 June 1784; BD.

43 BD; *Pigot and Co.'s national commercial directory* (1830), entries for Dorset and

Somerset; BG 7 June 1832, 3 Apr, 30 Oct 1834.

44 *Hampshire Chronicle*, 29 July 1776; FFBJ 28 Oct 1780, 27 Oct, 3 Nov 1781, 7 May 1785, 25 July 1789, 1 Aug 1801; BD; *Report from the Select Committee on post communication with Ireland*, PP 1831-32 (716), p. 74; *Mail coaches*, PP 1836 (364), p. 3; Bath RO, BC 134/75; BG 28 Apr 1831; *Great Western Railway Bill: Minutes of evidence*, Lords PP 1835 (81), p. 1331. Bristol-Brighton coaches from the Bush from 1820 had an overnight stop at Southampton, indicating a forwarding arrangement (BG 17 Aug 1820).

45 BG 23 Nov 1815, 18 Apr, 24 Oct 1816, 7 Dec 1820, 12 July 1821, 1, 8 & 15 July 1824, 30 Nov 1826, 12 July 1838; *Bath Chronicle*, 25 Mar, 15 July, 28 Oct 1824; BD; *Pigot and Co.'s national commercial directory* (1830), entries for Dorset and Somerset.

46 *Bonner & Middleton's Bristol Journal*, 24 June 1797; BG 7 June 1832; BD 1833. Sidmouth coaches from the Swan in 1833-7 seem to have branched from the Minehead coach at Bridgwater (BD).

47 BG 25 Oct 1821, 24 Apr 1823; BD; PP 1836 (364), p. 3.

48 *Mail coach contracts*, PP 1835 (313), p. 16; *The Bath and Bristol guide* (1750, 1753, 1755); FFBJ 13 Apr 1754; *Jackson's Oxford Journal*, 13 Oct 1764, 4 May 1765; FFBJ 28 Mar 1767, 2 Oct, 27 Nov 1784, 29 Oct 1785.

49 FFBJ 4 Feb, 30 Sept 1786; POST 96/21, f. 57; POST 96/13, pp. 100-1; POST 10/366, p. 115; above, pp. 95-6.

50 POST 10/366, p. 115; PP 1835 (313), p. 16.

51 BG 2 Oct 1817, 19 Sept 1822, 3 Apr 1823, 28 Apr 1825, 21 Aug 1834, 4 June 1835; BD; POST 10/203, p. 107; POST 10/256, 27 Dec 1826; PP 1835 (313), p. 27; FFBJ 17 May 1788.

52 FFBJ 20 June 1772; BG 5 July, 20 Sept, 8 Nov, 13 Dec 1810, 3, 17 & 24 Jan, 7 Mar, 2 May 1811.

53 BG 2 Dec 1813, 27 July 1820; BD. Leicester services from the Greyhound in 1833-6 were apparently a branch from a Birmingham coach via Alcester.

54 Nicholas Herbert, *Road travel and transport in Gloucestershire 1722-1822* (1985), pp. 137-8; *South Wales roads*, PP 1826 (278), pp. 20-1; NLW, transcript of diary of Lewis Weston Dillwyn, 20 May 1818, 22 July 1820, 23 Oct 1821, 14 Mar 1833; *The Cambrian*, 19 Mar, 1 Oct 1814.

55 FFBJ 26 May, 4 Aug 1787; POST 10/24, pp. 42-5; POST 10/25, pp. 47-8. See also POST 10/366, p. 100.

56 FFBJ 12 July 1788; BD; BG 26 June 1806, with *The Cambrian*, 4 Jan 1806; BG 12 Apr 1810; *The Cambrian*, 27 Sept 1817; BG 14 & 21 Dec 1820; Carmarthenshire RO, CDX/734, 18 Jan 1815; Bristol RO, 39951(1), 27 June 1828.

57 BM 13 July, 28 Oct 1822, 7 July 1823; *The Cambrian*, 5 Apr 1823; NLW, transcript of diary of Lewis Weston Dillwyn, *passim*; PP 1831-32 (716), p. 11.

58 *Report from the Select Committee on the Milford Haven communication*, PP 1826-27 (258), pp. 18, 61; *The seventh report of the commissioners appointed to inquire into the management of the Post Office Department*, PP 1837 (70), p.

53; PP 1826 (278), *passim*; PP 1831-32 (716), p. 101; Herbert Williams, *Stage coaches in Wales* (1977), pp. 107-10.

59 NLW, Vivian B133; Williams, *Stage coaches*, pp. 110-12. See also the 1831 timings in PP 1831-32 (716), pp. 8, 333.

60 BG 3 Dec 1840, 5 Aug 1841.

61 FFBJ 11 Oct 1794, 2 June 1798; BD; BG 13 July 1809, 5 Aug 1813; *The Cambrian*, 29 May 1830; *Monmouthshire Merlin*, 29 Sept 1832; BG 28 July 1831, 4 July 1833, 28 Aug 1834, 4 June 1835, 29 June 1837, 5 May 1842.

62 BD 1831, p. 294; FFBJ 11 Mar 1780, 24 Aug, 19 Oct 1782, 10 Feb, 3 Mar 1787; BD; above, pp. 191-2; BG 23 Apr 1829, 28 Aug 1834, 13 & 20 Aug 1835, 12 July 1838.

63 BG 8 Sept 1831; Frederick Baines, *On the track of the mail-coach* (1895), p. 49; *First Report from the Select Committee on postage*, PP 1837-38 (278), p. 120.

64 BD; *Liverpool Mercury*, 22 May, 11 Dec 1835. See *Cheltenham Chronicle*, 1 Dec 1836, for a similar link with the L'Hirondelle.

65 BD; BG 26 June 1828, 17 Dec 1829; Webb 2, pp. 38, 46; BM 15 May 1843; *Keene's Bath directory* (1829), p. 16. See also the undated bill at Berkshire RO, D/P 96/18/5.0; Dowden, *Journal*, vol. 5 (1988), pp. 1966-7.

66 FFBJ 13 Apr 1765; BD; BG 29 Aug 1822, 7 June 1832, 14 Apr 1836; Fig. 95; Alan Sutton (ed.), *The complete diary of a Cotswold parson: the diaries of the Revd. Francis Edward Witts 1783-1854* (2008), vol. 4, pp. 376-9.

67 BD; BG 6 July 1820; *Gloucester Journal*, 17 Feb 1827, 6 & 13 Dec 1828.

68 BG 10 Aug 1815, 4 July 1816; BD; Kenneth R. Clew, *The Kennet & Avon Canal: an illustrated history* (1968), p. 90; FFBJ 23 Sept 1780, 24 Dec 1791; *Salisbury and Wiltshire Journal*, 25 May 1835; BG 3 July 1834.

69 EFP 5 Feb 1824.

70 BG 3 Aug, 7 Sept 1809, 8 Feb 1810, 23 Aug 1821, 15 Aug 1822, 27 Sept 1827; *Taunton Courier*, 6 Dec 1810; *North Devon Journal*, 14 Jan 1830; BD; POST 10/110; *Mail coach contracts*, PP 1835 (542), p. 3.

71 BG 7 Sept 1809, 10 Apr 1834; PP 1836 (364), p. 3; BG 6 Nov 1823, 13 May 1824, 14 Apr 1836; BD.

72 Online index to *Bath Chronicle*, 8 Sept 1785 (Wells); BD; BG 28 July 1831 (Sherborne), 19 Apr 1832 (Yeovil), 5 July 1832 (Langport), 15 May 1834 (Calne), 18 June 1835 (Chalford).

73 EFP 26 Jan 1837; online index of *Bath Chronicle*, 22 May 1788. The 1837 figure for Bristol-Bath is probably derived from RLD, which for 1836 indicates 18.5 local services and 15.5 going further (ten to London).

74 RLD 1832, 1833; BD.

75 FFBJ 24 July 1779, 23 Sept 1780, 3 July 1784, 9 Apr 1796, 3 May 1800.

76 FFBJ 18 May 1782.

77 BD; BG 31 Aug 1815.

78 FFBJ 23 Apr 1814; Bryan J.H. Brown, *Weston-super-Mare and the origins of coastal leisure in the Bristol region* (1978), pp. 10-11; BD 1821, 1828; BG 26 May

1825, 26 June 1828, 9 Feb, 17 Aug 1837.

79 BG 9 May 1833; BD.

80 i.e. 1793-4, 1804-7 and 1811-13.

81 The figure for 1811-15 suggests they were higher then too, but is based on relatively few examples.

82 In the five-year periods from 1816 to 1840, average inside fares ranged from 87% to 112% of the London ones.

83 O. Bryan Morland, *An introduction to the infrastructure of the Industrial Revolution in Somerset* (1982), *passim*.

84 Based on research in progress on speeds and fares. Elsewhere, speeds were somewhat lower in the 1780s and 1790s, and fares were sometimes somewhat higher in the nineteenth century.

85 Cheltenham 11 examples 1820-36; Oxford 15 examples 1788-1835; Southampton six examples 1820-9.

86 Also, less convincingly, Aberystwyth in 1832.

87 Weymouth 14 examples 1819-39; Sidmouth and Lyme four examples 1830-4; Weston-super-Mare 11 examples 1820-39.

88 Also the Oxford mail in 1823 (5.9 miles per hour) but this was for technical reasons (see p. 226 above).

89 Only 44% to Birmingham in 1804-5 and 47% to Weston-super-Mare in 1835.

90 BG 6 Feb 1834; PP 1836 (364), p. 3.

91 RLD 1836; BM 17 June 1837; BG 26 Nov 1840, 4 Mar 1841.

92 BG 8 Dec 1814, 12 Apr 1821; EFP 25 July 1822, 26 June 1823.

6
Railways

PROPOSALS FOR RAILWAYS between Bristol and London began
to appear in 1824. The one that was eventually successful – the
Great Western Railway – was proposed in 1832, with Brunel as its
engineer, and obtained parliamentary authorisation in 1835. The line

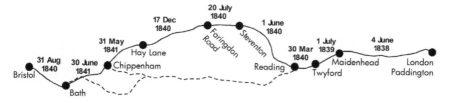

103 *Dates of opening of the Great Western Railway. The dashed line shows the
Bristol road from Reading to Chippenham and Bath.*

opened gradually, from 1838 to 1841 (Fig. 103).   The first part of
the Bristol and Exeter Railway, from Bristol to Bridgwater, opened
in 1841 and the line from Bristol to Gloucester, providing a link to
Birmingham, in 1844. The line from Birmingham to Gloucester,
completed in 1840, also had an impact.[1]

London coaches

EVEN BEFORE THE Great Western opened from London to
Maidenhead in June 1838, several Bristol coach firms announced

their intention of using it (Fig. 104). In practice, it took a little time, as the railway at first had limited ability to carry coaches. At first no-

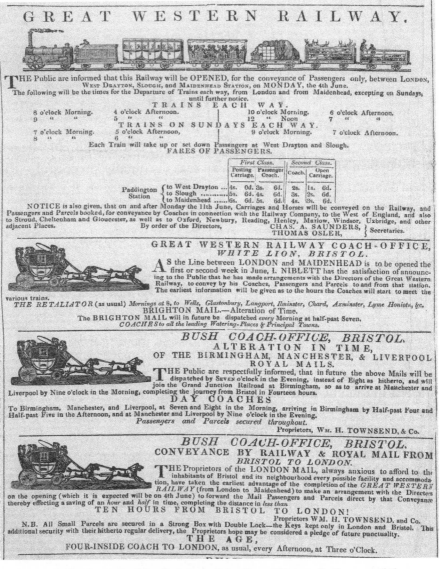

104 *The opening of the first part of the Great Western Railway, and the coachmasters' response, 1838. The mail coach to London in fact remained entirely on the road until April 1840. (Bristol Gazette, 31 May 1838.)*

Rev Francis Witts transferring from coach to railway at Maidenhead Station, 4 May 1839

The coach drove into the station yard where the passengers alighted, leaving their luggage with the coach which proceeds a little onwards, and reaches the level of the railway by a road constructed for the purpose: there the carriages are placed each on a railway truck, ready to be hooked on to the train when it comes to that point. In the meantime the passenger, furnished with an order from the coach proprietors to which the conveyance by which he came belongs, exchanges that order for a railway ticket to London, which purports to be worth 5s.6d. – We arrived ten minutes before the hour of starting, there is much less bustle of course than at the Birmingham and Manchester railroad stations, and no appearance of the transit of merchandize as yet ... The distance to London 22 miles (or rather the distance to Paddington) is traversed in 50 min. including stoppages the motion, I thought, rather less easy and gliding than on the grand junction railway: passed the Slough, Southall, Hanwell, Ealing and other stations. ... At the Paddington Station the coach is met by a pair of horses, the passengers resume their seats, and your journey is continued by the Edgware Road &c. to Oxford Street &c.

Source: Alan Sutton (ed.), The complete diary of a Cotswold parson: the diaries of the Revd. Francis Edward Witts 1783-1854 (2008), vol. 6, p. 294.

one seems to have thought of coaches meeting the trains at each end of the line; instead the coaches were loaded onto the trains. In July the newly-established Beaufort coach from Bath was said to be the only Bristol or Bath coach being conveyed by rail. The first Bristol coaches using the railway were Cooper's day coach in July 1838 (claiming to save two hours), the newly-established Eclipse in August, three more of Niblett's coaches in November and the New Company's day coach in December. New coaches established to take advantage of the railways included Townsend & Co's Eclipse using the Great Western in 1838 and the Economist using the London & Southampton Railway from Hartley Row Station to London, recorded only in 1838. By June 1839 all of Niblett's coaches were using the railway, and were advertised as taking ten hours.[2]

The faster coaches tended to make the earliest use of the railway. The main exception was the mail coach, which did not transfer to the railway until April 1840, shortly after the line opened to Reading. The Post Office may well have mistrusted at first the Great Western's ability to keep to time. The Great Western issued no timetables until the end of 1840 because, as its general manager explained later, 'At the opening in 1838 we found the engines were so inefficient that time-table working was hopeless; one or two engines might keep time, the other eight or ten were always out of time. So we suspended time-tables till the locomotive power became sufficient.'[3]

Another drawback of railways, quickly discovered, was the risk of fire. One of the Regulator coaches was burnt in October 1839 when cinders from the engine set fire to luggage on the roof. The coachman, Gooch, had remained inside the coach, and, despite the speed of the train (said to be 40 miles an hour), he clambered on to the roof, rescued most of the luggage and eventually, with the guard's help, put out the fire. The local newspaper noted that 'Great praise is due to the coachman and guard for the manner in which they acted throughout the affair'. A Bristol mail coach was less fortunate in April 1840 when its front boot was similarly set on fire. Parcels and luggage worth between £400 and £500 were destroyed, though the letters in the back boot were unharmed.[4]

THIRTY BATH and BRISTOL COACH HORSES, Harness, Cloths, Headstalls, &c.—To be SOLD by AUCTION, by Mr. DIXON, at his Repository, Barbican, on Friday, June 4, commencing at 12 o'clock precisely, the genuine and entire known good STOCK of Mr. William Lawes, of Chippenham ; comprising 30 well-bred, fine-shaped, fast, powerful horses, seven sets of four-horse harness, 30 cloths, and 30 headstalls, which have been working the new Company's fast day coach from Hungerford to Chippenham; positively for unreserved sale, in consequence of its being discontinued, and Mr. Lawes entirely declining the coach business. Colours—bays, browns, grays, blacks, roans, and chestnuts. The above valuable stock of seasoned horses is worthy the attention of the nobili y, gentry, job and post masters, commercial travellers, &c., as they are from 15 hands one inch to 16 hands three inches high, remarkably fine-shaped, beautiful steppers, with figure, fashion, power, and breeding rarely equalled in coachmasters' stocks, and are just taken from the above work, without exchange or addition. Among them are several elegant tilbury horses, some well known good hunters, and truly beautiful phaeton horses, as well as a number of useful powerful fa·t horses, calculated for omnibus, coach and cab masters, public companies, &c. On view, and catalogues had two days previous to the sale.

105 *The sale by William Lawes in 1841 of the 30 horses which had worked the New Company's day coach between Chippenham and Hungerford.*
(The Times, 29 May 1841.)

Once the Great Western opened beyond Reading in June 1840, it diverged from the old route through Newbury and Marlborough. Coachmasters then either had to abandon the trade from towns along the old route or to remain on the road for much of the distance and risk losing the through passengers. In fact, virtually all the coaches from Bristol or Bath to London which had remained entirely on the road transferred to the railway between April and September 1840 (the two mail coaches, the other two Bath coaches and probably The Age). The only exceptions were the New Company's night coaches. These remained on the road and simply ceased to run in July 1841.[5]

The Age, another slow coach, had started using the railway between London and Reading some time between December 1839 and February 1841. At the latter date it was run by King, an innkeeper at Devizes, James Foster, who was based at Newbury, and Sarah Ann Mountain, an important London coach proprietor. In July 1841, when the whole railway was open, it was transferred back to the road, at the same time changing from a four-horse to a two-horse coach. Other

William Henry Tucker from Bath to Bristol by railway, 8 September 1840

Went to Bath by coach ... and to Bristol by railway in twenty one minutes. Liked it extremely, the variety of rocks and plains, nocturnal caverns and sunlit hills suiting my varying mood.

Source: Helen Rogers (ed.), The diary of William Henry Tucker 1825-1850, *Wiltshire Record Society, vol. 62 (2009), p. 91.*

coaches re-established on the road were a Marlborough to London coach in April 1841 and Mountain & Co's Emerald between Bath and London in September 1841.[6] The purpose of continuing The Age at all must have been to serve the towns on the old road between Reading and Bath, but why it stopped using the railway between London and Reading is unknown. Perhaps low fares meant that the railway's charges were too high, or the Great Western was no longer interested in carrying coaches. The use of two-horse teams suggests that The Age carried relatively few passengers.

Mountain & Co emphasised in August 1841 that they were determined to continue covering the whole distance by turnpike road. The fares advertised were indeed 'very reduced', at 21s. and 12s. ('a much less fare than by railway'), but the speed may have been low. The economics of the coach must have been precarious. In November 1842 Peter Mountain, who had succeeded his mother, sold 50 horses previously used for the Age, and the coach was said to have been entirely discontinued. However, even this was not the end of Bristol to London coaching. A new coach, the Prince of Wales, was advertised in the same month, with the same fare, and was claimed to be superior to The Age (Fig. 106). Its proprietors were Nelson,

Gray & Co, one from a long-established London coach firm and the other a newly-established coachmaster at the Swan in Bristol. Fares were cut to 20s. and 10s. in April 1843, but low fares were evidently not enough: the coach last ran in the week of 16-20 October 1843, bringing to an end almost 200 years of stage coaching on the Bristol road.[7]

NOTICE TO THE PUBLIC.
A NEW FAST COACH, AT VERY LOW FARES.
"THE PRINCE OF WALES"

LEAVES the SWAN HOTEL, BRIDGE STREET, BRISTOL, every Evening (Sundays excepted), at ¼ before Five, through BATH, DEVIZES, and MARLBOROUGH, for the BELLE SAUVAGE, LUDGATE HILL, LONDON, returning thence every Evening at ¼ before 5, (Sundays excepted).

FARES—Inside, £1 1s. - Outside, 12s.

Parcels carried under the Railway Prices; no Booking charged.

Messrs. NELSON, GRAY, & Co. beg to inform the Public that the *Prince of Wales* will be conducted in a manner much superior to the old *Age*, and respectfully solicit their patronage.

106 Advertisement for the last Bristol-London stage coach, 1842. (Bristol Gazette, 10 November 1842.)

The end of Bristol to London stage coaches was inevitable following the opening of the Great Western Railway, and it is remarkable that even one coach continued for two years after the whole railway was open. What happened as regards the through passengers was perhaps similar to events on the Birmingham road in 1839, where Sherman kept on two night coaches in conjunction with Sarah Mountain. The fare was £1 inside and 12s. outside, compared with a minimum of £1 for rail. However, as Sherman explained, there was great difficulty keeping the coaches going:

> we do not book one inside passenger per coach on an average; we
> book more than the number outside. We have people come; they go
> away, saying, We can go by the railway for £1; ... we say we will book
> them as outsides, and put them in; but that makes the sharings so
> bad, that the workers [i.e. those horsing the coaches] are constantly
> giving notice to take off. ... What we carry now are mostly people who
> are timid people, and do not like to go by the railroad, except it is
> when we go with very low fares indeed; that induces the lower orders
> of people; the people we carry are so poor, the coachmen and guards
> say they get nothing besides the passage-money; their places are not
> worth having.[8]

Passengers who valued their time and were willing to pay
more for a faster journey inevitably transferred to the railway, and
no coach could hope to compete on speed. On the other hand, The
Age and Prince of Wales coaches were just about able to compete
on price, despite the Great Western having lower third-class fares

107 Reading Station, 1852

than the London & Birmingham. The railways at first showed little interest in the poorer passengers and did nothing to attract them. The Great Western's passenger trains carried only first- and second-class passengers; third-class passengers travelled instead by the goods trains in open trucks. Moreover, whereas none of the passenger trains were scheduled to take longer than four hours 45 minutes in 1841, the two goods trains a day took eight hours ten minutes and ten hours ten minutes. Even this cost 12s.6d in 1841, but that was 6d more than an outside place on The Age, and 2s.6d more than the Prince of Wales later charged. When a young Halcomb expressed sympathy for the passengers in an open truck being lashed by rain, his father, the former coachmaster Thomas Halcomb, replied sternly, 'Sorry for them! Why? In the olden time these people would have had to walk to London, and now they can ride', but in fact it is more likely that they would formerly have been lashed by rain on top of one of the cheaper stage coaches. Eventually, following an Act of 1844, the Great Western reduced its third-class fare to 9s.10d and passengers were provided with cover, but the two trains a day carrying third-class passengers still took more than nine hours.[9] By then the Prince of Wales had already ceased to run, and evidently there were not enough passengers to and from the towns still distant from the railway or seeking the cheapest possible fare to keep a coach going.

The disappearance of stage coaches had serious consequences for some of the towns and villages bypassed by the railway, such as Devizes, Marlborough, Newbury, Thatcham and Hounslow. The most creative response was at Marlborough, where the Halcombs were among those who promoted the foundation of Marlborough College. It now incorporates the former Castle Inn.[10]

108 *The three railway classes, 1847. These engravings illustrated an article about the Epsom races, but show well the different accommodation provided for each class. What they do not show is that third-class trucks were attached to goods trains rather than to the faster passenger trains.* (Illustrated London News, *22 May 1847.*)

Regional and local coaches

R EGIONAL SERVICES BEGAN to be cut back substantially in 1841, with the opening both of the Great Western throughout and the Bristol and Exeter line as far as Bridgwater in June that year. From June 1841 or shortly afterwards, Exeter, Barnstaple, Minehead and Lyme were served from the railhead at Bridgwater, and two months later 105 coach horses were sold by Niblett of Bristol and Lane of Bath as a result. Competition remained intense between Bridgwater and Exeter, but the line gradually opened further, reaching Exeter in 1844.[11] In the opposite direction the railway was at first some distance from Bristol. From 1837 coaches were advertised as meeting trains at Birmingham, and from 1840 passengers were conveyed to the newly-established railhead at Cheltenham, soon superseded by Gloucester, from which trains took them to Birmingham and beyond. Coaches to Gloucester became more frequent, until in 1844 the line from Birmingham opened to Bristol. The last mail coach towards Birmingham set off with the coachman and guard dressed in black and the horses bearing funereal plumes.[12]

One last attempt was made to create a new coaching business at Bristol, by William Gray at the Swan. In 1842, in addition to the Prince of Wales to London, he had a mail coach to Stroud. In 1843 he started a new coach to Clevedon, entirely by road, which he said was to do away with the inconvenience of removals between coach and train. It took an hour and a half, whereas Niblett's service, using rail as far as Yatton, was advertised as taking an hour. Gray also had Hereford and Cheltenham coaches, and in 1843 reduced their fares, claiming that the notoriously high fares on those routes could only have been maintained by a monopoly. Again his rival was Niblett, and the same applied when Gray established a new coach to Brecon in 1844. Evidently it was Niblett who prevailed, as none of Gray's services are recorded after 1844 except the Clevedon one (for the last time) in 1845.[13]

The Bush closed in 1844, and by 1846 almost all the remaining services at Bristol were in Niblett's hands at the White Lion. John Bland at the Rummer had one to Southampton, but it was by road only between Chippenham Station and Southampton (and later only between Chippenham and Salisbury Stations). Niblett still advertised an impressive range of services, but many of them set off from Bristol by train. The last coach services of any length were Niblett's to Swansea and Brecon. The Cymro to Swansea became the mail coach in 1845 and continued until 1850, when Chepstow and Swansea were linked by railway. Niblett continued to advertise a Swansea service until 1856, for there was still no direct rail link between Bristol and South Wales, but from 1850 it must have been largely a railway journey. Niblett's Brecon service lasted until 1854, making it Bristol's last long-distance coach. Among the local services, omnibuses to Thornbury (all that remained of the service to Wotton-under-Edge and Dursley) continued until at least 1862, and Prewett's in 1859 was said to proceed at a 'steady trot' of six to seven miles per hour, but by 1863 passengers from Bristol to Thornbury were travelling as far as Patchway Station by train. All that then remained were omnibuses to Shirehampton and Portishead.[14]

The last coachmasters

IT WAS LATER said that 'Few people are aware of the misery caused by railways to innkeepers, coachmen, guards, postboys, ostlers, and horse-keepers, as it all came to pass so suddenly. Nor could anybody foresee exactly the effects they would have'. That may well have been true of many coachmen and other staff, especially at towns and villages dependent on road traffic, but at least a few of these were successful in finding new occupations. William Mills, who had driven Niblett's coaches to Newbury and then to Hereford, briefly ran his own coach linking Monmouth to the Bristol steam packets at Chepstow and then settled down as an innkeeper at Monmouth, dying in 1879.[15] The mail coach guards were the most fortunate, being direct employees of the Post Office. Moses Nobbs, guard to various mail coaches, including the Bristol to Portsmouth one, remained with the Post Office, eventually taking charge of the receipt and despatch of the mails at Paddington. He retired in 1891 and died six years later.[16]

As for the coachmasters, they had plenty of notice that railways were to be built and were well aware that their businesses would be 'annihilated' by them. Some, like Niblett and Townsend at Bristol, had invested in railways by 1837.[17] Consequently, most adapted successfully. The fate of the London coachmasters is already well-known. The greatest of them, William Chaplin, saw what was coming, sold his coach interests, took a long break in Switzerland to think about the future and then re-invested his money in railways, becoming Chairman of the London & Southampton Railway (later the London & South Western Railway). He also secured an exclusive arrangement with the London & Birmingham Railway for carriage of parcels from its stations, in partnership with another former coach proprietor, Benjamin Horne. Sherman was slightly slower to adapt and lost by it. John Nelson moved into the omnibus business and prospered. Sarah Mountain seems to have been willing to carry on the fight against the railways, but died in 1842.[18]

At Bristol, John Townsend died in 1841, aged about 75. His son, William Henry Townsend, was in serious financial difficulty by the end of 1841, owing £4,678 to Niblett, and transferred all his coaching assets to Niblett. Nevertheless, the following year he managed to purchase what was left of the late William Lane's coaching business at Bath, and was still a coachmaster there in 1845.[19] Niblett proved the greatest survivor, maintaining a viable business based on the Lion Hotel (formerly the White Lion and White Hart), where he claimed to have entertained members of the British, French, Russian and Prussian royal families. His coach trade declined, but he booked goods and parcels, ran omnibuses to the railway station, Hotwells and Clifton and provided horses and carriages for posting. In the 1840s he described the Lion as the 'Universal Royal Mail and City Railway Office'. He also ran Conygre Farm at Filton, and won prizes for his cattle. He eventually retired from managing the hotel in 1859, after working there for more than 54 years, but even then carried on business as 'Posting Master and Carrying Agent' at the White Lion Booking Office. He died in December 1860, aged 68.[20]

John Bland also adapted successfully to the railway age. In addition to coaches, he had a substantial goods business, and he continued to use vans and railways to serve a wide area of the West Midlands and Manchester. His obituary noted that his enterprise was not restricted to railway carrying: for many years he 'horsed several collieries, conducted the business of a very large and exceedingly well-managed farm, and was also largely engaged in the timber trade, and in some steam saw mills'. The farm was at Sully in Glamorgan, where he lived, but he 'was almost a weekly visitor to Bristol, and for many years past he always kept his own apartments at the Rummer hotel'. He died in 1870.[21]

Less is known about the Bath coachmasters. Members of the Lane family continued to run coaches until 1842, unprofitably in the last few years, and then sold what remained of the business to William Henry Townsend, who had married a Lane. When Moses Pickwick died in 1869, aged 87, it was said that he had accumulated a large fortune which he subsequently lost, but how he lost it is not recorded.[22]

It was harder for the middle-ground coachmasters to continue in business, particularly those outside towns, but the only bankruptcy seems to have been that of Eleanor Botham at the George and Pelican,

Speenhamland. Even in 1841 she was working a Frome coach, in partnership with Sarah Mountain, and a Marlborough coach called the Optimus. She was declared bankrupt in April 1841 and evidently had not reduced her commitments fast enough as the coach trade disappeared. Among her expenses she included £2,800 as the cost of maintaining her establishment without profit for four years (presumably from 1837), blaming the Liverpool Railway for destroying the Irish trade and the Great Western for destroying the trade on the Bristol and Bath road. £600 was accounted for by the keep of 100 horses from December 1840 to April 1841. Even supplying post-horses had become unprofitable because competition had resulted in lower prices, to which she attributed a loss of £555. Among various other losses and expenses, one seems to sum up her situation:

> Loss on 100 horses being thrown out of work coaches going to the rail at short notice & same sold by auction £1000.[23]

Nevertheless, according to the Duke of Beaufort, 'Mrs Botham died at a ripe old age, respected by all who knew her.'[24]

In contrast, Maria Fromont proved, characteristically, a survivor. She sold her 90 horses working the New Company's coaches in July 1841 and concentrated on running Thatcham Farm and another farm at Wargrave. She had substantial property at Thatcham, including the King's Head, and at Hare Hatch. She died in 1866, aged 90, leaving an estate worth up to £4,000.[25]

As for Thomas Cooper, when the coaches were taken off, Chaplin obtained for him the post of stationmaster at Richmond upon Thames, where he served until at least 1861, living there apparently alone. By 1871 he had retired and was living in Richmond as a lodger. He died there in 1873, aged 78.[26] A few old coachmen still survived, but Cooper was the last link with the world of the coachmasters on the Bristol road.

Notes

1   E.T. MacDermot (rev. C.R. Clinker), *History of the Great Western Railway* (1964), vol. 1, pp. 1, 13; Leslie James, *A chronology of the construction of Britain's railways 1778-1855* (1983).

2   Webb 2, pp. 38-9, 41; BG 19 July, 23 Aug, 18 Oct, 1 Nov 1838, 27 June 1839; *The Times*, 13 Oct, 17 Dec 1838.

3   BG 22 Aug 1839, 30 Apr 1840; POST 10/117; MacDermot, *Great Western Railway*, vol. 1, p. 329.

4   *The Times*, 22 Oct 1839 (col. 6b); Webb 2, p. 43.

5   Webb 2, pp. 42-4; *The Times*, 21 & 27 July 1841.

6   BG 5 Dec 1839, 4 Feb 1841; *Reading Mercury*, 24 July 1841 (col. 2g); Webb 2, pp. 46-7; *The Times*, 23 Sept 1841.

7   BG 4 Feb 1841, 17 Feb, 10 Nov 1842; *Oxford dictionary of national biography*, Sarah Mountain; *Salisbury and Wiltshire Journal*, 30 May 1836; *Reading Mercury*, 24 July 1841 (col. 2g); BM 7 Aug 1841, 1 Apr, 21 Oct (col. 8d) 1843; *The Times*, 14 Nov 1842, 20 Nov 1843.

8   *Report from the Select Committee on turnpike trusts*, PP 1839 (295), pp. 8, 10.

9   MacDermot, *Great Western Railway*, vol. 1, pp. 333-5, 338-9; Wiltshire Heritage Museum, MS 1360-1, cutting from *Wiltshire, Berkshire and Hampshire County Paper*, 3 Sept 1915; *Exeter Pocket Journal* (1845). In 1842 Great Western third-class fares were recorded as 1.83 pence per mile, indicating 18s. between Bristol and London (MacDermot, *Great Western Railway*, vol. 1, p. 334).

10 Webb 2, pp. 46-8; Wiltshire Heritage Museum, MS 1360-1.

11 BG 5 Aug, 16 & 30 Sept, 9 Dec 1841, 17 Mar 1842; BD 1842-5; *The Times*, 24 Aug 1841; Lord Algernon St Maur, 'Old coaching days', in Duke of Beaufort (ed.), *Driving* (1890), pp. 205-6.

12 BG 7 & 14 Sept 1837, 9 & 16 July, 12 Nov, 3 Dec 1840; BD; Herbert Williams, *Stage coaches in Wales* (1977), p. 113.

13 BD 1842-5; BG 20 Apr, 15 June, 17 Aug 1843, 25 Apr, 2 May 1844.

14 BG 28 Mar 1844; BD 1846-62; BM 11 July 1846, 19 May 1849; *The Cambrian*, 11 Jan, 16 Aug 1845; Williams, *Stage coaches in Wales*, p. 115; BG 8 June 1846; BM 17 Sept 1859, 19 Sept 1863. The Brecon service was discontinued in 1845 and resumed in 1849.

15 BM 7 Feb 1879.

16 St. Maur, 'Old coaching days', p. 197; BM 7 Feb 1879, obituary of William Mills; Charles G. Harper, *Stage-coach and mail in days of yore* (1903), vol. 1, pp. 264-71.

17 *Report from the Select Committee on internal communication taxation*, PP 1837 (456), pp. 1, 5; *First Report from the Select Committee on railroad communication*, PP 1837-38 (257), pp. 92-3; *Railway subscription contracts*, PP 1837 (95), Nos. 28, 30.

18 C.G. Harper, *Stage-coach and mail in days of yore* (1903), vol. 2, pp. 208-10, 222-3, 235; PP 1839 (295), pp. 11-12; Harris, pp. 143-5, 147, 157; above, pp. 263-4.

19 Bath RO, 08022/23; census 1841; TNA, C 14/1259/L86; BG 29 Sept 1842; BM 12 July 1845.

20 BD; BM 28 May, 4 June 1859, 15 & 27 Dec 1860; census 1841.

21 BG 7 Oct 1841, 17 Mar, 7 Apr 1842, 18 Jan 1844; BM 12 Nov 1870.

22 TNA, C 14/1259/L86; TNA, C 14/407/L42; BM 30 Jan 1869.

23 TNA, B 3/788; *Reading Mercury*, 4 Apr 1840.

24 Duke of Beaufort, 'The Brighton, Bath, and Dover roads', in Beaufort, *Driving*, p. 244.

25 *The Times*, 19 & 27 July 1841; Principal Probate Registry, will of Charlotte Maria Fromont 1866; 1861 census; Berkshire RO, transcripts of monumental inscriptions, Thatcham.

26 Harper, *Stage-coach*, p. 180; census 1851, 1861, 1871; Principal Probate Registry, will; register of deaths, 1873.

7
Conclusion

THE STORY OF Bristol's stage coaches can be briefly summarised. The first stage coach to London almost certainly ran in 1657, and the number of coaches per week to London increased from eight in the 1680s to 69 in 1834-8, thereafter declining to nil in 1843. Growth was concentrated in the late1770s/early 1780s and the mid-1820s. Average overall speeds increased from 3.1 or 3.8 miles per hour (depending on the season) in the period up to the 1750s to 8.4 in the 1830s, with the fastest coach, the mail coach, reaching 10.3. Again the increases were concentrated, though less strongly, in two periods: the 1750s to the early 1780s and the late 1810s/early 1820s. Higher speeds were accompanied by only a small increase in fares, reflecting a considerable increase in productivity. Fares in the 1830s were little more than a quarter of what they would have been but for improvements in roads, horses and vehicles since the 1750s. The story can be divided into five periods: the pioneering phase from the 1650s to the 1670s, a period when little changed from the 1670s or 1680s to the 1750s, a period of speeding up and increasing productivity from the 1750s to the 1780s resulting in rapid growth, a period of stagnation from about 1790 to 1815 and a final period of speeding up and growth from about 1815 to 1840.

A network of regional coaches also developed, starting in 1701 or earlier with the first such coach recorded anywhere, between Bristol and Oxford. The network started to grow significantly in the 1770s and very rapidly from about 1808 to 1839, by which date there were about 280 services per week extending 20 miles or more from Bristol. The earliest regional services used unturnpiked or only recently turnpiked roads, which are likely to have been more challenging than the London road. Even after turnpiking these roads seem to have been poorer, and there was also in most cases a more precarious trade, with some roads unable to sustain competition. Consequently services were on average somewhat slower than London coaches but had similar fares. In the nineteenth century, however, the gap was closed, so that by the 1830s the average speeds and fares of Bristol's regional coaches were similar to those of London ones, though there was much variation among them.

The impact of faster coaches

D ID IT MATTER that stage coaches speeded up from between three and four miles per hour overall to between eight and nine miles per hour? Even the coaches of the 1820s and 1830s would seem extremely slow to the modern traveller, and from the same perspective the increase in speed seems trifling. Nevertheless, speeds more than doubled. In the case of Bristol to London, it meant that instead of a journey of two or three days, stopping overnight, one city could be reached from the other in just one day, or an evening and a night. Combined with a relatively small increase in fares, and an increased range of services from fast and expensive to cheap and slow (with especially cheap outside fares), that was enough to increase demand massively. Some of that travel replaced journeys which would have been undertaken by other means, for example on horseback or even on foot, but there can be little doubt that better stage coach services brought about a considerable increase in travelling.

Some coach travel was leisure travel, and its growth was therefore an aspect of increasing consumption and an indication of rising standards of living. Increasing leisure travel was demonstrated most clearly by the growth of services to seaside resorts and spas, including Bath. In this way stage coaches contributed to the growth of such resorts and spas. Services to Bath and Cheltenham tended to be fast, though in Bath's case there were also two-day services uniquely late because an easy journey was more suitable for the unwell. Services to seaside resorts such as Weymouth and Weston-super-Mare tended to be slow, and perhaps in these cases cheapness was more prized than speed. In fact almost any journey not undertaken mainly or wholly for economic purposes falls into the leisure category, which therefore includes many journeys to London and other visits to friends or relations, such as James Woodforde's coach journeys. Stage coaches contributed to what was described in 1823 as 'the perfect mania that the English have for moving about from one place to another'.[1]

There was also business travel, the earliest clear examples being Ned Ward's fictional merchant going to Bristol in 1700 and Matthew Boulton travelling via Bristol and Exeter to the Cornish mines in 1779. Traders went to London for the markets and exchanges and to meet those they traded with. Much business could be done remotely, through correspondence or intermediaries, but there was much greater likelihood of a strong and mutually beneficial relationship if the principals could meet from time to time, just as is the case today, and conducting business directly rather than through intermediaries was simpler, safer and cheaper. In this way the stage coaches contributed to the development of a national market and a more efficient economy. They also did so by carrying letters, parcels and luggage. Rapid delivery of letters, especially once mail coaches were established in 1784, meant that information about markets and prices could be obtained while still current and orders from remote customers could be fulfilled quickly, making it easier to secure and retain such customers. Most goods conveyed by road went in carriers' waggons, but, where speed was valued, stage coaches might be used, especially for smaller and lighter items. A glimpse of the importance of this parcels traffic to businesses is provided by Edward Fromont's reference in 1802 to 'samples, patterns, and other similar packages'. Even heavy goods might be carried by coach if urgently needed or conveyed cheaply. One of the reasons for Thomas Cooper's downfall was said to be his failure to charge for overweight luggage, which resulted in Bristol merchants using his coaches to bring home heavy goods bought in London.[2]

In many of these ways the importance of faster coaches and increased coach travel lay in spreading information, ideas and assumptions more quickly and pervasively, which had a major impact on the nation's economic, cultural and political life. Not only were people with the knowledge and opinions inside their heads travelling more, but letters, London newspapers and books printed in London were conveyed by coach.[3] The importance of rapid conveyance of information to economic life has been noted already. As for cultural life, it was observed in 1761 that 'the manners, fashions, amusements, vices and follies of the metropolis now make their way to the remotest corners of the land ... along the turnpike road'.[4] Faster coaches and increased travelling helped to break down local, regional and national differences between and among the peoples of Great Britain, formerly 'separated from each other and among themselves by different folklores, different sports, different costumes, different building styles, different agricultural practices, different weights and measures, and different cuisines'.[5] The impact on political life was also significant. The *Scotsman* noted in about 1809 that 'The post, the press, and the stage-coach, have made it easier to unite twenty millions of men in a common cause in our own days, than it was to unite the fiftieth part of the number in the days of Philip of Macedon'.[6] The rise of the anti-slavery movement in 1787-8 provides a good example, just after the main period of speeding up of stage coaches and the establishment of mail coaches carrying letters and London newspapers.[7]

Bristol's stage coaches in context

THERE ARE FEW aspects of the history of Bristol stage coaches which clearly distinguished them from stage coaches elsewhere in the country. The economics of coaches must have been broadly the same everywhere, because they were shaped everywhere by the horse. Improved breeds of horse and improved vehicles, for example with better springs, could be moved from one area to another, and with so much of the coaching trade serving London any innovations must always have spread quickly. There were nevertheless some reasons for variation: the quality of roads varied, the level of tolls varied, provender prices varied (especially when the coasting trade and imports were disrupted by war), and above all the level of competition varied. It is in their attitude towards competition and their expansion of the market through faster or cheaper services that coachmasters were most likely to have made Bristol's stage coaches distinctive. Examples include each decision to set up a new service, especially Fromont's establishment of slow coaches, and Clift's unwillingness to collude.

However, such decisions were more likely to affect the short term and the timing of change rather than the longer-term development of stage coaching, and that is what we find when it is possible to compare Bristol's coaches with those elsewhere. This is particularly clear in respect of the changing speeds and fares of Bristol's coaches, which followed similar patterns to the national averages, including the decline of seasonal variation in speeds. It is less clear as regards the rate of growth, which was also affected by the different rates at which towns grew. However, the seven other towns or cities with a good run of local directories (Birmingham, Exeter, Leeds, Liverpool, Manchester, Southampton and Worcester) all experienced a doubling or more, and in at least five of these cases a trebling or more, in the number of services in the 1770s and 1780s, though the timing within that period was sometimes earlier or later than in Bristol.[8] The quarter-century of stagnation is likely to have been almost universal, since provender became dear everywhere, though Leeds, Liverpool and Manchester all saw some growth in services in the early nineteenth century. The five towns with informative local directories in the nineteenth century all (except Leeds) saw significant growth in services in the period 1815-30, again with the timing varying within that period, and all (possibly except Manchester) saw little or no growth in the 1830s. Bristol's regional network is harder to compare with those of other areas, since few have been studied in detail.[9]

All this has implications for the effectiveness of turnpike trusts at different periods. Until the 1750s, both on the Bristol road and elsewhere, they seem to have been fairly ineffective in improving the roads and had little impact on coach services. However, the productivity of Bristol's London coaches grew significantly and apparently continuously from the 1750s to the 1780s and then again in the early 1820s. That growth reflected steel springs, better horses and improved roads, but use of steel springs and change in the character of stage coach horses had been heavily dependent on improved roads. The growth in productivity was therefore largely a tribute to the effectiveness of the turnpike trusts from the 1750s to 1780s and in the 1820s. Effectiveness in the latter period clearly reflected the influence of McAdam's methods of road repair and a more determined attitude towards road improvement and the reduction of gradients. Effectiveness in the earlier period is more of a surprise, but evidently reflected the dogged pursuit of mostly small-scale improvements and an increasingly systematic attitude towards road repairs and improvements. It was not necessarily universal, but national figures indicate that the timing and extent of productivity growth in stage coaching was similar elsewhere, both then and later. Nationwide, fares fell by the mid-1780s to about 54% of what they would have been without road and other improvements, compared with about 48% on the Bristol road. After that there was little change until a further period of growth in the 1810s and 1820s, bringing fares down to about 29% of what they would have been, compared with about 28% in the Bristol road's case.[10] The evidence from the Bristol road that the turnpike trusts were highly effective in the period from the 1750s to the 1780s and increased their effectiveness further in the period around 1820 is therefore consistent with the national evidence.

Each coach route was different to some extent, and it would be helpful to have more local studies, but the quality of the evidence for Bristol coaches and the absence of any features suggesting they were exceptional mean that they provide the key to understanding the development of stage coaching as a whole. The Bristol evidence makes it possible to see not only what changed but also how and why those changes occurred. With the help of improved roads, horses and vehicles, the coachmasters were able to provide much faster coach services for little extra cost, with immense economic, cultural and political consequences.

Notes

1   P.G. Patmore, quoted in Paul Langford, *Englishness identified: manners and character 1650-1850* (2000), p. 37.
2   Above, pp. 156, 175.
3   Linda Colley, *Britons: forging the nation 1707-1837* (2009 edn.), pp. 225-6.
4   Quoted in Edwin A. Pratt, *A history of inland transport and communication in England* (1912), p. 96.
5   Colley, *Britons*, p. 14.
6   *Ibid.*, p. 224.
7   Adam Hochschild, *Bury the chains: the British struggle to abolish slavery* (2006 edn.), pp. 213-16.
8   The most rapid growth was in the mid-1770s in Exeter and Southampton

and the late 1780s at Manchester. Some use has been made of newspaper advertisements here in addition to local directories.

9   M.J. Freeman, 'The stage-coach system of South Hampshire', *Journal of Historical Geography*, vol. 1 (1975), pp. 264, 266, does not provide separate figures for London and regional coaches.

10 Based on work in progress drawing extensively on newspaper advertisements.

Appendix 1: Counting Bristol's stage coaches

THE BEST SOURCE for numbers of services is trade directories, but they are full of traps for the unwary and need to be treated with suspicion and compared with other sources, especially advertisements, whenever possible. The main problem is that the way they present their information multiplies the apparent number of coaches, and that this distortion becomes worse over time. They do this both by repeating services which could be booked from more than one inn in the entries for each inn, and by repeating services which served several places (including places reached by connecting coaches) under the names of each place. The duplication is often far from obvious. Any figures derived from directories which take no account of these problems will certainly be wrong, whereas any that seek to overcome the problems, as in this book, inevitably contain a subjective element. The problems diminish once coaches start to have names, but not all directories included them.

Newspaper advertisements are also useful, not only as a check on the directory information but also on their own in the period before local directories begin, when coach firms were few and advertisements were reasonably frequent and comprehensive. Advertisements in local newspapers of other places and local directories for other places can provide valuable information too, such as those of Exeter and Birmingham in Bristol's case.

London services

L ONDON DIRECTORIES LISTING stage coaches exist from 1681 onwards, but many coaches, especially Bristol and Bath ones, are listed at more than one London inn, often with slightly different departure times or other details, so that it is hard to determine whether more than one coach is being referred to. For example, Glasier & Co's machines, advertised at Bristol in March 1777[1] as six times a week from four London inns (each sharing three of the services), appear in the *New Complete Guide* for 1777 under those four inns and also four others, three times a week at each, with variations in the timing and the description (machines in one case but otherwise just coaches).

Therefore, while London directories have been used for the first century or so, later figures are derived mainly from Bristol directories, when available, and otherwise from newspaper advertisements. Sometimes assumptions have had to be made about exact numbers in a particular year, especially about whether a service listed at two or more Bristol inns was in fact a single service, though this is only occasionally in doubt. Also it is sometimes unclear whether a coach described as daily ran on Sundays. Nevertheless, the overall picture is undoubtedly reliable.

It is necessary to define 'coaches between Bristol and London' in order to take account of coaches from London passing through to a further destination (Milford Haven) or stopping just short with easy onward access (Bath). Mail coaches from London to Bristol and Bristol to Milford Haven were horsed under separate contracts, and are therefore regarded as separate services here.[2] Bath is more of a problem because in practice there was little difference between a coach travelling the whole way between London and Bristol and a

London to Bath coach which transferred passengers to a Bath-Bristol coach (often in the same ownership) at Bath. The risk is that the figures could be distorted by changes in the way coachmasters chose to organise and advertise their services as opposed to a real change in the number of services, and indeed in the nineteenth century Bristol-London services became more numerous and Bath-London ones less numerous. Therefore an attempt has been made to count Bath to London services as well, though this has proved impossible for most years from 1781 to 1808 (Fig. 21). The main sources used for Bath services have been newspaper advertisements (only sometimes distinguishing Bath-only services), Bath directories (rarely helpful), coach lists in *Cary's new itinerary* from 1810 to 1828 and stage coach duty lists in *Robson's London directory* from 1832 to 1839.

Regional and local services

LOCAL DIRECTORIES CAN no more be taken at face value than London ones. Sometimes they under-record services. In particular, *Matthews's new Bristol directory* was sometimes slow to record new services, such as Luce's Birmingham coach of 1796 (listed in 1807), Bessell's Leicester coach of 1810 (listed in 1814) and Clift's Weymouth service of 1834 (listed in 1837).[3] It seems also to be patchy for local services. However, new services except local ones seem almost invariably to have been advertised, so this is not a significant problem other than for the local coaches.

There is one other way in which the directories might have under-recorded coaches: through coachmasters having more than one coach setting out for the same destination at the same time. This would not be easy to identify – the only possible example found is Birmingham coaches from the Bush in 1785[4] – but it is unlikely ever to have been common, and would have become even rarer with time as coachmasters became keener to maximise the apparent number of services operated.

All the other problems of local directory information significantly exaggerate the number of services. Like the London directories, Bristol's often record a service at more than one inn, either because it was shared between several inns or because the coach called at a second or third inn on the way out of the city. Where a service used different inns on alternate days, it might be listed only for those days or as a daily service at both inns.[5] Times for the same service often vary slightly, making it harder to determine whether they refer to one coach or two. This was sometimes because inns were some way apart but apparently sometimes because of carelessness. By the 1830s there seems to have been a deliberate practice of making the stated departure times for different places slightly different, usually by a quarter of an hour, apparently in order to make the range of destinations served more impressive. For example, in 1835 the White Lion claimed to have mail coaches at 5.30 pm to Hereford and Oswestry, 5.45 pm to Chester and 6 pm to Shrewsbury, Holyhead and Liverpool, but this was a single mail coach to Liverpool.[6] In one exceptional case, Manchester coaches from the White Lion from 1814 to at least 1839, the listing seems to reflect an arrangement whereby the White Lion booked Manchester passengers on Birmingham coaches from a different inn, reflecting a compromise over Birmingham coaches.[7]

As for potential double counting of coaches listed for several places, this is far more of a problem than in London directories because of the greater variety of possible destinations and links. It arises in four main ways:

(1) Listing of intermediate places, such as Southampton for a Gosport, Portsmouth or Brighton coach.

(2) Inclusion of connecting services from a nearby place, especially Bath. In this case a link could give access to a wide range

of destinations. Some services originating in Bath, for example to Frome, Weymouth, Poole, Gosport and Oxford, were recorded in Bristol directories as services from Bristol but in directories for other places as services from Bath.[8] By the 1830s there were similar links via Cheltenham to Liverpool and probably Oxford.[9]

(3)   Inclusion of connecting services from a relatively distant destination.   For example, when coaches were advertised to Birmingham, Manchester and Liverpool, fares, timings and proprietors were almost invariably given only for Bristol to Birmingham, and the Birmingham to Manchester or Liverpool services were occasionally acknowledged as separate, though Manchester and Liverpool were nevertheless often separately listed in Bristol directories. Similarly, Exeter coaches were often advertised as serving Plymouth and Devonport, and Hereford coaches as serving Shrewsbury and Holyhead, and those places were often separately listed too.

(4)   Listing of branches from Bristol services. For example, Fromont & Co's Minehead services were a branch from their Exeter coach at Bridgwater and Clift & Co's Barnstaple services were a branch from their Exeter coach at Tiverton, though listed in Bristol directories as services from Bristol. An interesting case is the entries in Bristol directories from 1828 for the Exeter mail coach, which was in fact separate mail coaches from Bristol to Barnstaple and Bath to Exeter, meeting and exchanging passengers at Taunton.[10]

Similar considerations applied at other places as regards services ostensibly to Bristol. For example, the Everlasting and Eclipse coaches from Kidderminster to Bristol were listed in a directory covering Kidderminster in 1822-3, but no such coaches, nor any services to Kidderminster, were listed in Bristol directories, and the passengers were evidently transferred at some point to a different coach.[11] Coaches might describe themselves as 'Bath and Bristol' ones without their owners having any link to one of the two cities: an advertisement of 1797 for a Birmingham to Bath coach, claiming to be the only direct service, stated that 'All other coaches go to Bristol only, where passengers take all chances of getting forwards next morning.'[12]

While it is difficult to turn directory information into numbers of services, the task is not hopeless. Advertisements and the directories of other places help greatly in interpreting the information in Bristol directories. Clues *within* the Bristol directories are departure times, especially whether departure times for apparently separate coaches changed similarly at the same time, whether a coach was named (a named coach was more likely to be serving the place listed) and the route (an indirect route sometimes indicates a linking arrangement).

The directories were of course telling passengers what they needed to know to reach, say, Liverpool or Minehead. Passengers evidently disliked being transferred between vehicles, presumably because of the disturbance and delay, but in the earlier period this might happen even with a direct service. Arguably, if a coach from Bristol carried numerous Liverpool passengers, it *was* a Liverpool coach, even if a separate partnership provided the service beyond Birmingham. However, on that basis, since nothing is known about passengers' final destinations, there would be no way of determining whether a coach was a Liverpool, Manchester, Birmingham or indeed Gloucester one. Also, if a coach from Bristol conveyed passengers both for Exeter and Barnstaple, with coaches owned by the same firm diverging at Taunton, it was arguably both an Exeter and a Barnstaple coach, but that does not alter the fact that only one coach set off from Bristol. In order to count stage coaches at Bristol and to have some chance of comparing one year with another, it is essential to count only coaches in and out of Bristol itself, as has been attempted here.

Robson's London directory

THE COACH LISTS in *Robson's London directory* in 1832-9 are lists of coaches paying stage coach duty, supplied by the licensing authority, rather than normal directory-type information. Each coach appears only once, so there is no risk of double-counting. They provide valuable evidence about the actual pattern of services, though their peculiarities need to be borne in mind: journeys each way are counted separately, doubling the apparent number, and, as each service is recorded only in one place rather than at both termini, entries for other towns and cities have to be examined too to identify all services at a particular place. Services passing through, such as Exeter to Cheltenham via Bristol, are not recorded in connection with the place passed through at all.

The lists of London services appear to be comprehensive, and indeed these lists are the best record of London services ever published. However, the record of regional services seems less comprehensive, with absences such as Bristol to Swansea and apparent under-recording on other routes, such as Bristol to Exeter. In other cases it matches exactly what interpretation of the directory entries suggests. The reason for under-recording is unclear, but may reflect the greater difficulty of enforcing the law where coaches followed numerous different routes as opposed to a few main roads out of London. Perhaps there was also some difficulty in gathering the regional records for publication. As regards local services, *Robson's London directory* is more comprehensive than local directories, at least in Bristol's case, though this partly reflected the fact that some services which were not really stage coach ones were caught by the requirement to pay duty.

Notes

1   FFBJ 8 March 1777.
2   *Report from the Select Committee on the Milford Haven communication*, PP 1826-27 (258), p. 60.
3   FFBJ 5 Nov 1796; BG 20 Sept 1810, 3 April 1834.
4   BD 1785; FFBJ 18 June 1785, 14 Oct 1786.
5   e.g. the Times coach to Exeter in 1836.
6   BD 1836; PP 1836 (364), p. 2.
7   The White Lion coach is always listed in Matthews's directory under Manchester but not Birmingham, always with a time the same within a quarter of an hour of the Duke of Wellington coach (sometimes changing in the same years), and is never advertised by the White Lion or listed in Birmingham directories, although the Duke of Wellington is stated there to use the Bush and the White Lion.
8   e.g. above, pp. 222, 224.   For branches to Bath from Exeter-Bristol and Weymouth-Bristol services respectively, see *English Reports*, vol. 130, p. 753; *Dorset County Chronicle*, 18 June 1835.
9   Above, pp. 226, 237.
10   BG 15 Feb 1810; EFP 5 Feb 1824; *Mail coaches*, PP1836 (364), p. 2.
11   *Pigot and Co.'s London & provincial new commercial directory, for 1822-3* (1822).
12   ABG 15 May 1797.

Appendix 2: Speeds, fares and productivity

Parts of this book are based on spreadsheets bringing together data on coach speeds and fares from 1658 to 1846 (but largely from 1750 onwards) derived from newspaper advertisements and directories – 324 references giving speed or fare or both for Bristol-London coaches and 573 likewise for other Bristol coaches. This appendix explains how those spreadsheets and the graphs in this book based on them were compiled and examines some of the issues they raise, including the issues involved in seeking to measure change in productivity.

Sources

The main sources were *Felix Farley's Bristol Journal* from 1752 to 1800, the *Bristol Gazette* from 1800 to 1846 and *Matthews's new Bristol directory* from 1793 to 1842 (annual from 1812). Additional material has been drawn from newspapers of Bath, Birmingham, Exeter, Gloucester, London, Sherborne, Swansea, Taunton, Worcester and elsewhere, including some from the three main digitised collections (the Burney Collection, British Newspapers 1800-1900 and *The Times*).

No coach has been entered more than once a year unless either the speed or the fare changed within that period. Speeds and fares for intermediate places have been ignored, only those for the full route being used, except in a few cases when only an intermediate speed or fare is available. Evidence from Bristol directories has been entered only for every other year.

Miles

A NALYSIS OF SPEEDS and fares depends on knowing reasonably accurately the mileage covered. Roads were of course being improved during the period dealt with here, but, as I have argued elsewhere, this usually had little effect on overall mileage, since improvements such as reduced gradients were as likely to increase the mileage as to reduce it.[1] Miles are taken from *Cary's new itinerary* for 1819.

There were of course variations in route. For Bristol to London in 1819 there were the old route through Sandy Lane (121 miles and four furlongs), the later ones through Chippenham (122 miles and one furlong) and Devizes (122 miles and six furlongs) and one via Andover and Devizes instead of Reading (124 miles and three furlongs). The mileage varied at most by only 2.3% (potentially changing a 38s. fare from 3.8 to 3.7 pence per mile), and in fact none of the Bristol and Bath coaches used the Andover route except in 1765 and 1779-86,[2] or after the 1750s the Sandy Lane route. None of the four routes changed in length by as much as a mile between Cary's editions of 1798 and 1828. 122 miles is used here for all Bristol-London coaches. A standard mileage is also used for other routes, unless coaches followed an indirect route such as Exeter via Axminster or Hereford via Gloucester.

Speeds

THE SPEEDS USED here are overall or end-to-end ones, ignoring the fact that coaches stopped for passengers to eat and horses to be changed. The travelling speeds, when the coach was actually moving, were somewhat higher. However, in the few cases included where a coach stopped overnight, those hours are not counted, since stopping overnight or not largely reflected passengers' preferences rather than any operational need and the extra hours did not affect the overall cost of the service.

Most coaches stopped at several places in London, including booking offices in Piccadilly. Typically half an hour was allowed between Piccadilly and the inn in the City where the journey ended, so when only the time in Piccadilly is indicated, half an hour is added here. The other adjustment made, for services which crossed the Severn, is to deduct three-quarters of an hour assumed to have been taken by the ferry at the New or Old Passages (on the basis of the hour allowed for the mail coaches at the New Passage, but bearing in mind that three miles of the journey was covered during the New Passage crossing).[3]

Sometimes, instead of departure and arrival times, a number of hours is given, and sometimes both forms of timing are given. Where both are given they often do not quite match up, but the discrepancy is rarely more than half an hour, and the explanation is sometimes that the number of hours rounded down the last half hour or so or omitted the half hour between the Piccadilly booking office and the main London inn.[4] Where both are given, arrival and departure times are used in preference to timings expressed in hours.

One puzzling feature is that up and down journeys frequently took a slightly different length of time, though again rarely varying by more than an hour. Possible reasons include variation in stopping times where, for example, time was needed for breakfast in one direction but not the other, and steep hills affecting more seriously coaches in one direction. In the case of Sherman's Wonder coach between London and Shrewsbury in 1836, the up coaches took 15 minutes longer than the down ones, reflecting the fact that in six of the eleven stretches of route the up coaches took from one to five minutes longer; the Wonder's up and down timings were sometimes adjusted by differing amounts, reducing the difference by 27 minutes between 1825 and 1834.[5] Where different up and down timings were given the average is used here.

Before the railway era, time was not of course the same in London and Bristol. In fact the difference from London time, 20 minutes, was greater than anywhere else.[6] This may explain some of the variations in timing between up and down journeys, but makes only a small difference (about 2.5%) to a journey of 13 hours.

Until the 1780s journey times were usually expressed in days. Had there been a standard coaching day it would be possible to turn these into hours, but there was not. The difference between a flying coach and an ordinary one was entirely the length of time on the road during the day, and many coaches advertised as taking one day in fact set off the previous evening, occasionally as early as 8 pm. Journey times expressed in days are therefore not used here. Nor are vague timings such as 'in time for dinner' or 'early in the morning'.

In some cases where newspaper advertisements give a fare but not a speed, the speed has been taken instead from the Bristol directory when there is good reason to believe the fare and speed applied at the same time (e.g. when the date of the fare falls between the publication of successive directories giving identical hours or timings). Fares might fluctuate, but hours were changed much less frequently.

While fares rarely varied at all between the seasons, advertised speeds varied significantly by season until the 1770s, as discussed in the text. The few speeds available up to the 1770s therefore have to be considered separately for summer and winter.

The reliability of advertised speeds

THERE WOULD HAVE been little advantage in advertising completely unrealistic speeds, so it is reasonable to take advertised timings as a guide to actual timings, but that is not to say that any individual advertised timing can be wholly relied on, or that every journey took exactly the advertised time. Sometimes a new firm did advertise an unrealistic timing, and two of these have been ignored here (Gevaux & Co's 16 hours in 1775, soon amended to 18 hours, and Pocock & Co's 14 hours in 1784).[7] Timings given for the same coach sometimes varied, for example as given at different inns or in different newspapers or directories, though rarely by more than half an hour. In the eighteenth century coachmasters sometimes referred to complaints about delays on the road or emphasised that their coaches would stop only to change horses, implying that that was not always the case.[8]

More significantly, scheduled times which were realistic in good times might not be achieved if the load was heavy or the roads were bad. In 1827 Waterhouse admitted that his other coaches were not as punctual as the mails: 'sometimes they get a heavy load, and if the roads are heavy by frost I think it is impossible for the horses to get through at certain times, to keep their time quite so regularly as the mail-coaches do'. Chaplin stated of his coaches in 1836-7 that 'in fine weather, they travel well; but with full loads and heavy road they decrease in speed, and are not punctual, like the mails'; 'There is summer travelling in the post-coaches, and winter travelling; the time of its arrival in the winter is quite uncertain, it may be eleven o'clock, it may be one'.[9] This is broadly confirmed by the limited evidence of timings given in passengers' diaries (Appendix 4). Sometimes the actual timing matched the advertised one, but often it was an hour or so longer.

The other doubt about advertised timings is whether they were representative, especially when they were fewest, from the 1790s to the 1810s. Around that time there was a widening gap between the speeds and fares of the faster and slower coaches, creating a risk that only the fastest advertised their speeds and the cheapest their fares, distorting the averages. Evidence on a national basis suggests that this occurred only to a small extent, and the slower Bristol coaches are in fact generally well-represented in advertisements giving speeds. Also, from 1810 the advertised times can be compared with the more comprehensive information in *Cary's new itinerary*.

Cary's timings

THE COACH LISTS in *Cary's new itinerary* from 1810 to 1828 give timings for the majority of London coaches, and there was a new edition every three years or so. Cary's timings normally match fairly well those given in advertisements, but the information is less accurate in 1821 (at least for Bristol) and less complete in 1826 and 1828. When up times are given, from 1810 to 1821, the departures are often an hour or so adrift from those in Bristol directories, but rarely more. Cary's up and down timings often differ by several hours (three hours in one case), with neither being consistently longer or shorter than the other.

Similar information is given in Alan Bates, *Directory of stage coach services 1836* (1969). No information is provided about sources, other than a reference to 'a multitude of directories, coaching bills and newspaper advertisements'. In fact the material is almost exclusively from *Robson's London directory*, with some additional information about mail coaches. The main exception is the journey times given for most coaches. In Bristol's case these are accurate. However, the source has not been traced.

Fares

FARES FLUCTUATED, BUT not as wildly as has sometimes been suggested. It is true that there were occasional drastic fare reductions in order to force a new competitor off the road, and that sort of fare was of course especially likely to be advertised, but such fares were not very common. There is a more general risk that advertised fares in any period might be unrepresentative, as seems to be the case for Bristol to London in 1816-20, with only six fares available relating to just three coaches. With regional fares there is the added problem that fares were higher on some roads than others, and the representation of different roads in the sample varies from one period to another. That problem has been addressed by compiling figures based on just the main regional routes where fares were normally around the average. Otherwise the main remedy is to have an adequate number of examples. From 1750, there are seven or more examples of Bristol-London fares in each five-year period except 1756-60, 1771-5, 1791-5, 1796-1800, 1806-10 and 1816-20 (three, six, three, one, nil and five examples respectively). Fares are most plentiful for 1786-90 and 1826-30 (30 and 33 examples respectively). There are fewer than seven fares available for Bristol's regional services only in 1751-5, 1756-60 and 1776-80. 16 or more regional fares are available for nine five-year periods, the highest number being 33 in 1781-5.

There is one indication, from 1828, that down fares could be higher than up ones (see p. 119 above), but that was for a mail coach. Up mail services were less popular than the down ones because some reached London inconveniently early in the morning, though that

did not apply in the Bristol case.[10] Such variation was perhaps why
the Magnet coach in 1824 proclaimed 'No extra charge in fares from
London.'[11] No other evidence of up and down fares varying has been
found, but to be certain that they did not it would be necessary to
have more advertisements for the same coach appearing in Bristol
and London newspapers at the same time.

Measuring productivity

WHAT IS ATTEMPTED here is to measure over time the impact on
the stage coach's productivity of better roads, horses, vehicles
and organisation (especially the first of these), and to determine
which were the periods of greatest improvement. Essentially this
is about the relationship between what went in (especially horse
provender and labour) and what came out (movement of passengers
over a number of miles at a particular speed), discounting changes in
the prices of the inputs. The input costs, fares and speeds of coaches
in 1653-1750 are the starting point for the calculation. The method
is, for each coach for which both speed and fare are known, to take
the average fare of 1653-1750, multiply it according to the increased
cost of inputs in the year concerned, multiply it again according to the
estimated increase in costs for the higher speed, and then compare
the result with what the fare actually was. The outcome is what was
actually paid as a percentage of what the journey at the same speed
would have cost had there been no improvements in roads, vehicles,
horses or organisation since 1750.

Three ingredients are needed for this calculation:

- Evidence of fares and speeds, as described above. The only
  evidence used is that providing both speed and fare for the same
  service at the same date, since either on its own can be misleading:

a low fare may reflect an unusually low speed rather than greater productivity, and a high speed may similarly have been made possible by a high fare rather than greater productivity. However, given the scarcity of evidence in the earlier period, fares are estimated for 1753-5[12] and speed estimated for 1763 (Table 1).

- A breakdown of the coachmaster's costs. One dating from 1688-9 is used here, giving the following proportions: oats 48.3%, beans 19.4%, hay 15.5%, wages 7.8% and industrial prices 8.9%.[13] Recalculating the figures from 1787-91 (when the evidence of speeds and fares is especially good) to the 1830s on the basis of a breakdown of 1760-1 (Fig. 6) made virtually no difference to the figures; doing the same with a breakdown of 1829 made very little difference, the productivity figure for 1828-38 being only a percentage point higher.[14]

- Indexes of the various costs. Those used here are as follows: Clark's series for oats, beans and hay; the Phelps Brown-Hopkins series for wages; O'Brien's series for industrial prices to 1820; and, for industrial prices after 1820, Tooke's series for English iron and the Royal Hospital, Greenwich series for coal.[15]

Of course, there are several complications and a number of assumptions have to be made, as follows:

- It is necessary to convert the overall speeds indicated by advertisements into travelling speeds, since an important part of the calculation is the increased cost of a greater travelling speed, whereas making refreshment stops shorter cost no extra. Advertisements suggest that the usual stops were for breakfast (if departure was at 7 am or earlier), dinner, and supper (if the coach was running through the night). The length of stops varied from one period to another and from slower to faster coaches. On the basis of an advertisement on another route in 1791, typical stops in the second half of the eighteenth century may have been half an hour for breakfast, an hour for dinner and three-quarters of an hour for supper.[16] The Bristol mail coach at first stopped only for 20 minutes (later 15 minutes in one direction only),[17] and the Balloon coaches can hardly have allowed more time. In the 1820s and 1830s stops were typically 15 or 20 minutes for breakfast and 20 to 30 minutes for dinner,[18] though the slower coaches perhaps allowed more time. A day coach such as the York House coach from Bath to London in the 1830s might stop for 20 minutes for breakfast and half an hour for lunch, whereas night coaches long before that had only one stop for a meal.[19] Here, for London to Bristol coaches, the following adjustments are made to allow for stops: to 1763, 1½ hours per day; mail coaches at any period 15 minutes; from 1776 to 1815, one hour for any journey taking 18 hours or less and 1½ hours for 20 hours or more; from 1818 onwards, ¾ hour for 17 hours or less and one hour for journeys longer than 17 hours. This is somewhat arbitrary, but fortunately does not have a major effect on the outcome. Strictly something should be taken off for changes of team – perhaps 20 minutes for ten changes at two minutes each in the 1830s and a similar time earlier (for slower changes but fewer of them and a higher proportion coinciding with refreshment stops). However, the timings are uncertain and the effect of doing so would be small; it would change the figure by 1.2 percentage points in 1790-1 and 1.3 in 1836-8, and would not affect the timing of the increase in productivity. This adjustment has therefore not been made.

- A higher speed cost more than a lower one, and that needs to be quantified for each example. In particular a higher speed required greater labour from the horses, so the share of costs which varied in proportion to the number of horses kept is increased here in proportion to the increased number of horses needed for the higher speed; the cost of coachmen is kept constant and the cost of coaches and harness is increased in the same proportion as the number of horses as a notional estimate of increased wear and tear. Evidence on the work done by horses at different speeds is provided by Fourier and Brunel.[20] Fourier's figures indicate that the work done decreased at a constant rate as speed rose from five miles per hour to ten miles per hour, but slightly less rapidly both below and above that range. Taking the work done at 3.75 miles per hour as 100, the decline was to 7.45 at 11.25 miles per hour. Brunel's evidence indicates a constant rate of decrease at least from 5.5 miles per hour to 7.8 (he is somewhat imprecise about the higher speeds), and assuming a constant rate the work done would have declined from 100 at 3.85 miles per hour to 25.3 at 11 miles per hour. Brunel's figures, with a slower decrease in work done as speed increased, correspond better to the evidence of actual speeds and fares: taking the resulting index figures for 1824-34 (when the evidence is best – 59 examples) and grouping the examples by speed into four bands (7.0-7.3 miles per hour up to 9.6-10.0), Brunel's evidence results in productivity index figures almost the same for each group, whereas Fourier's result in the index figures falling continuously from the lowest-speed band to the highest, from 26.4 to 19.0. Brunel's figures are therefore used here rather than Fourier's. A puzzling aspect is that both sets of figures indicate an accelerating increase in costs as speed rose, whereas actual fares in 1824-34 indicate if anything the opposite. The reason could be the increased proportion of costs which did not vary according to speed (stage coach duty and tolls), amounting to about 25% by 1830. Chaplin stated in 1837 that an extra mile per hour increased total cost by 13 to 20%,[21] while the figures used here indicate increases from 13 to 29% for each rise of one mile per hour from five to nine.

- The base used for the comparison can have a considerable effect on the outcome. Here, because of the quantity of evidence and the stability of fares and speeds throughout the period, the fares and travelling speeds of stage coaches nationwide from 1653 to 1750 are used as the base (3.85 miles per hour, as the average of 4.3 in summer and 3.4 in winter; 2.34d per mile inside, excluding East Anglian examples). There is no reason to regard the Bristol route as untypical: four travelling speeds in summer from 1725 to 1755 ranged from 3.6 to 4.7, and all recorded fares up to 1750 were from 2.0 to 2.5d per mile (sometimes the lower figure for three-day coaches and the higher for two-day coaches).[22]

- Whereas in 1653-1750 speeds varied greatly between summer and winter, that variation had largely disappeared by the late 1770s. It is therefore appropriate to use average speeds for summer and winter in 1653-1750 to compare with speeds in the later period regardless of season. However, the speeds and fares used for 1753 and 1763 (but not 1755) are summer ones, so in these cases the speed used as the base for 1653-1750 is the summer one of 4.3 miles per hour.

- Two new items were added to the breakdown of costs in the eighteenth century – tolls and duties. Tolls are not a problem: the better roads they paid for meant that fewer horses were required, and fares reflected both the fewer horses and the tolls, in effect providing a net figure. But this does not apply to duties on stage coaches, first levied in 1779, since there was no corresponding benefit; duties are comparable to an increase in cost. Duties are included in the calculation here by taking their estimated proportion of total costs in 1830 (12.5%),[23] adjusting the absolute amount in each year to reflect changes in the level of the duties,[24] and deducting it from fares. The effect is to reduce fares and therefore to increase the level of productivity growth.

- The composition of the coachmaster's income changed over

time as the number of outside passengers increased. In 1833-4 between Bristol and London, outside fares accounted for from 43 to 57% of a full load, except for the mail coach (Table 2). Outside fares were most often 50% of inside fares at first, but ranged from 45 to 60% and occasionally beyond (especially in 1818-33 when there seems to have been particularly strong competition over outside fares; the five-year averages from 1816-20 to 1831-5 were from 46 to 48% of inside fares). The problem is that in the eighteenth century there was often no outside fare stated, and there was often only one outside passenger, creating a risk of the outside fares given being eccentric. Here, in order to ensure consistency, when there is only an inside fare that is taken as it is; when both are given the figure used is half of the total of one inside fare and two outside fares.

- Fares are matched here to harvest years (October to September), but any new fare may relate to provender prices (or expected prices) at a particular moment rather than the annual average. This is only a significant problem when fluctuations in provender prices were unusually extreme, as in 1800, and may account for some of the variations in index figures at such times.

- From 1825 many Bristol-London coaches operated on a 'no fees' principle, whereby coachmen and guards were not allowed to accept gratuities and must instead have been paid more by the proprietors. Not having to pay gratuities constituted a benefit to passengers which is not reflected in the level of fares. According to Harper, tips to mail guards were 2s.6d from inside passengers for a 100-150 mile journey. If each of two coachmen was given the same, the total was 19% of a 40s. fare. All the direct evidence is from the eighteenth century. In the case of James Woodforde from 1775 to 1795, gratuities on various routes ranged from 4.6% to 11.1% and averaged 7.5%, and other examples in that period are around the same level.[25] Here the fares of no fees coaches (the two companies' and Niblett's) are reduced by 10%.

- Night running is not counted here as an increase in productivity, though apparently regarded as a benefit by most passengers, since it was mainly a reflection of customer preferences and cost little or no extra; indeed coaches were increasingly running during the night in the early eighteenth century, well before turnpikes had had any significant impact.[26] There may have been some link through better roads reducing the danger of night-travelling, but it does not seem to have been a strong one.

Even after making these adjustments, the increase in productivity can only be tracked fairly roughly, but this is to be expected: coachmasters sometimes significantly reduced fares to beat off a competitor, or conversely might raise them collusively when competition was muted; high fares might reflect the reliability or the

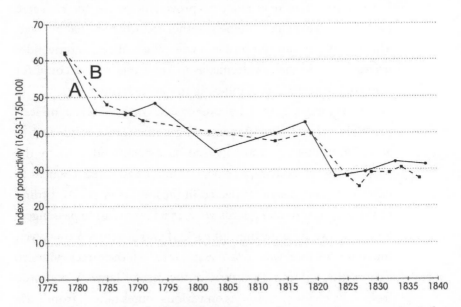

109 *Productivity growth of Bristol's London coaches, 1775-1840, comparing index figures derived from the five-year averages of all known fares and speeds (line A) with the index figures from Fig. 25 based on individual examples of coaches (line B).*

prestige of a particular service (as in the case of Cooper's coaches in the 1830s); and relating fares to an annual figure for costs which is also a national figure is fairly imprecise. On the other hand, the quantity of evidence in the 1780s and the late 1820s and 1830s means that the assessment of productivity then is reasonably robust.

One way of checking the reliability of the figures is to perform a similar process for the five-year averages of all recorded fares and speeds. For this purpose overall speeds are multiplied by 1.05 to convert them into approximate travelling speeds. This is less reliable evidence, because the speeds and fares are not necessarily for the same coaches, but it makes up in bulk for what it lacks in quality. Periods for which there are not at least three speeds and at least three fares are excluded (1756-1775, 1795-1800 and 1805-10).[27] The figures are reassuringly similar for the two processes, though those derived from all speeds and fares are more erratic (Fig. 109).

Both methods – individual examples and five-year averages – have also been used to plot the growth of productivity in Bristol's regional services (Fig. 102). As regards individual examples, four with fares 60% or less of the five-year averages have been excluded, as have two South Wales examples with fares 129% or more of the averages, leaving only 47 examples. As regards the five-year averages, periods not having at least three speeds and three fares have been excluded (i.e. the period up to 1770, together with 1791-5 and 1801-5).

Notes

1   Gerhold, p. 239.
2   Above, pp. 62, 65; online index to *Bath Chronicle*, 5 Jan 1786 (for Bath-London mail coach).
3   POST 10/366, pp. 100-3.
4   e.g. BG 3 May, 7 June 1827 (Sovereign and Monarch); BD 1837, p. 29 (Monarch).
5   *The seventh report of the Commissioners appointed to inquire into the management of the Post-Office Department*, PP 1837 (70), p. 74.

6   POST 10/366, p. 20. The difference was said to be only ten minutes in 1827 (*Report from the Select Committee on the Milford Haven communication*, PP 1826-27 (258), p. 60).

7   FFBJ 22 Apr 1775; *Morning Chronicle*, 20 Feb 1784. Occasionally the timing for London, Bath and Bristol coaches is actually for London-Bath (e.g. *The Times*, 8 Nov 1828).

8   e.g. FFBJ 29 Oct 1774, 12 April 1788.

9   *Mail coach contracts*, PP 1835 (313), p. 47; PP 1837 (70), pp. 71, 107.

10 PP 1835 (313), p. 78.

11 BG 27 May 1824.

12 Fares in the flying coaches were 24s. in 1753, 26s. in 1754, 'usual prices' in 1755 and 25s. in 1756; 25s. is therefore used for flyers; Bath evidence in 1748-9 and 1752 is that fares in three-day coaches were only 78-80% as much; on the basis that flying coaches were no dearer to run than three-day ones, average fares of the two are used, i.e. 22s.6d.

13 TNA, E 112/598/541. See Dorian Gerhold, 'Productivity change in road transport before and after turnpiking, 1690-1840', *Economic History Review*, vol. 49 (1996), p. 513; the provender cost has been re-divided here into oats, beans and hay instead of just oats and beans.

14 The breakdown of 1830 is from Samuel Salt, *Statistics and calculations essentially necessary to persons connected with railways or canals* (1845), p. 83. The figure was adjusted to reflect relative changes in costs between 1787-91 and 1829 (tolls being arbitrarily reduced by a third).

15 Gregory Clark, 'The price history of English agriculture, 1209-1914', *Research in Economic History*, vol. 22 (2004), pp. 70-4, 85-9; E.H. Phelps Brown and S.V. Hopkins, 'Seven centuries of building wages', *Economica*, new ser., vol. 22 (1955), pp. 195-206; P.K. O'Brien, 'Agriculture and the home market for English industry, 1660-1820', *English Historical Review*, vol. 100 (1985), pp. 792-5; Thomas Tooke, *A history of prices, and of the state of the circulation, from 1793 to 1837* (1838-57), vol. 2, p. 406; *ibid.*, vol. 3, p. 297; *Report on wholesale and retail prices in the United Kingdom in 1902*, PP 1903 (321), p. 11.

16 *Newcastle Courant*, 2 Apr 1791.

17 POST 10/366, pp. 19, 23; POST 10/203.

18 e.g. Figs. 90, 92; *The Cambrian*, 20 Oct 1821; BG 11 April 1839. See also PP 1837 (70), pp. 72-4.

19 Duke of Beaufort, 'The Brighton, Bath and Dover roads', in *ibid.*, *Driving* (1890), p. 242; above, p. 150.

20 R.H. Thurston, *The animal as a machine and a prime motor* (1894), p. 52; William Youatt, *The horse, with a treatise of draught* (1843), p. 531.

21 *Report from the Select Committee on railroad communication*, PP 1837-38 (341), p. 92.

22 Gerhold, pp. 224-6, 233-5; *The Bath and Bristol guide* (1753, 1755); Charles E. Davis, *The mineral baths of Bath* (1883), p. 48n.

23 Based on Salt, *Statistics and calculations*, p. 83. Theo Barker and Dorian Gerhold, *The rise and rise of road transport, 1700-1990* (1993), p. 17, wrongly includes mileage on coaches as tax.

24 Recorded in *Report of the Commissioners of Inland Revenue*, PP 1870 (406), pp. 28-9; 1779 c.51; 1783 c.63; 1796 c.16; 1804 c.88; 1815 c.185; 1822 c.95; 1832 c.120.

25 Charles G. Harper, *Stage-coach and mail in days of yore* (1903), vol. 1, p. 253; John Beresford (ed.), *The diary of a country parson: the Reverend James Woodforde* (1924), *passim*; Basil Cozens-Hardy (ed.), *The diary of Sylas Neville 1767-1788* (1950), pp. 55-7, 266; Birmingham City Archives, MS 3782/12/107/11, 18 Nov 1779; Cardiff Central Library, MS 3.552, account.

26 Gerhold, pp. 154-5.

27 Costs and duties have been weighted to reflect the years in which fares are recorded.

Appendix 3: Actual and advertised times between Bristol and London, 1777-1838

Source	Date	Journey (and coach)	Times	Adjusted hours	Advertised time
1, 17	Mar 1777	Bristol-London (Gevaux & Co's diligence)	1am-8pm	19	18 (2am-8pm)
2	July 1777	Bristol-London	9pm-6.30pm*	22	
3	Dec 1781	Bristol-London	4am-10pm	18	
2	May 1782	Bath-London	10pm-9pm (h)	23	
2, 17	May 1786	London-Bristol (Balloon)	7pm-c.12.30 (u)	17½	18 (Dec 1786, Apr 1787)
2, 17	May 1786	Bristol-London (Balloon)	3.30pm-8am	16½	18 (ditto)
4, 17	June 1786	London-Bath (Balloon)	6.45pm-10am	15¼+2	18 (ditto)
4, 18	Sept 1789	Bath-London (Royal Blue)	4pm-11am	19	16 (Bath; 4pm-8am)
4	June 1793	London-Bath (White Hart)	5am-10pm	17	
5	May 1795	London-Bath	c.4.30-8.30*	16½	
4	June 1795	London-Bath (White Hart)	4am-c.9.30pm	17½	
4	Oct 1795	Bath-London (White Hart)	4pm-10am	18	

Source	Date	Journey (and coach)	Times	Adjusted hours	Advertised time
6	Dec 1801	London-Bath	4am-11pm	19	
7, 17	Jan 1802	Bath-London (opposition coach; Fromont's?)	2pm-8am	18	16 (Bath; 2pm-6am; July 1801)
8, 19	Jan 1815	Bath-London (Exeter Mail)	4pm-c.7am (u)	15	14¾ (Bath; 4.15pm-7am)
9, 19	May 1818	Bristol-London (Mail)	4pm-c.7.45 (h)	15¾	15 (4pm-7am)
8	Jan 1821	Bath-London (York House)	3pm-9am	18	
9, 20	May 1822	Bristol-London (Mail)	4pm-c.7.45pm (h)	15¾	14½ (4pm-6.30am; late 1821)
9, 20	July 1823	Bristol-London (Mail)	4pm-c.7.30am (u)	15½	14½ (4pm-6.30pm)
9	Nov 1823	Bath-London	6.30am-9pm	14½	
10	Apr 1824	London-Bath (White Lion)	6.45am-c.7.30pm	12¾	
10	June 1824	London-Bath	c.7.30am-c.9.30pm	14	
11	July 1824	London-Bath	13 hours*	13½	
12, 21	Mar 1826	London-Bath (Company's)	7am-7.30pm (u)	12½+2	14¾ (7am-9.45pm)
12	Mar 1826	Bath-London (Company's)	2.30pm-9.15am (u)	18¾	
13, 22	May 1827	London-Bath (York House)	6am-6.30pm	12½	12 (Bath; Sept 1828)
8	June 1827	London-Bath	c.4pm-7pm*	15½	
14	Aug 1827	London-Bristol	5pm-9am	16	
15	Oct 1828	London-Bristol (Company's)	4.30pm-8.45am	16¼	
9, 21	May 1831	London-Bristol (Emerald)	c.8am-c.9.45pm (u)	13¾	13½

Source	Date	Journey (and coach)	Times	Adjusted hours	Advertised time
9	Sept 1831	Bath-London	7am-c.7pm (u)	12	
9, 21	Oct 1831	London-Bristol (Emerald)	8am-c.10pm (u)	14	13½ (8am-9.30pm)
8, 21	May 1833	Bath-London (Regulator)	8.10am-c.9pm*	13¼+1½	14
8, 20	June 1833	London-Bath (Monarch)	6pm-6am*	12½+1½	14½ (late 1833)
9	June 1833	Bath-London (White Hart)	7.15am-7.45pm (h)	12½	
9	Feb 1834	Bristol-Reading	10am-7pm	9	
9	Apr 1834	Bath-London (Exeter Mail)	6.30pm-6.30am (h)	12	
9, 22	Mar 1835	Bath-London (York House)	7am-6.30pm (h)	11½	11 (Bath; Mar 1836)
9, 20	Sept 1835	London-Bristol (Emerald)	8am-10pm (u)	14	13 (late 1835)
9, 23	Feb 1836	Bath-London (White Hart)	7.15am-8pm (u)	12¾	11 (Bath)
9, 20	May 1836	London-Bristol (Emerald)	c.8am-c.9.45pm	13¾	13¼ (late 1836)
9, 22	June 1836	Bath-London (Regulator)	c.8.30am-c.8.45pm (h)	12¼	11 (Bath)
16, 20	July 1836	Bath-London (Company's)	8.30am-8.30pm	12	12¼ (Bath; 9am-9.15pm)
9	Mar 1837	London-Bristol	8am-9.55pm	14	
9, 20	June 1838	Bristol-London (Regulator)	7am-c.8pm*	13½	13 (late 1837)

[see notes and sources pp.313-14]

Notes

The hours in the last two columns are comparable. They are either actual and advertised Bristol-London times, or (if 'Bath' is indicated in the last column) actual and advertised Bath-London times, or (if '+2' or '+1½' is indicated in the penultimate column) actual Bath-London times with time added for the Bristol-Bath stretch and advertised Bristol-London times.

Times: Times are asterisked if the diarist joined or left the coach in Piccadilly, which cut about half an hour from the journey. '(u)' indicates that the place of joining or leaving the coach in London is unknown; '(h)' indicates that the time of arrival in London is when the diarist reached his home or lodgings.

Adjusted hours: Half an hour is added if the diarist joined or left the coach in Piccadilly. '+2' (or '1½' in the 1830s) is indicated when an actual Bath-London journey is being compared with advertised Bristol-London times.

Advertised time: 'Bath' indicates that the time given is between Bath and London; all others are between Bristol and London.

Sources

1. George Atkinson Ward (ed.), *The journal and letters of Samuel Curwen* (4th edn., 1864), pp. 111-12.
2. NLW, transcript of diary of William Dillwyn, 1774-5, 1777, 1781-90.
3. Birmingham City Archives, diaries of Matthew Boulton, MS 3782/12/107/12.
4. John Beresford (ed.), *The diary of a country parson: the Reverend James Woodforde* (1924), vol. 2, p. 255, vol. 3, p. 139, vol. 4, pp. 39, 209-10, 239-40.
5. Cardiff Central Library, diary of Rev D. Powell, MS 3.552.
6. Earl Leslie Griggs (ed.), *Collected letters of Samuel Taylor Coleridge*, vol. 2, *1801-1806* (1956), p. 778.
7. Alan Sutton (ed.), *The complete diary of a Cotswold parson: the diaries of the Revd. Francis Edward Witts 1783-1854* (2008), vol. 2, p. 497.
8. British Library, journals of John Skinner, Add 33,649, 24 Jan 1815, Add 33,658, 27-8 Jan 1821, Add 33,697, 1 June 1827, Eg 3100, 14 May, 18 June 1833.
9. NLW, transcript of diary of Lewis Weston Dillwyn, 1817-38.
10. Wilfred S. Dowden (ed.), *The journal of Thomas Moore*, vol. 2 (1984), pp. 725, 743.
11. Nathaniel Sheldon Wheaton, *Journal of a residence during several months in London* (1830), p. 287.
12. London Metropolitan Archives, diary of Mr Wolley, Acc 0611/05.
13. Cardiff Central Library, journal of tour, MS 2.325, p. 1.
14. NLW, journal of tour by Captain Lloyd, MS 786A.
15. Bristol RO, diary of C.J. Thomas, 39951 (1).
16. Devon RO, memoirs of Henry Ellis, 76/20/5, pp. 65-7.

17. FFBJ 27 July 1776, 5 July 1777, 16 Dec 1786, 28 Apr 1787, 4 July 1801.
18. Online index to *Bath Chronicle*, 1 Jan 1789.
19. POST 10/366, pp. 15, 19.
20. BD 1822-4, 1834, 1836-8.
21. BG 27 Apr 1826, 21 July 1831, 28 Mar 1833.
22. *Bath Chronicle*, 18 Sept 1828, 24 Mar 1836.
23. Alan Bates, *Directory of stage coach services 1836* (1969), p. 3.

Appendix 4: Horses used for Bristol and Bath coaches, 1828-43

Date	Coach	Owner (and residence)	Road covered	No. of horses (& sets of harness)	Miles & furlongs	Overall speed (mph)	Horses per double mile	Miles per week per team
July 1828	Mail	William Waterhouse (London)	Hounslow-London	10	12.5	9.1	0.79	88
Apr 1828	Mail (Bath and Bristol)	Mr Botham (Salt Hill)	Theale-Hounslow (both coaches)*	40	34.2	9.1	1.17	60
Apr 1833	Mail (Bristol)	George Collins	Maidenhead-Slough	6 (1h)	5.4	9.4	1.09	77
Mar 1833	Cooper's Old Company, day & night	Thomas Cooper (Thatcham)	Bristol-Theale	170 (40h)	75.2 twice	9.0 & 8.4	1.13	62

Date	Coach	Owner (and residence)	Road covered	No. of horses (& sets of harness)	Miles & furlongs	Overall speed (mph)	Horses per double mile	Miles per week per team
„	„	Richard Lovegrove (Reading)	Theale-Brentford	70	36.4 twice	9.0 & 8.4	0.96	73
„	„	Thomas Cooper (Thatcham)	Brentford-London	16 (4h)	10.3 twice	9.0 & 8.4	0.77	
„	„	[Whole route]	Bristol-London	256	122.3 twice	9.0 & 8.4	1.05	66?
Apr 1840	York House (Bath)	W.H. Botham (Salt Hill)	Maidenhead Thicket-Hounslow	18	18.5	10.9	1.03	
„	„	„	Hounslow-London	10	12.5	10.9	0.79	88
Nov 1838	Regulator		Theale-Twyford	12 (2h)	9.7	9.4	1.22	69
July 1839	Regulator & Monarch		Twyford-Maidenhead	18	7.6	9.4 & 8.4	1.16	72

Apr 1831	Monarch	Richard Lovegrove (Maidenhead)	Maidenhead-Colnbrook	8	9.2	8.1	0.86	65
Nov 1838	Monarch	John Nelson (London)	Slough-London	22†	23.6	8.4	1.08	
Apr 1840	Monarch & Eclipse	W.H. Botham (Salt Hill)	Reading-Twyford	8	5.1		0.78	72
July 1829	[New] Company's [day & night?]	Mr Walkden	Knowl Hill-Slough	17 (4h)	9.4 twice	8.4 & 6.6	0.89	67
May 1841	New Company's day	William Lawes (Chippenham)	Chippenham-Hungerford	30 (7h)	28.5	8.7	1.05	67
Dec 1838	New Company's day	W.H. Gilbert (London)	Slough-London	20	23.6	8.7	0.84	83
July 1841	New Company's night ('one side')¶	H. Dibben (London)	Slough-London	10 (2h)	23.6 (halved)¶	6.8	0.84	83
July 1835	Age		Twyford-Slough	10	13.2 (DES)	7.9	0.88	80

Date	Coach	Owner (and residence)	Road covered	No. of horses (& sets of harness)	Miles & furlongs	Overall speed (mph)	Horses per double mile	Miles per week per team
Nov 1843	Prince of Wales	Mr Davies (Devizes)	Devizes-Marlborough	10 (2h)	14.0 (DES)		0.83	84
Oct 1838	Unidentified day coach		Maidenhead-Hounslow	20	16.5		1.20	58
Nov 1839	Unidentified day coach		Theale-Twyford	12 (3h)	9.7		1.23	69

Sources for first five columns: *Report from the Select Committee on the Whetstone and St Albans turnpike trusts, PP 1828 (546), p. 9; The Times,* 14 Apr 1828 (with POST 10/203, pp. 1, 5), 4 July 1829, 4 Apr 1831, 4 Feb, 4 & 11 Mar, 10 Apr 1833, 28 July 1835, 3 Oct, 10, 12 & 22 Nov, 17 Dec 1838, 15 July, 6 Nov 1839, 21 Apr 1840, 29 May, 21 July 1841, 20 Nov 1843.

Note: 'DES' in the sixth column indicates daily except Sunday; all other coaches were daily. Overall speeds are indicative only, as a few are taken from several years away from the date in the first column. In the final column, the number of teams is sometimes an assumption, but usually based on the principle that ten horses were needed to keep two teams at work.

*Botham's horses are said to be those used on the Bath, Bristol and Exeter mails, indicating two separate coaches to Bristol and to Exeter via Bath, but the number of horses seems more appropriate to a single coach.

†The 22 November advertisement indicates 29 horses, including some used on the Magnet coach to Weymouth between London and Hounslow; the 10 November advertisement, though not indicating owner or places, refers to 22 horses from the Monarch, and evidently relates to the same sale.

¶ 'One side' indicates that Dibben horsed only every other journey.

Index

Bold type indicates an illustration.

Lightning Source UK Ltd.
Milton Keynes UK
UKHW041024231118
332791UK00001B/171/P